Filmmaking For Dummies®

A Recipe for Filmmaking: Coo... Production Team

I like to compare the positions of each crew member to pre... ...The following chart lists the common positions found on a typical film production team:

D0117100

Position	Responsibility
Writer	Writes the list of ingredients
Executive producer	Pays for the cost of the dinner
Line producer	Finds where to get the best deals
Producer	Purchases the groceries, helps choose the brands
Casting director	Chooses the food that's ripe for the picking
Location scout	Locates the dinner location
Transportation	Transports the guests to the table
Director	Takes all the ingredients and cooks them into a great meal
Assistant director	Assists the chef
Script supervisor	Makes sure the chef follows the recipe
Director of photography (cinematographer)	Makes the food look really good
Sound mixer	Records all the crunches and lip smacking
Boom operator	Gets the microphone in close to hear all the crunches and lip smacking
Gaffer	Lights the food to look good (sets the mood with a candlelit dinner)
Grips	Help with the utensils for eating the meal
Production assistants	Act as waiters and busboys
Make-up person	Brushes on healthy colors to prepare the food to look appetizing
Wardrobe person	Dresses the food to look tasty
Production designer	Enhances the setting and decorates it for dinner
Prop master	Supplies the appropriate tableware, including plates and glasses
Stunt coordinator	Rigs the exploding champagne bottles and smashing of silverware
Editor	Serves the meal in continuity (appetizer first, entrée next, dessert at the end)
Composer	Creates the right music atmosphere for enjoying the meal
Post-production supervisor	Cleans up the mess

Filmmaking For Dummies®

Important Things to Remember Before You Begin to Shoot Your Film

You need to prepare certain things before setting foot on your set. Following this checklist can increase your chances of having a successful shoot:

- Make sure the money's in the bank (is your investor for real?).
- Hire a great cook or caterer.
- Buy insurance (for crew, equipment, and locations).
- Book a professional still photographer for film stills (needed for advertising and posters when you set up distribution).
- Secure location permits if necessary (so the police don't bust you).
- Make sure all contracts are signed with cast, crew, and location owners, and get releases from everyone on camera — especially background people.

Ways to Enhance the Production Value of Your Film

To enhance the production value of your film:

- Barter for things you can't afford to pay for. "Give me this, and I'll give you a credit or show your product or location in my film!"
- Use big locations. Expansive looks expensive.
- Use large crowds to make your film look like a bigger production. Instead of only 3 people standing in line, have 100!
- Move the camera.
- Get in a high shot or two. Shooting from an apartment balcony works great.
- Use an aerial shot to open up your film. If you can't afford to rent a helicopter, license stock footage to use in your film.
- Make sure you get believable performances from your actors.
- Get a crisp, clear recording of your actors' dialogue.
- Get professional music. A great composer can do wonders on your music score.
- Hire a cinematographer with a good eye. He'll make your movie look impressive — what you see is what you get.

Checking Twice Before Heading Out to a Shoot Location

Before you head out on location, make sure you have everything you need:

- Map to the location
- Camera
- Sound recorder
- Microphones
- Extra batteries
- Lights
- Extension cords
- Masking tape, duct tape, rope
- Tripod
- Actors' wardrobe
- Film or video stock
- Storyboards and the shot list
- Copy of the script

For Dummies: Bestselling Book Series for Beginners

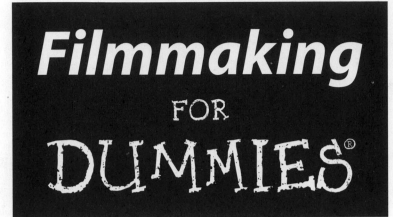

Filmmaking FOR DUMMIES®

by Bryan Michael Stoller

Foreword by Jerry Lewis

Wiley Publishing, Inc.

Filmmaking For Dummies®

Published by
Wiley Publishing, Inc.
111 River Street
Hoboken, NJ 07030
www.wiley.com

For general information on our other products and services or to obtain technical support, please contact our Customer Care Department within the U.S. at 800-762-2974, outside the U.S. at 317-572-3993, or fax 317-572-4002.

Wiley also publishes its books in a variety of electronic formats. Some content that appears in print may not be available in electronic books.

Library of Congress Cataloging-in-Publication Data:

Library of Congress Control Number: 2003101939

ISBN: 0-7645-2476-3

Manufactured in the United States of America

10 9 8 7

1B/ST/QX/QT/IN

WILEY   is a trademark of Wiley Publishing, Inc.

About the Author

Bryan Michael Stoller is an international-award-winning filmmaker who has produced, written, and directed over 80 productions that include short comedy films, half-hour television shows, music videos, commercials, and feature films. Bryan and his films have been featured on *Entertainment Tonight* and *Access Hollywood,* as well as in many newspapers and periodicals, including *The Los Angeles Times, Premiere Magazine, The Hollywood Reporter,* and *People Magazine.*

Bryan's film career began at the early age of 10, when he hosted the network series *Film Fun* with his little sister Nancy on *The Canadian Broadcasting Corporation.* In 1981, Bryan moved to Los Angeles to attend The American Film Institute.

His comedy shorts entitled *Undershorts* have appeared on ABC's *Foul-Ups, Bleeps & Blunders* hosted by Don Rickles and Steve Lawrence, and NBC's *TV's Bloopers & Practical Jokes* with Dick Clark and Ed McMahon. Bryan's parody, *The Linda Blair Witch Project,* starring Linda Blair possessed by famous comedians, streamed on Steven Spielberg's *CountingDown.com* Web site.

Bryan's work has appeared on major U.S. networks including NBC, ABC, HBO, and DirecTV. His top-rated episode of George Romero's *Tales from the Darkside* continues to run as a late-night favorite in syndication.

His films have screened at MIFED in Italy, the Cannes Film Festival in France, and the American Film Market in Santa Monica, California. His screenplays have also won acclaimed awards at the Burbank Film Festival and the Santa Clarita International Film Festival.

You can find Bryan's award-winning film *Undercover Angel,* which stars Yasmine Bleeth *(Baywatch, Nash Bridges),* Dean Winters (HBO's *OZ*), James Earl Jones, Casey Kasem, and Emily Mae Young (of Welch's Juice commercials), at any Blockbuster video store. The film has aired on UPN, Lifetime, and PAX TV.

In his 2001 mockumentary *Hollywood Goes to Las Vegas,* Bryan's dream of meeting actress Sandra Bullock finally came true. The program also included appearances by Haley Joel Osment, Nicolas Cage, John Travolta, Chris Rock, Sylvester Stallone, and Academy Award–winner Russell Crowe.

In various other productions, Bryan has also directed George Carlin, Howie Mandel, Gilbert Gottfried, Barbra Streisand, Drew Barrymore, Jerry Lewis, and Dan Aykroyd. Dolly Parton wrote and recorded four original songs for one of Bryan's films.

King of Pop Michael Jackson is co-directing with Bryan in the big-screen adaptation of Jennings Michael Burch's book, *They Cage the Animals at Night*. Bryan adapted the screenplay for Mel Gibson's Icon Productions.

Bryan enjoys being a mentor as he continues to teach filmmaking seminars for The Learning Annex in the United States, as well as the Summer Film Institute and Alan Morissette's "What Do I Do Now?" seminars in Canada. He also teaches film and acting techniques regularly at various industry schools in the Los Angeles area, including Action in Acting, APS, The Casting Break, and the Creative Actor's Alliance.

For more information on Bryan, check out his official Web site at `www.bryanmichaelstoller.com`.

Dedication

To my Mom, who claims the film credit, *Producer of the Director,* on all my movies. To my Dad (who played the "ambassador" in my movie *The Random Factor*) — I miss you. And to my dog, Little Bear, who can't wait to get a copy of this book — he'll just eat it up, literally.

Author's Acknowledgments

The undertaking of this book has been very much like that of producing a movie. And of course, like the production of a film, this book wouldn't have been possible without all the help and support of such wonderful individuals.

I'd like to thank Natasha Graf, my Acquisitions Editor, for her kindness and understanding, and for believing in me. I'd also like to thank Alissa D. Schwipps, my Senior Project Editor, who made the writing of this book such an enjoyable experience. She never ceased to amaze me with how she juggled so many things while deciphering my words in an organized and coherent fashion. If she ever wants to co-produce a movie, I hope she gives me a call.

Additional thanks goes out to family and friends who were there for support and feedback, including my sisters, Nancy and Marlene, and my friends, Gary Bosloy, Russel Molot, Tim Peyton, Peter Emslie, Tina and Alan Fleishman, Kamilla Bjorlin, and Steffanie Thomas. To my dear friends Frank Tyson and Michael Jackson — thank you for allowing me to spend some writing time up at Neverland Ranch. Thanks to Alan Samuels, Philip Silver, and Jeremy Grody for reviewing some of the technical aspects in the sound chapters; Gloria Everett for being a sounding board on the budget and scheduling chapters; Cara Shapiro for reviewing the accuracy of the chapter on distribution; my agent, Caren Bohrman; my attorney, Michael E. Morales; and A.J. Brandenstein and Tamara Cholakian for valuable advice. And I couldn't forget Noah Golden for his dedicated assistance. And last but not least, thanks to Robert Caspari for being a true friend and a genius in his own right, and for his expertise on the technical review of this book.

And a special thanks to Jerry Lewis. It shows that life is magical when one of your favorite actor/filmmakers writes a foreword to your book!

My Cine-cere thanks to you all,

Bryan Michael Stoller
Studio City, California
www.bryanmichaelstoller.com

Publisher's Acknowledgments

We're proud of this book; please send us your comments through our Dummies online registration form located at www.dummies.com/register/.

Some of the people who helped bring this book to market include the following:

Acquisitions, Editorial, and Media Development

Project Editor: Alissa D. Schwipps

Acquisitions Editor: Natasha Graf

Copy Editor: Laura B. Peterson

Acquisitions Coordinator: Holly Grimes

Technical Editor: Robert Caspari

Senior Permissions Editor: Carmen Krikorian

Editorial Managers: Jennifer Ehrlich, Michelle Hacker

Editorial Assistant: Elizabeth Rea

Cover Photos: © Getty Images

Cartoons: Rich Tennant, www.the5thwave.com

Production

Project Coordinator: Kristie Rees

Layout and Graphics: Amanda Carter, Seth Conley, Mary Gillot Virgin

Proofreaders: Laura Albert, Andy Hollandbeck, Angel Perez, Carl William Pierce, Kathy Simpson, Brian H. Walls, TECHBOOKS Production Services

Indexer: TECHBOOKS Production Services

Special Help: Tere Drenth, Elizabeth Kuball, Pamela Mourouzis

Publishing and Editorial for Consumer Dummies

Diane Graves Steele, Vice President and Publisher, Consumer Dummies

Joyce Pepple, Acquisitions Director, Consumer Dummies

Kristin A. Cocks, Product Development Director, Consumer Dummies

Michael Spring, Vice President and Publisher, Travel

Brice Gosnell, Publishing Director, Travel

Suzanne Jannetta, Editorial Director, Travel

Publishing for Technology Dummies

Andy Cummings, Vice President and Publisher, Dummies Technology/General User

Composition Services

Gerry Fahey, Vice President of Production Services

Debbie Stailey, Director of Composition Services

Contents at a Glance

Table of Contents

Foreword

Gertrude Stein said, "A rose, is a rose, is a rose," and Jerry Lewis says, *Filmmaking For Dummies* is a kind of book, a kind of book, a kind of book that all new and old film students can learn from.

It's the brainchild of Bryan Michael Stoller, whose company is Stellar Entertainment, and from the looks of this book, he's consistent.

He began in Canada at the age of 10 and knew then that he had to do it all, and he does — writes, produces, directs, and keeps away from acting because that's Jack Nicholson country, and no one ever wants to be there.

I met Bryan on the set of a film I was making at the time called *Slapstick*. It should have been called *Helter Skelter*. . . . Never have so many been killed by one bad idea.

But this kid Bryan worked his little heart out filming behind-the-scenes footage of *Slapstick,* and if the studio had been smart, it would have released what he shot! We might have had a winner.

Although our meeting was over 20 years ago, I still recall watching one of his early films in my trailer dressing room between shots and I can remember how impressed I was. And I knew he was good. . . . And I am never wrong when *I'm jealous.* So read on, you fledglings, and see if his book can help you fly to stardom.

—Jerry Lewis
Actor, comedian, and author of *The Total Film-Maker*

Introduction

. . . .

*W*elcome to the wonderful world of filmmaking. Whether you love the escape of watching movies or the excitement, challenge, and magic of making a film yourself, this book is an informative, entertaining guide to help you realize your dream. For the beginning filmmaker, this book is your primer and reference guide to making a film. For the seasoned professional, it's a perfect refresher course (with many new ideas) before starting your next big flick.

This book is not only for the professional filmmaker, but for anyone interested in making film, whether you're an actor, a factory worker, or an office employee, and whether you're unemployed, retired, or independently wealthy. This book will inspire you to reach for your filmmaking goals — and it will be a great adventure along the way! *Filmmaking For Dummies* comes out of my filmmaking experiences — both my successes and my mistakes — and is bursting with helpful information and secret tips to assist you in making your own successful film.

In 1987, I directed an episode of *Tales from the Darkside* titled "The Bitterest Pill." The show was about a crazy inventor who created a pill that gave him total recall. The premise of the episode was that "knowledge is power." A little, innocent-looking pill allowed you to remember everything you ever saw, ever heard — right back to the day the doctor pulled you from the womb and slapped you on the behind! With *Filmmaking For Dummies,* you gain the knowledge and thus the power to be a filmmaker. Whether you're a great filmmaker depends on how you apply this knowledge. Like the pill in my *Tales from the Darkside* episode, this book will give you all the knowledge you need to get started (it's up to you to recall it) and is your prescription for filmmaking — so read it and call your distributor in the morning!

About This Book

I've written this book with almost 30 years of hands-on experience (I started young and naïve at the age of 10), and so I know everything I talk about in this book through trial and error. I can save you a lot of time, trouble, and money because I've been there before — this book helps make your first time on the set seem more like you've been there before, too.

This book contains valuable information on:

- ✔ Writing or finding a screenplay
- ✔ Raising financing for your film
- ✔ Budgeting and scheduling your film
- ✔ Hiring the right actors and crew
- ✔ Planning, shooting, and directing your film
- ✔ Putting your film together in the editing room
- ✔ Finding a distributor to get your film in front of an audience
- ✔ Entering (and maybe even winning) film festivals

The new age of filmmaking includes the advent of digital technology, so throughout this book, all creative elements apply to both film and video production. Technically, film and video are different, as I address in each particular example — but you soon realize that the similarities are beginning to beat out the differences.

Conventions Used in This Book

To help you pick out information from a page, I use the following conventions throughout the text to make elements consistent and easy to understand:

- ✔ Web addresses appear in a special font (like `www.bryanmichael stoller.com`), so you can easily pick them out.
- ✔ New terms appear in *italics* and are closely followed by an easy-to-understand definition. Movie titles and the names of TV shows also appear in italics.
- ✔ **Bold** highlights the action parts of numbered steps or keywords in bulleted lists.
- ✔ Sidebars, which look like text enclosed in a shaded gray box, consist of information that's interesting to know but not necessarily critical to your understanding of the chapter or section's topic. If you do stop to read a sidebar, you'll either gain something you'll appreciate or at the very least be entertained.

Foolish Assumptions

I assume in this book that you have some knowledge of the Internet and have access to the Web sites I list (or someone you know does). I direct you to some pretty nifty sites to get free downloads, special software deals, and fun stuff to look at. Keep in mind, however, that Web addresses can quickly change or become obsolete, so be prepared to find a few that may lead to a black hole in cyberspace.

I assume you also like to watch movies and are interested in how they're made so that you can make some of your own. I also take into account the fact that you may be a beginner with a camcorder or a seasoned professional who wants to make an independent film.

This book can't possibly cover every aspect of running a camera and putting together a film. So, if you don't know the difference between a camera's eye-piece and the lens, and which end to look through, pick up other books that are more specific to the technical aspects of filmmaking. You may also want to pick up other *For Dummies* books that complement this one, such as *Digital Video For Dummies* by Martin Doucette, *Screenwriting For Dummies* by Laura Schellhardt and John Logan, and *Breaking into Acting For Dummies* by Larry Garrison and Wallace Wang (all published by Wiley). After you start making your own films, you may need to read these books: *Stress Management For Dummies* and *High Blood Pressure For Dummies*.

How This Book Is Organized

This book is divided into six parts — from the screenplay, all the way to the distribution — and of course the ever popular Part of Tens. These six parts are each self-contained, so they help you understand the filmmaking experience, regardless of what order you read them in. If you're more interested in finding material or writing a screenplay, Part I will be of interest to you. If you want to know more about distribution before you decide to make a film, then you'll want to look at Part V first.

Part I: Filmmaking and Storytelling

This part introduces you to the world of filmmaking and the excitement behind it. You see all the different genres to choose from to help you decide which one works best for your film. This part also helps guide you to the right material, whether a short story, a news article, a true biographical story, or a completed screenplay.

Part II: Gearing Up to Make Your Film

This part shows you where to find financing for your film so that you can schedule and budget accurately. The preproduction process also includes finding the perfect location for the setting of your film, and finding the perfect crew. You audition actors and choose performers who will bring life to the characters in your screenplay. While you're gearing up for the actual shoot, you're also organizing your ideas for your shots on paper in the form of sketched images called *storyboards*.

Part III: Ready to Roll: Starting Production on Your Film

In this part, I introduce you to the magical box that captures your story on film or video — it's called the camera. In a non-technical style, I explain how the camera and lens work. You see how lighting is more a science than just pointing some lamps in a particular direction. Sound is an important element to your production, and after reading this part, you may notice your hearing has become more acute.

This part also helps you work with your actors to get the best and most believable performances in front of the camera. I also cover the multifaceted job of the director — from a technical and creative sense. Now with the new age of digital technology, anyone with a video camera can go out and make a film (with virtually no budget).

Part IV: Finishing Your Film in Post

In this part, you discover the magic of non-linear editing and how you can even possibly salvage bad scenes and make them work in postproduction. With new computer software and editing technology, you can turn your home computer into a powerful postproduction editing system — and affordably, too! In this part, you also begin working with a composer to set your film to music, enhancing the visuals with sound effects, and employing other post-production sound techniques that make your film sound great. Special visual effects don't have to be expensive, and you see how you can do many effects with the camera without exploding your budget. This stage in production is also the time to thank everyone who worked on the production by giving them the appropriate recognition in the opening or ending credit roll of your film.

Part V: Finding a Distributor for Your Film

This part deals with one of the most important aspects of the filmmaking process because, without distribution, no one will ever see your masterpiece, and your investors will never make their investment back — with no chance of a profit. You may want to read this part first so that you're aware of the commercial elements your film needs in order to get a distributor who can sell it successfully in the domestic markets (the U.S. and Canada), as well as the international territories. Along with finding the right distributor, you may also want to enter your film in film festivals to try to garner some award attention. (Film festivals can help attract a distributor if you haven't found one at this point.)

Part VI: The Part of Tens

For Dummies books are famous for The Part of Tens. Here, I share ten great tips on how to find talent for your film, along with how to raise attention through proper publicizing after your film is finished. I talk from experience about ten ways to save you time, trouble, and money — maybe even save your production. I also list the ten best magazines and newspapers to keep you informed on the entertainment industry and to help you find some great material for your film.

Icons Used in This Book

Icons (little pictures in the margins) are used throughout this book to bring attention to things that you may find helpful or important.

This icon shares tips that can save you a lot of time and trouble.

This icon is a friendly reminder of things that you don't want to forget about when making a film.

This icon makes you aware of things that can make a big difference in planning or shooting your film. In other words, follow this warning.

This icon alerts you to important words or phrases that you need to know as a filmmaker. You can walk-the-walk and talk-the-talk after these icon alerts.

This icon reveals secrets only you'll know from reading this book. These secrets will lead you to helpful filmmaking information not known by the masses. But don't tell anyone — it's a secret!

Where to Go from Here

Unlike watching a film from beginning to end, you can open this book in the middle and dive right in to directing your film. *Filmmaking For Dummies* is written in a non-linear format, meaning you can start anywhere — even go backwards — and read what you want to know in the order you want to know it. This means that you can start on any chapter in this book and move around from chapter to chapter in no particular order — and still understand how to make a film.

Part I
Filmmaking and Storytelling

The 5th Wave   By Rich Tennant

©RICHTENNANT

WASH

"It's Mr. Tarzan. He's got another screenplay. It's sort of a *Breakfast at Tiffanys* meets *The Philadelphia Story* meets *When Animals Attack.*"

In this part . . .

You're reading this book because either you want to be a movie mogul or you already are one. You've chosen an exciting career or hobby and this part puts the world of filmmaking into perspective for you and sets you on track for a cinematic adventure.

In this part, I introduce you to the different film genres so you can decide what kind of story you want to share with an audience. I also guide you through a crash course on the process of writing an original screenplay — or finding a commercial script and getting the rights to produce it.

Chapter 1

So You Want to Be a Filmmaker

In This Chapter

▶ Recognizing how independent films differ from studio pictures

▶ Getting an overview of the filmmaking process

*F*ilm is a powerful medium. With the right script under your arm and a staff of eager team players, you're about to begin an exciting ride. The single most important thing that goes into making a successful filmmaker is the passion to tell a story. And the best way to tell your stories is with pictures. Filmmaking is visual storytelling in the form of shots that make up scenes and scenes that eventually make up a complete film.

You have the power to affect people's emotions, make them see things differently, help them discover new ideas, or just create an escape for them. In a darkened theater, you have an audience's undivided attention. They're yours — entertain them, move them, make them laugh, make them cry. You can't find a more powerful medium to express yourself.

As a filmmaker, you have to decide what you enjoy doing most. Do you like putting things together and making them happen? Then you'd probably make a great producer. Do you like things just a certain way, can you envision things as they should be, and do you love working with people? Then your calling may be directing. Or do you love telling stories, and are you always jotting down great ideas that come to you? If so, then writing screenplays may be for you. You can be referred to as a "triple-threat" in filmmaking if you write, produce, and direct. Having some understanding of what the other people on your crew do — like the cinematographer, the producer, the editor, the dolly grip, and the prop or wardrobe person — is important. Understanding what each person on your team does will improve your working relationship with them and, in the end, make a better film.

Independents Day versus the Hollywood Way

An independent film is often a low-budget film (costing anywhere from $5,000 to $1 million) because the filmmaker has to raise money to make the film on his or her own and not be dependent on a studio for the financing. Many films circulating the film-festival circuit are independent films, produced independently of the studios. These films are little gems that didn't have a string of studio executives sending script notes to the filmmaker and ruining the film before anyone even set foot on the set. If a major film studio puts up the money for a film, the studio — not the filmmaker — ultimately ends up calling the shots.

You can find both advantages and disadvantages to making a studio picture or an independent film. On an independent production, your film ends up on the screen the way you envisioned it, but you don't have much of a budget. A studio picture has larger financial backing and can afford to pay the astronomical salaries that actors demand, as well as pay for seamless special effects and longer shooting schedules (the studio has more money to spend, allowing you to spend more days filming to get the best footage), but the film ends up the way the studio envisions it — and in the most commercial way. The studio looks at dollars first and creativity second. They look at the market statistically. What are the demographics for this type of film? Who's starring in it? Will it make a good profit? Many independent filmmakers discover that, although having and making money is nice, being independent allows them to tell a story in the most creative way.

However, an independent film doesn't always have to be a low-budget or no-budget film. George Lucas is the ultimate independent filmmaker. He's independent of the studios and makes his own decisions on his films without the politics or red tape of a studio looking over his shoulder. *Star Wars* may not seem like an independent film, but that's exactly what it is — even though you may have difficulty seeing yourself as one of Lucas's peers.

Developing Your Sense of Story

Without a great story, you can't possibly end up with a great film. Finding the right story makes all the difference, which means that choosing the right material is more important than anything else. Great film careers have been built on making the right decisions about a story more than having the right talent and skills.

JARGON ALERT

Digital filmmaking: The future of making films

Today, you can shoot your film in several different formats. You can choose *analog* video or *digital* video or use a completely different format by shooting with a traditional film camera using super-8 or 16mm film, or the choice of studio productions, 35mm motion-picture film stock.

In this age of digital technology, almost anyone with a computer and video camera can make a film. You can purchase (for around $3,500) or rent a 24-frame progressive digital camcorder (like the Panasonic AG-DVX-100 — see Chapter 10 for more on cameras) that emulates the look of motion picture film, without incurring the cost of expensive film stock and an expensive motion-picture camera.

If you can't afford one of these digital cameras, you can purchase computer software that takes a harsh video image shot with an inexpensive home camcorder and softens it to look more like it was shot with a motion-picture film camera. Many new computers come preloaded with free editing software. In Chapter 16, I give you tips on starting your very own digital-editing studio. You can also find out more information on the world of digital filmmaking in *Digital*

Video For Dummies by Martin Doucette (published by Wiley). You can uncover more camera information in Chapter 10.

High Definition (HD) TV is a new technology that takes the video image one step farther. The picture is much sharper, richer, and closer to what the human eye sees as opposed to what the video camera shows you. Watching HD video is like looking through a window — the picture seems to breathe. The new HD digital cinema cameras (the ones used by George Lucas) combine HD technology with the 24-frame progressive technology to emulate a unique film-like picture quality in an electronic environment, without the use of physical film. Unfortunately, HD digital is still expensive (much more costly than using a regular digital camcorder); the cameras are extremely expensive to purchase, and daily or weekly rental rates are usually beyond what the independent filmmaker can afford. HD also requires special monitors and viewing equipment that processes the high resolution in this new technology, making this medium too complicated and expensive to be part of the independent filmmaker's equipment.

So where do you find the good ideas to turn into films? An idea starts in your head like a tiny seed, and then it sprouts and begins to grow, eventually blossoming into an original screenplay. Don't have that tiny seed of an idea just yet? Turn to Chapter 3, where you develop strategies for finding ideas or taking a story or book and turning it into a screenplay. In that chapter, I show you how to *option* (have temporary ownership of) existing material, whether it's someone's personal story or a novel that's already been published.

REMEMBER

You have a story in you. If something is a curiosity, is constantly on your mind, or is troubling you, write about it. See Chapter 3 for tips on turning your idea into a feature-length script (at least 90 pages). You'll find yourself answering many of your own questions — you may even solve your problem. Best of all, you could very well end up with a screenplay.

Surfing sites for filmmakers

You can find a virtually unlimited number of Web sites dealing with filmmaking and independent films. Becoming a filmmaker includes plugging yourself into informative outlets that help you be more aware of the filmmaker's world. Here I list six sites that may be helpful to you as a low-budget filmmaker:

✔ **The Internet Movie Database** (www.imdb.com) is a valuable information source used by Hollywood executives. It lists the credits of film and TV professionals and anyone who has made any type of mark in the entertainment industry. It's helpful for doing research or a background check on an actor or filmmaker.

✔ **The Independent Feature Project** (www.ifp.org) is an effective way to get connected right away to the world of independent filmmaking.

✔ **In Hollywood** (www.inhollywood.com) is a research site updated weekly that offers current information on film projects.

✔ **The Association of Independent Video and Filmmakers** (www.aivf.org) is an organization that (as the name suggests) supports independent filmmakers. At the Web site, you can find subscription information to *The Independent* (a magazine geared toward the independent filmmaker), discounts on film-related books, festival updates, crew classified ads, and other membership perks.

✔ **IndieTalk** (www.indietalk.com) is a discussion forum for filmmakers. Here you can post and read messages about screenwriting, finding distribution, financing, and lots of other topics. It's a great site for communicating with other independent filmmakers.

✔ **Amazon.com** (www.amazon.com), an Internet store where you can purchase movies and books, has a plethora of information for the independent filmmaker, from films available for sale on VHS and DVD to cross-referencing actors, directors, producers, and all related movie memorabilia.

Financing Your Film: Where's the Money?

After you've turned your idea into a completed screenplay, you can't get it made (produced into a film) unless you have the financing. In Chapter 5, I give you some great tips on how to find investors and how to put together a *prospectus* to attract them to fund your film. You also find out about other money-saving ideas like bartering and product placement.

In Chapter 5, I even show you how to set up your own Web site to help raise awareness for your film, attract investors, and eventually serve as a promotional site for your completed film. Raising money isn't as difficult as it sounds if you have a great story and an organized business plan. You can find investors who are looking to put their money into a film for the excitement of being involved with a film and/or the possibility of making a profit. Even friends and family are potential investors for your film — especially if your budget is in the low-numbers range.

On a Budget: Scheduling Your Shoot

Budgeting your film is a delicate process. Oftentimes, you budget your film first (this is usually the case with independent low-budget films) by breaking down elements into categories — such as crew, props, equipment, and so on — the total amount you have to spend. Your costs will be determined by how long you'll need to shoot your film (scheduling will determine how many shoot days you'll have), because the length of your shoot will tell you how long you need to have people on salary, how long you'll need to rent equipment and locations, and so on.

When you know you can only afford to pay salaries for a three-week shoot, you then have to schedule your film so that it can be shot in three weeks. You schedule your film's shoot by breaking down the script into separate elements (see Chapter 4) and deciding how many scenes and shots you can shoot each day, so that everything is completed in the three weeks you have to work with. An independent filmmaker doesn't usually have the luxury of scheduling the film first (breaking it down into how many days it will take to shoot) and then seeing how much it will cost. You also should have a budget and even a possible schedule as ammunition to show a potential investor.

Planning Your Shoot, Shooting Your Plan

Planning your film includes envisioning your shots through storyboarding, by sketching out rough diagrams of what your shots and angles will look like (see Chapter 9). You can storyboard your films even if you don't consider yourself an artist. Draw stick characters or use storyboard software, like Storyboard Quick or the 3-D Storyboard Lite, which gives you a cast of characters along with a library of props and locations.

You also need to plan where you'll shoot your film. You research where you're going to film much like planning a trip — then make all the appropriate arrangements like figuring out how you're going to get there and the type of accommodations if it's out of town. Regardless of where you're shooting, you'll need to sign an agreement with the location owner to make sure you have it reserved for your shoot dates. Also, you'll have to choose whether to film at a real location, on a sound stage, or in a virtual location that you conjure up inside your computer.

Film feeling

Audiences experience distinct psychological effects when looking at film or video. Film tends to have a nostalgic feeling, like you're watching something that has already happened. Video elicits the feeling that it's happening right now — unfolding before your eyes, like the news.

Many people love old movies, not just because of the great storytelling, but because of the sentimental feeling they get, especially with old black-and-white films or even the color films of the 1960s. Steven Spielberg made *Schindler's List* in black and white to help convey both the film as a past event and the dreariness of the war. The medium on which you set your story — whether it be actual film celluloid on which the images are developed, videotape, or digital with a film-style look — has a specific feel and effect on your audience.

Hiring Your Cast and Crewing Up

Your film crew becomes your extended family (although maybe a dysfunctional one). You spend many days and nights together — through good and bad times — so hiring people who are passionate about your project and willing to put their all into it is important. You may have to defer salary to your crew if you're working on a tight budget. (Find out how to do that and more in Chapter 7.)

Acting is not as difficult as you may think. People are born natural actors and play many parts on the stage of life. Everyone is constantly in front of an audience — or performing monologues when alone. In Chapter 8, I lead you step by step through the process of finding a great cast to bring your screenplay to life. I also fill you in on acting secrets so that you can direct your actors and get the best performances.

Filming in the Right Direction

Making a film requires special equipment, like *cranes* (tall apparatuses on which you place the camera for high shots), *dollies* (which are like giant skateboards that you put the camera on for movement), camera systems, and so on. Without the proper lighting, you'll leave your actors in the dark — literally. Lighting can set a mood and enhance the entire look of your film.

In addition to seeing your actors, you need to be able to hear them as well. This is where the art of sound comes in. Microphones need to be placed close enough to the actor to get a good sound recording, but not too close as to have the microphone creep into the shot. The skill of recording great sound comes from the production sound mixer.

If you're taking on the task of directing, you'll become a figurehead to your actors and crew. You'll need to know how to give your actors direction and what it takes to bring the best performance out of them.

In terms of telling your story visually, you'll need to understand a little about the camera. Much like driving a car, you don't need to understand how it works, but you need to know how to drive it (your cinematographer should be the expert with the camera and its internal operations). The camera is a magical box that will capture images so that you can effectively and visually tell your story to the world.

Seeing the light

The eye of the camera needs adequate light to "see" a proper image — whether it be appropriate exposure for a film camera, or enough light to get a proper light reading for a video camera. Chapter 11 gives you the lowdown on lighting. Lighting can be very powerful and can affect the mood and tone of every scene in your film. A great cinematographer combined with an efficient gaffer (see Chapter 7) will ensure that your film has a great look.

Being heard and scene

Production sound is extremely important because your actors must be heard correctly. Your sound mixer, who's in charge of primarily recording your actors' dialogue on set, needs to know the right microphones and sound-mixing equipment to use, as you see in Chapter 12.

Actors taking your direction

The director's job is to help the actors create believable performances in front of the camera that lure the audience into your story and make them care about your characters. Directing also involves guiding your actors to move effectively within the confines of the camera frame. Chapter 13 guides you in the right direction with some great secrets on how to warm up your actors and prepare them to give their best on the set.

Threatening film

Chris Gore runs an e-mail newsletter called *Film Threat Magazine.* If you're a filmmaker or want to be a filmmaker, you need to be on this mailing list. You'll find interesting reading including information on film festivals, box office updates, and brutally honest movie reviews, along with actor and filmmaker interviews. Get more information at www.filmthreat.com.

Shooting through the camera

Directing the camera requires some technical knowledge of how the camera works and what each lens and filter does, which I explain in Chapter 10. Chapter 14 addresses how to frame your shots and when to move the camera. In that chapter, you also discover the skills that make up a successful director and how to run a smooth, organized set.

Cut It Out!: Editing Your Film

Editing your film gives you a chance to step back and look at the sequence of events and all the available shot angles in order to shape and mold them into the most effective production. You can even repair a bad film (or at least make it better) during the editing process. Editing is the time when you'll really see your film coming together. It's a fascinating phase of filmmaking and can be very rewarding as you watch your baby come together piece by piece.

Nonlinear editing software is now available for virtually any computer (starting at $50), and it allows you to edit anything from a home movie to a professional theatrical-length piece (90 to 120 minutes). The technology of nonlinear editing allows you to cut your shots together in virtually any order. You can easily see different variations of cutting different shots together, rearrange them, and move or delete in between scenes in a concise and easy-to-understand manner. Chapter 15 tells you what the new digital technology makes available to you for editing your film on your desktop.

Listening to your film

At the editing stage, you add and create the audio, dialogue, sound effects, and music as you see and "hear" in Chapter 16. Titles and credits are important, too, and I discuss them in Chapter 18.

Simulating film with software

If you can't afford to shoot your movie on film, you can use a technology by FilmLook (www.filmlook.com). FilmLook runs your video footage through special processors, electronic settings, and so on, and creates the effect that your image was shot on film.

Software programs can also make your video footage look more like film. These programs emulate grain, softness, subtle flutter, and so on. Bullet software available at www.redgiantsoftware.com can convert your harsh video footage to look like it was shot on film. The video-to-film process converts 30-frame video to a 24-frame pulldown, adding elements to create the illusion that your images were photographed on film as opposed to shot on video.

Using software that makes your video footage look like film takes time for the computer to process. Depending on what software you use, the processing time could take hours or days just to turn video footage into something that looks more like film. With a 24-frame progressive video camera, you get the film image immediately as you shoot. (See Chapter 10 for more information on 24-frame progressive video.)

Distributing Your Film and Finding an Audience

The final, and probably most important, stage of making a film is distribution. Without the proper distribution, your film may sit on a shelf and never be experienced by an audience. Successful distribution can make the difference between your film making $10 (the ticket your mother buys) or $100 million at the box office. *The Blair Witch Project* may never have generated a dime if it hadn't been discovered at the Sundance Film Festival by Artisan Entertainment.

There's no business like ShowBiz Expo

ShowBiz Expo is one of my favorite conventions. Four times a year, Mind Ventures offers regional conventions in Miami, Chicago, Los Angeles, and New York. Thousands of people flock to the expo to schmooze with fellow filmmakers, network, and see the latest developments in equipment technology (and in some cases, even experiment with the technology, hands-on). It's like a giant toy store for filmmakers. The convention runs for three days, and you can get a free pass (worth $50) by pre-registering at the expo Web site (www.showbizexpo.com).

Even mediocre films have done well commercially because of successful distribution tactics. And great films have flopped at the box office because the distributor didn't carry out a successful distribution plan.

Here are several suggestions on how to find a distributor for your film:

- ✔ Send out your screenplay before shooting your film and see if you can get distribution interest based on the script.

- ✔ Send out screening cassettes of your completed film to distributors with the potential that one will acquire your film and distribute it.

- ✔ Enter your finished film in film festivals like the Sundance Film Festival (see Chapter 20) and let a distributor discover *you*.

- ✔ Have a premiere screening for your film and invite distributors and industry people to the big event.

- ✔ Set up a publicity stunt (see Chapter 22) to attract the attention of a distributor.

Check out Chapter 19 for more tips and secrets to finding a distributor.

Chapter 2

Genres in General

*I*n the mood for a quiet romantic comedy or an action-packed adventure? Feel like a good scare with a suspense or horror movie? How about a sci-fi epic to take you to new worlds? Next time you walk into a video store, think about what genre interests you — not only to watch, but also what film genre you want to make.

In this chapter, I introduce you to all the various genres of film and tell you which ones are the most popular at the box office — and which ones are best to avoid when deciding to shoot your film. Understanding the various genres and what characteristics make up each one helps you decide on the best story for you as a filmmaker to produce.

Most films combine several genres, as you can see from the examples given in this chapter. If you want to make people laugh and feel good, obviously a comedy is the way to go. If you want the audience to escape from everyday troubles and tribulations, a magical fantasy makes a great getaway. If you just want to excite your audience and take them on a whirlwind ride, then produce an action picture that plays like a never-ending roller coaster. Pick a genre that you enjoy watching.

In this chapter, I also introduce you to the *media categories* of filmmaking, from commercials, music videos, shorts, and industrials to documentaries and feature-length films, and I address the benefits of each. Not everyone can start out successfully by making feature films; other categories give you a chance to get your feet wet before you make the leap to full-length features.

Exploring Film Genres

A *genre* is a category that contains a particular style or form of content. In filmmaking, each genre has its own set of rules and characteristics.

John Truby, a prominent screenwriting consultant, puts out writers' software called Blockbuster. You can also purchase additional software packages for Blockbuster that guide you through specific tips and examples that help make up each separate genre (www.truby.com).

The following are commonly recognized genres:

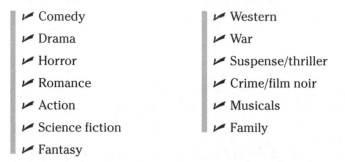

- ✔ Comedy
- ✔ Drama
- ✔ Horror
- ✔ Romance
- ✔ Action
- ✔ Science fiction
- ✔ Fantasy
- ✔ Western
- ✔ War
- ✔ Suspense/thriller
- ✔ Crime/film noir
- ✔ Musicals
- ✔ Family

The time period of your story is not a genre but a setting that can fit with virtually any genre. A *period piece* is a story set in the days of yesterday (a story set in the future is considered fantasy or science fiction). *Road to Perdition,* for example, is film noir but also a period piece. *The Green Mile* (in the fantasy, horror, and suspense genres) is a period piece, too, as is *Catch Me If You Can.* Unless you're doing a studio-financed picture with a healthy budget, avoid period pieces, period. They require special art direction, wardrobe, and props dealing with that specific time period.

Genres can also be crossed together to create a variation in genres. A romance can be crossed with a comedy to become a romantic comedy, like *You've Got Mail.* A comedy crossed with a crime genre gives you *Who Framed Roger Rabbit* (combining animation *techniques*). *Minority Report* is a science-fiction/suspense/thriller crime drama.

Booking comic heroes

From the colorful pages of comic books, super-heroes have claimed their own type of story. Not traditionally classified as a genre, the comic-book-hero film can be classified as an adaptation from comic book to film. These stories usually fall into the fantasy and science-fiction genres, and almost always the action genre as well. That's why the toy replicas you buy of your favorite superheroes are called *action figures.*

The Incredible Hulk is classified as science fiction because the film explains how Dr. David Banner becomes the Hulk (as extraordinary as it may be). *Batman* is more of a fantasy because his history doesn't include a scientific explanation. Other popular comic-book heroes successfully pulled from the pages of comics and placed on the silver screen include *Spiderman, Superman, X-Men,* and *Daredevil.*

Making 'em laugh with comedy

Comedy can be dry humor, slapstick, or just plain silly fun. Comedy works with other genres, including romance, science fiction, fantasy, Western, and even drama. Many comedies branch out into a series of films based on the success of the original concept, such as *Airplane, The Naked Gun,* and the *Austin Powers* films. Here are some other comedies to laugh about:

- ✔ *Home Alone*
- ✔ *There's Something about Mary*
- ✔ *Tootsie*
- ✔ *Scary Movie*

Scary Movie is a perfect example of a film *parody* — a subgenre that pokes fun at other movies. My parody film *Miss Cast Away* crosses *Cast Away* with *Miss Congeniality* — what happens when a planeload of beauty contestants crashland on a deserted island? Other popular parodies include *Loaded Weapon* (spoofing *Lethal Weapon* movies), and many of Mel Brooks's movies including *Young Frankenstein, Blazing Saddles* (parodying Westerns), and *High Anxiety* (which parodied Hitchcock's *Vertigo*).

Dark subject matter mixed with comedy is known as *black comedy.* A black comedy can include dark elements combining pathos, pain, sickness, and death with comedic undertones. Often, a black comedy has twisted humor in the characters and situations, as exemplified in films like *Fargo, Adaptation,* and *About Schmidt.*

Comedy is difficult for some filmmakers to conceptualize and comes naturally to others. Comedy requires proper structure, comedic timing, gimmicks, and unique setup and situations. Choose this genre only if comedy is something that is natural for you. You don't want the audience laughing *at* you; you want them laughing *with* you.

If your film is a comedy, make sure that you set it up as one so the audience knows right away that it's okay to laugh. Don't wait until the film has rolled for five or ten minutes before introducing a comic gag or a humorous piece.

Getting dramatic about it

Drama is one of the broadest genres. A dramatic story has serious issues that usually deal with a character's struggle that could put him or her into a life-or-death situation. Drama is often combined with other genres, except for outright comedy (then it becomes a *dramedy,* covered later in this section). Drama can work well with the horror, crime, thriller, science fiction, Western, and even fantasy genres. Many dramas successfully include romance, such as *Titanic* and *A Beautiful Mind.* Other dramatic films include

- ✔ *The American President*
- ✔ *Gangs of New York*
- ✔ *The Hours*
- ✔ *Schindler's List*

Dramedy is a phrase coined for a drama mixed with elements of comedy. Dramedy is different from black comedy in that it is much lighter, and the characters are more logical in their actions. The movie (and the TV show) *The Odd Couple* made for a great dramedy by contrasting two individuals with opposite personalities. *MASH* also made for a great dramedy with the underlying story of war combined with characters who kept their sense of humor to survive.

Even in times of tragedy, dramas need humor. No audience would sit through a drama and come out of the theater unscathed unless the film provided some comic relief. Audiences want that relief; they need to breathe between the tragic moments. The movie *Rainman* had a touch of comic relief in Dustin Hoffman's character, Raymond; the comic relief broke the tension at times when the story became too serious.

Nail-biting through horror films

Alfred Hitchcock pulled out all the stops in horror with his film *Psycho.* Steven Spielberg scared people out of the water for years with *Jaws.* M. Night Shamaylan successfully spooked audiences in *The Sixth Sense.* Audiences love being terrified and on the edge of their seats — in the safety of a movie theater. Horror uses the element of shock value that works by surprising the audience. When I was a kid, I hid under my little sister Nancy's bed and waited until she was tucked in for the night; then I jumped out and scared her — she was horrified. Here are a few titles that'll bring some chills to your bones:

- ✔ *The Exorcist*
- ✔ *Halloween*
- ✔ *Scream*
- ✔ *The Shining*

A *slasher* film is a subcategory of the horror genre that often includes shots showing the killer's point of view, vulnerable teenage girls (usually virgins at the beginning of the picture who get murdered as soon as they lose their virginity), and very naïve victims. Slasher films also tend to be very graphic. *Friday the Thirteenth* is a great example of a slasher film.

Horror films do well overseas, mainly because of the graphic images that translate visually in any language. Many domestic audiences like the sight of blood, too, as long as it's not their own.

Less is more when it comes to shooting horror films. The robot shark that kept breaking down during production of the film *Jaws* worked to Steven Spielberg's advantage, because the less we saw of the shark, the more suspenseful and frightening the threat became.

Getting romantic

For the sensitive (myself included), a good romance makes for a great date movie and fills the bill when you're in the mood to be romanced. I especially like fantasy romances, like *Ghost, Somewhere in Time,* and *Lady Hawk.* Romance stories rely on character development and rarely on fancy special effects. The story is the star. Romance mixes well with comedy, too, as in *When Harry Met Sally* and *My Big Fat Greek Wedding.* You'll be swept away by these titles:

- ✔ *An Affair to Remember*
- ✔ *The Bridges of Madison County*
- ✔ *Moonstruck*
- ✔ *Sleepless in Seattle*

There's always an audience for a good romance. If you cry at the movies when the guy finally gets the girl, that means you're sensitive, and a romance may be the perfect genre for you to undertake.

Getting physical: No talk and all action

Action movies like *Indiana Jones and the Temple of Doom* are a treat for the eyes with the energy of a sporting event. With a good action picture, you can turn off the sound and enjoy the visuals without having to follow the dialogue. Audiences with a competitive nature enjoy action films with a lot of physical conflict. Action-packed examples include

> ✔ *Die Hard*
>
> ✔ *The Matrix*
>
> ✔ *Mission Impossible*
>
> ✔ *Speed*

Action does extremely well internationally. Everyone likes a good action piece, especially when it doesn't rely on a detailed story with heavy dialogue that can get lost in translation.

Shooting action scenes can be dangerous. Always have a trained stunt coordinator and a pyrotechnician on set if your film involves any explosions or gunfire.

Separating fact from (science) fiction

Audiences appreciate an escape and the opportunity to ask, "What if . . . ?" So science fiction has always been popular at the box office. If a film's subject stems from a scientific explanation (even if it's a rather fantastic explanation), it falls into this genre. Science fiction also includes interplanetary worlds with aliens and monsters and plays on the idea that we may not be alone in the universe. Here are some titles that are considered science fiction, even though you probably didn't study them in science class:

> ✔ *Close Encounters of the Third Kind*
>
> ✔ *Jurassic Park*
>
> ✔ *Men in Black*
>
> ✔ *Star Wars*

Science fiction stories can be very expensive to produce and are normally out of reach for a low-budget independent film. However, computer-generated creatures and effects are making it easier.

Indulging your fantasy

The fantasy genre combines fantasy worlds and magical elements that could never exist in today's world (this is what separates this genre from science fiction). Comic-book characters like Superman in the fictional city of Metropolis are part of the fantasy genre (see the sidebar "Booking comic heroes" for more on movies made about comic-book characters). For a fantastical adventure, take a look at these titles:

> ✔ *Ghost*
>
> ✔ *Harry Potter: The Chamber of Secrets*
>
> ✔ *It's a Wonderful Life*
>
> ✔ *Lord of the Rings*

Making a film in the fantasy genre can be expensive if you have to create worlds that don't exist. Some effects (with some ingenuity) can be done inexpensively, as I show you in Chapter 17.

A fantasy story doesn't always require special effects. In *It's a Wonderful Life,* the story sets up a fantastical situation without having to weigh down the visuals with special effects.

Go West, young man: Westerns

Westerns were popular years ago but seem to have gone West over the years. Clint Eastwood can still make a Western that audiences will flock to see, though, and John Wayne Westerns will always be popular on TV, especially late at night and on rainy Sunday afternoons. George Lucas updated the Western and put it in outer space with his *Star Wars* franchise. Find a ghost town, some horses, and a couple of cowboy hats, grab a sarsaparilla, and you've got yourself a Western like

> ✔ *The Good, the Bad, and the Ugly*
>
> ✔ *The Magnificent Seven*
>
> ✔ *Unforgiven*
>
> ✔ *The Wild Bunch*

A Western may be inexpensive to shoot if you have a couple of horses and a ghost town at your disposal, but Westerns aren't the most commercial of film genres today and are considered more of a risk. And for that reason, many distributors steer away from acquiring them.

Going to war

War movies have always been popular. It's the good team versus the bad team — with lots of gunfire and explosions (which can be expensive for an independent filmmaker). These films do well internationally as well as at home. War is a global theme; no matter what country or language, everyone can relate and get caught up in a good war movie.

War movies are categorized as action films in video stores. Mel Gibson's films *We Were Solders* and *Braveheart* are classified under the war/action genre. Here are some other films worth fighting for:

- ✔ *Black Hawk Down*
- ✔ *Glory*
- ✔ *Saving Private Ryan*
- ✔ *Apocalypse Now*

War films seem to do better at the box office when the world is not dealing with a war or with pending war issues. When there's talk of war, the studios tend to oversaturate the market, which makes the films less successful at the box office. The film becomes too close to reality, and people just don't need more of what's going on in the real world.

Thrilling audiences with suspense

Suspense thrillers keep you on the edge of your seat. A good suspense film is like a ball rolling downhill, picking up speed — the audience doesn't know where and when it's going to stop. Alfred Hitchcock was the master of suspense with such films as *North by Northwest*. Horror and crime films incorporate the suspense genre effectively as well. A suspense/thriller can also mix in science fiction, as in *Signs* and *Minority Report*. Other titles that'll keep you in suspense include

- ✔ *Fatal Attraction*
- ✔ *Rear Window*
- ✔ *The Fugitive*
- ✔ *Dial M for Murder*

A good suspense thriller relies on a great script. You don't need to rely on special effects or even fast-paced action to have a good suspense thriller. This genre can be done on a low budget — you just need to intrigue your audience with a story that they love to see unfold.

Stealing the audience's attention: Crime pays

Audiences have always been intrigued by police dramas, detective tales, and mobster stories because an audience likes to piece the clues together and doesn't want to know all the answers right away. Many crime dramas fall into a subgenre known as *film noir* (which conjures up images of darkness and shadows in the 1940s). The film *Dick Tracy* is a prime example of the crime genre and film noir. *Batman* is a science-fiction comic-book action story in the film-noir style. Other titles include

- *China Town*
- *The Godfather*
- *The Untouchables*
- *Road to Perdition*

The independent filmmaker on a limited budget should avoid this genre, especially if it's a film-noir period piece. Crime genres usually contain visual elements that can be expensive for a small film. Guns, explosions, expensive wardrobe, and blood effects (which ruin the expensive wardrobe) can all contribute to a higher-cost production.

Moving musicals

A musical film is like a real stage show combined with the magic of moviemaking — and without the intermission. Musicals seem to be making a comeback, with *Moulin Rouge* and the Academy Award–winning *Chicago* earning high praise and doing well at the box office. Classic musicals include *The Sound of Music, My Fair Lady,* and *The Wizard of Oz* (which is also a great film in the family genre). Many of Disney's animated films, like *Beauty and the Beast,* are also considered musicals. Here are some other musicals that will have you shouting, "Bravo!":

- *A Chorus Line*
- *Grease*
- *Oliver!*
- *West Side Story*

Film soundtracks are big business. Sometimes the soundtrack does better financially than the film from which it came. Eminem broke records with his soundtrack from the film *8 Mile.* Selecting the right music for your film, including original songs, can make your film sing. Check out Chapter 16 for more information on movie music, songs, and soundtracks.

Keeping kids in mind: Family films

A family picture often contains positive family values that both children and adults can enjoy. Family films encompass many genres, except for war, crime, and graphic horror. The *Harry Potter* films are classified as family entertainment but also fall into the fantasy genre. Jim Henson's Muppet films are examples of the family genre at its best. Other great movies to watch with your family include

- *Monsters, Inc.*
- *Beauty and the Beast*
- *Beethoven*
- *The Wizard of Oz*

The family genre lends itself well to the technical category of cartoon animation. Animation is a style that young people immediately accept as friendly, safe, and inviting.

Categorizing Your Genres

Your production not only is part of a particular genre or combination of genres, but also falls under one of the following media categories:

- Feature film
- Documentary
- Short film
- Television program (sitcom, drama, and so on)
- TV commercial
- Public service announcement (PSA)
- Music video
- Industrial

Featuring films

Most filmmakers dream of making a feature film that will be projected in a movie theater to a captive audience. If you're planning on theatrical distribution for your film (see Chapter 19), you may want to shoot on 16mm or 35mm motion-picture stock. However, you can shoot your film with the new 24p digital video cameras, but you'll have to blow up the footage to a 35mm print later, which can be quite expensive. The hardest thing about making a feature film is that it has to be feature-film length (meaning at least 90 minutes long). Also be prepared to spend a lot more time making a feature film than you would if you were making a TV commercial, short film, or documentary.

Documenting documentaries

Documentaries are based on factual people and events, as opposed to the fictional characters and stories used in feature filmmaking. In rare situations, a documentary may receive a theatrical release, such as *Roger and Me* and *Bowling for Columbine* by filmmaker Michael Moore. The feature documentary *The Kid Stays in the Picture,* based on Robert Evans's autobiography, received rave reviews from many film critics.

If a documentary puts a fictional, humorous spin on its subjects, it can be categorized as a *mockumentary,* like *This Is Spinal Tap* and *Best in Show.* I did a mockumentary called *Hollywood Goes to Las Vegas* about a filmmaker (I hired myself) who wants to meet Sandra Bullock at a film convention and who encounters Russell Crowe, George Carlin, Haley Joel Osment, and John Travolta along the way.

Shooting short films: Keep it brief!

Producing a short film is a good way to get your foot in the door. I've made over 50 short films called *Undershorts* that have appeared on *TV's Bloopers and Practical Jokes* with Dick Clark and Ed McMahon and *Foul-ups, Bleeps, and Blunders* with Don Rickles and Steve Lawrence. You can check out my *Undershorts* at www.bryanmichaelstoller.com.

Short films lend themselves well to the new technology of streaming over the Internet. They're short enough in length — usually one to four minutes — and can be quickly streamed or downloaded for immediate viewing. One of my short parody films, *The Linda Blair Witch Project,* can be streamed on the Internet at http://countingdown.com/theater/short_films/detail/ 316272/. You can submit your own short film to CountingDown.com for consideration.

Shorts can be utilized as interstitials on television. *Interstitials* are short films that fill in the gaps between regular programming — usually on cable channels that don't run commercials. My comedy shorts have appeared as interstitials on HBO and various other pay and cable channels.

Animating animation

Animation is a technique that works with most genres (and combinations of genres), especially family films. Often, though, animation is more fitting for comedy or light humor. Fantasy and science fiction stories are also good candidates for animation, because drawing fantastic worlds or outer-space environments is easier (and cheaper) than actually creating them in a convincing setting. Filmmakers have the following animation techniques to choose from:

✔ **Traditional cel animation:** Disney's films in this style, from *Snow White and the Seven Dwarfs* to *Lilo & Stitch,* are popular. Individual drawings (up to 24 images for 24 frames a second) are inked onto clear acetate cels and photographed against painted backgrounds. Animated flipbooks use the same principles as cel animation.

✔ **Stop-motion animation:** Gumby and Pokey are two of my favorite stop-motion characters (see the following figure). I started my filmmaking career emulating Gumby movies on super-8 film when I was 10 years old. *Chicken Run* is a stop-motion feature film that utilizes clay characters. The clay models are moved slightly into different positions by an animator in between single frames taken by the motion-picture camera. Stop motion is a fairly inexpensive technique and a good way to learn about animation.

✔ **Computer animation:** Computer animation has replaced the popular three-dimensional stop-motion techniques used in the past years. Successful computer-generated image (CGI) films include *Shrek, Toy Story, Ice Age,* and *Monsters, Inc.*

✔ **Flash animation:** Flash animation is a new technique that utilizes limited animation over the Internet. This inexpensive animation has a staccato and jerky motion to it and often has simplified drawings with thicker lines (see the following figure). It's an inexpensive and fun way to animate a short film and have it viewed by a large audience via the Internet.

Check out `http://looneytunes.warnerbros.com/web/all_new_toons/index.jsp?ID=lt_unplained_07&fromtout=homepage_a` to see a great Looney Tunes flash cartoon in action.

Arthur Clokey

Directing television programs

Breaking into producing or directing television shows is a lot harder than making an independent feature film. With television, you have network executives and a lot of red tape to deal with.

Directing commercials

Many big-time feature directors have come from a commercial background, such as Michael Bay, who directed *Bad Boys, Armageddon,* and *Pearl Harbor.* A 30-second commercial is quick to produce, and the pay can be very lucrative. When I was 16, I was producing, directing, and writing several TV commercials a month out of my basement studio. Check with the TV stations and advertising agencies in your city to see whether you can produce some local commercials for them.

Minding your PSAs: Public service announcements

TV networks have an obligation to air *public service announcements,* also referred to as *PSAs,* for campaigns dealing with health and safety issues. PSAs include antismoking and antidrug commercials, don't-drink-and-drive campaigns, and environmental messages. The FCC requires TV stations to run public service announcements that are usually commissioned by various government agencies. Try making an inexpensive PSA on a subject that you're passionate about — this is your chance to make a statement. Shoot it with a video camcorder. If it's well made, your local TV station may air it.

Feel like dancing?: Music videos

Music videos are another great way to break into filmmaking. Find a local band and offer to shoot their first music video. Music videos can be shot inexpensively and are a fun way to experiment and play with visuals — and they're a great way to tell a story without dialogue.

Industrials: Industrial strength

An *industrial* is usually a film commissioned by a corporation showing how its products are manufactured. Industrial films can also be shot as training films for employees to find out more about the company and the products they represent. Industrials are often very technical and instructional in nature. Check out local corporations in your area to see whether they may be interested in having you produce an industrial video for them.

Chapter 3

Pining For, Penning, and Pitching a Great Story

*I*n order to make a film, you must first find an interesting *screenplay* (a properly formatted manuscript that follows industry guidelines), or at least a great story idea. And where do screenplays come from, you ask? Well, anywhere actually. You can put out feelers in the industry to let writers know you're in the market for a screenplay, or you can write one of your own. You can find fascinating articles in your local newspaper, funny stories in magazines, and intriguing biographies that are just begging to be made into screenplays.

In this chapter, I show you the secrets to structuring the elements of your screenplay and developing characters that your audience will care about. You also see how easy it is to acquire stories or even the rights to a published book, if that's the route you want to take. Finally, you discover how to pitch your story ideas to a studio executive or potential investor in the hopes of getting your story made into a film.

Finding the Perfect Screenplay: That's the "Ticket"!

Finding a screenplay is not difficult — it's finding a good one that's not easy. But if you look carefully, you can find many talented, up-and-coming writers who have good or maybe even great scripts under their arms just waiting to be made into films. Or, if you find a great story from a published book, you can adapt it into a screenplay.

Keep in mind that the beginning filmmaker should select or write a story that is realistic to shoot as a first-time movie. Don't choose material that's too ambitious. Keep the locations and characters to a minimum and keep away from special effects (they can be costly and time consuming).

The right way to find a writer

How do you find screenplay writers? Here are some ideas:

✔ Put an ad in one of the entertainment trade papers such as *Backstage West* (www.backstage.com) or *The Hollywood Reporter* (www.thehollywoodreporter.com) to let writers know that you're seeking an original screenplay for production.

✔ Read screenplay magazines such as *Creative Screenwriting* (www.creativescreenwriting.com) and *Scr(i)pt Magazine* (www.scriptmagazine.com) and look for articles on writers. Check the classified sections and request available screenplays being advertised by writers.

Screenplay magazines usually list writers' newsletters and writers groups that you can join in order to find writers who have a screenplay ready to turn into a film.

✔ Attend writing seminars advertised in the various writers' magazines or in the classified sections of trade papers like *The Hollywood Reporter,* or that you find out about from a writers' group, and network with the people in attendance, in addition to the speaker. Many attendees probably have a script they're peddling.

✔ Send an e-mail to everyone you know (we all have a screenplay in us), telling them you're looking for a great screenplay or idea for a great film. After the word spreads, especially on the Internet, you'll start getting submissions.

✔ Contact agencies that represent writers. (You can request a list of agencies from the Writer's Guild of America at www.wga.org.) Send a query letter or call, and tell the agency that you're looking for scripts. Be sure to give them an idea of your budget range — how much money you have to make your film (a little or a lot?). See Chapter 4 for more information.

✔ Check the library and bookstores for directories such as *The Hollywood Creative Directory* (*www.hcdonline.com*) that list established writers who may have a great spec script sitting in their closets, or young new writers eager to have you produce their work. A *spec script* is a speculative screenplay that a writer has written without being commissioned by someone to write it — in the hopes of it being considered for production. It's usually a story the writer is extremely passionate about.

Networking for a script

The Writer's Script Network is a great Web site that brings new and even seasoned writers (and their unproduced screenplays) together with filmmakers and producers. Searching for a script doesn't cost the producer or filmmaker anything, but you do have to qualify for free membership. You can apply for membership at its Web site (www.writerscriptnetwork.com). Acceptance is at the discretion of the Writer Script Network. However, anyone can subscribe to the free e-mail newsletter available on the site.

As a member, you gain access to writers' contact information and can contact writers directly with no agent or middleman. You can

even download screenplays (as PDF files, a format that most computers accept — if yours doesn't, go to www.adobe.com/acrobat to download Adobe Acrobat Reader, free of charge). The network has a robust search engine that can find very specific types of screenplays. If you're looking for a sci-fi genre with a female lead that takes place on another planet and has some comedy undertones, but you want it to be a low to medium budget, click a few buttons, and away the search goes. The site also has listings of short screenplays available for production if you don't have the funds to do a full-length film.

A novel idea: Working with an adaptation

One of the best ways to get a studio deal in Hollywood is to find a great book and option the rights to it. When you *option* a book, you're temporarily leasing the rights to it, giving you exclusive permission to adapt it to a screenplay and to shop it around as if you owned it. In a sense, you do own it — for a limited amount of time. An option can be as short as four months or as long as two years or more.

Literally hundreds of thousands of books are out there. Go to the library or a secondhand bookstore. You're sure to stumble across a little gem that somebody has missed. Scan the racks for something that could work as a film. You could even take a short story and adapt it into a full-length feature film. Many of Stephen King's short stories were adapted into full-length films. King's short story *Rita Hayworth and the Shawshank Redemption* became the feature film *The Shawshank Redemption,* and his novella *The Body* was released as the theatrical film *Stand by Me.*

The popularity of the book will determine whether you can get an inexpensive option. If it's an older book, the chances of getting an inexpensive option are very good — especially if you can contact the author directly.

When you option the rights to a novel, you draw up an agreement (preferably have an attorney do it) and you name a purchase price to be paid if and when you sell the novel to a studio or produce it yourself. You can often option for

$1 and set a purchase price that is paid only when the film is produced. Often the purchase price of a script is 10 to 15 percent of the budget on an independent production, plus any agreed upon royalties on the picture's profits. You're probably saying to yourself, "Why even pay a dollar?" Any monetary amount makes it a legal agreement. Plus, I had a writer once whom I optioned a story from for $1, and he was able to treat himself to a fast-food hamburger — I felt good that I helped a starving artist.

Writing Your Own Screenplay

If you can't seem to find the perfect screenplay, then why not try writing your own? "Because I'm not a writer," you say. To that I say, "Just try." In Los Angeles, everyone, no matter what they do for a living, seems to be writing a screenplay. When you pass people on the street, you don't say "Hello." You say, "How's your screenplay going?" Usually people answer, "Great! Thanks for asking. How's yours?" Don't be intimidated by the numbers. Even though a ton of screenplays are out there, most of them aren't worth the paper they're typed on. If you can converse with people and relate incidents and stories verbally, you can probably put your words on paper, so give it a try. I highly recommend the book *Screenwriting For Dummies* by Laura Schellhardt and John Logan (published by Wiley).

Start by perusing newspapers and magazines to trigger ideas for your story, or think about subjects that interest you and that you want to see on the big screen. Choose a story that keeps the reader glued to the page where they can't put it down because they need to know what happens next. Try to get the reader glued to the page by your great story — not with a strong adhesive.

Before you start writing your screenplay, you should familiarize yourself with some of the basics of what makes up good story structure. You also need to decide if you're ready to tackle a feature-length screenplay or ease your way in by doing a short story first. Regardless of whether it's a short story or a feature-length one, similar story principals apply with regards to structuring your screenplay.

Structuring your screenplay

Feature films are usually structured into three acts. The acts are like the life to birth listing on a person's biography: 1900–1989. The first year is Act One, the birth; the hyphen is Act Two, the life and adventures of a person; and the final year is Act Three, the death. Here's a happier example: In Act One the dog chases the cat up the tree. In Act Two, the cat is stuck in the tree, and an attempt is made to get it down safely. Act Three is the resolution of how the cat gets rescued.

Creating conflict

Conflict is what propels a story into motion. Without conflict, you have no action. Every day you deal with conflict, good or bad. Paying bills, getting stuck in traffic, having an argument with your spouse, missing your plane, getting a flat tire, being too rich — these are conflicts. Conflict usually starts when your *protagonist,* the lead character, encounters friction, a problem. Your character then deals with and tries to solve this problem. If the story is a good one, he or she eventually solves this problem or doesn't solve this problem, but either way the protagonist grows from it. A good story has your protagonist a changed person at the end of the film.

Conflict can also be an opposing character, the *antagonist,* like Patrick Swayze's co-worker in *Ghost,* whose greed leads him to have his friend murdered. Or it can be the elements of nature, such as Tom Hanks's character in *Cast Away* being stranded on a desert island, or the deadly tornado that Helen Hunt faced in *Twister.* In *Titanic,* a historic and tragic event that was a natural disaster took the lives of many innocent passengers; the film also had a human antagonist in the form of Rose's fiancé. Conflict can also occur when the antagonist and protagonist want the same thing — money, custody of their child, the same woman, and so on.

When creating conflict in your screenplay, keep the following ideas in mind:

- ✓ **You don't want your story to be predictable.** What fun would that be for your audience?

- ✓ **Your story should be believable.** A story loses credibility if the answer to the hero's problem conveniently falls out of the sky. (This is called *deus ex machina,* a convention from Greek stage plays where a god is lowered in a chair from above, conveniently solves the situation, and then is cranked back up to the heavens. It works in cartoons and silly comedies, but not in most genres, especially dramatic pieces.)

- ✓ **Think outside the box.** Once a truck got stuck under a low bridge. The whole town came out to push and pull, but to no avail. The truck seemed permanently wedged under the bridge. Then a little girl, who was watching the firemen and townspeople pushing and pulling, stepped forward and said, "Why not let the air out of the tires?" She was thinking outside the box.

    People want to be surprised. I loved the twist in *The Sixth Sense* when Bruce Willis turns out to be a ghost. (I hope you've seen the film. If not, I apologize now for ruining it for you.)

- ✓ **Studios like high-concept ideas.** *High-concept* means something out of the ordinary. *Jurassic Park* with dinosaurs being brought back to life in a theme park is a high-concept idea. *Spider-Man* is high concept — a man is bitten by a scientifically altered spider and becomes a human spider.

Another high concept is when Jeff Goldblum in *The Fly* accidentally merges with a fly to become a 6-foot insect with horrifying results. Hey, what a great idea for a sequel, *The Fly Meets Spider-Man* — and it's high-concept!

Follow the Law of Threes. If you want to establish a developing relationship in your story, you need at least three situations where your characters interact. If a relationship builds too fast, your audience will think it's contrived (too convenient). Think of it as the third date. The first date is a little awkward, the second date is a little more comfortable, but by the third date, you're starting to feel that this new relationship may be reality. A great example of the Law of Threes is the three brief encounters between Elliott and E.T. in *E.T. the Extra-Terrestrial* before they befriend each other. First, Elliott hears something in the shed; then Elliott goes to the forest; and, finally, Elliott sits outside on a lawn chair in front of the shed and is approached by E.T. This gradual lead-up to their bond makes it more acceptable, believable, and effective for the audience.

Developing characters

You're taking a drive out to the country. Whom do you want to ride with you? Call up some of your favorite people and have them go along for the drive. Make it an enjoyable journey, not just a destination. The same is true with the characters in your film. Make them interesting enough that the reader will want to go with them on a ride, no matter what the destination is. Make them good company! Give your characters personality.

Your characters should be real and well rounded outside the scope of your screenplay as well. Does the audience care about these characters? The audience can then see them as no one else in the story sees them — their true selves are revealed by what they do when they're alone. Follow them around in your head and see what they do.

Drafting your screenplay: Putting it all together

The process of writing a screenplay includes writing a first draft. You need to remember that it's only a first writing session, and there will be changes. Knowing this helps your ideas flow from your thoughts to the page, and you won't be concerned about editing your words. You're free to put any and all of your ideas on paper at this first-draft stage.

Keeping focused

Writing is fun, but it also requires discipline if you want to turn out a commercial screenplay to produce yourself or sell to a studio. In order to accomplish your dream of writing a screenplay, certain things will help you reach your goals:

✔ **Set a deadline and stick to it.** Tell everyone that you're writing a screenplay, and tell them the date you plan on finishing it. Give yourself a reasonable time (at least a couple months, if not more) to write a solid first draft. If you beat your deadline, people will be more impressed. Broadcasting your deadline forces you to sit down and write because everyone will be asking you how your screenplay is going, and you don't want to let everyone down now, do you?

✔ **Force yourself to sit down and write within a reasonable schedule.** If you set a goal of writing three pages a day, you'll make your deadline of a first draft in a little over one month. The worst thing you write down on paper (or type on your computer) is always better than the best thing you didn't write down. I'm often amazed at how much better my writing is than I thought it would be, even when I feel that I'm forcing it.

✔ **Get over writer's block.** Writer's block is a familiar condition, but it's really nothing more than procrastination. Don't convince yourself that you have this symptom called writer's block. You'll only make yourself feel intimidated. Instead think of writer's block in your vocabulary as being only a neighborhood of successful writers (and you're one of the writers who lives on that block).

✔ **Always know that writing is rewriting.** Rarely does a person write a letter, story, or screenplay that is ready to be read by all. Knowing that you can rewrite what you wrote is a comfort — even the most brilliant of writers rewrite, often more than beginning writers do! You can, and often will, go back and edit what you've written.

✔ **Just start the venture — start writing.** Look at it as crossing the bridge. Just cross halfway. Now that you're in the middle, it's the same distance to go back where you started — so why not go the same distance but at least finish crossing the bridge?

If you have trouble getting a first draft down on paper, pick up some index cards. Cards are an excellent way to put your film together, and they can make writing a first draft much easier. Here's how it works:

1. **Write on an index card a scene that you envision in your film.**

   You only have to write the location and a brief summary of what the scene is about. If it takes place at the exterior of the diner, you would write: *Ext. Diner — Tim finds out that Sheila works at the diner outside of town.*

2. **After you've written all the scenes you've thought of, lay the cards out on the floor.**

   Spreading out the cards helps you stand back and look at the whole picture — much like a traffic helicopter.

3. **Fill in the missing pieces.**

   This part of the process is like doing a jigsaw puzzle — you have to find the perfect pieces to fill in the holes. When you get a brilliant idea for a missing scene, write it on an index card and slip it in where it belongs between two other cards.

4. **Translate the final order of the scenes into a screenplay format.**

The advantage of using index cards is that they create a non-linear environment for experimenting with your story and the order of events. You can rearrange each scene in any order until the story begins to fall into place.

Using cards can also be useful in adapting a book into a screenplay. When I adapted Jennings Michael Burch's book for Mel Gibson's Icon Productions, the task of turning a 293-page book into a 100-page screenplay was overwhelming. I broke the book down into separate incidents or events and turned them into individual scenes on over 400 index cards. I arranged the cards and then decided which scenes to keep and which scenes to discard. I rearranged the order of some cards and saw which scenes needed to be consolidated. It made the adapting process much easier.

When you're finished with your first draft of your new screenplay, put it down and walk away. That's right — just walk away. You're too close to it when you've just finished it to start considering rewrites. You need a break — get away from your screenplay, take a vacation for a few days, or even a few weeks, before you begin rewriting. When you return, you have fresh eyes and can see things more objectively. If you revise too soon, you won't want to change a word — and odds are, you probably need to.

Watching words: Closed captions

Want to watch a movie and see the script at the same time? Most TVs nowadays have a closed-caption function that allows you to watch a film or TV show and read along. Closed captioning was established for the hearing impaired, but it's also a great way to study the actual written words while you watch the actors and scenes play out. It lets you compare what you see written on the bottom of the screen — and how delivered dialogue by the actor is written on the page. It makes you realize that everything the actor says is scripted and how the written word is delivered in a natural way following the script verbatim.

Registering your script via the Internet

The main reason for registering your screenplay is to show that you had the idea first — that it is original with you on a certain date. This way, if someone steals your idea or has a similar idea *after* the date that you registered it, you have proof that you had the idea first.

The Writer's Guild of America now has online registration. You can submit your screenplay via an e-mail attachment to the WGA. You pay by credit card and immediately get an online receipt, which you can print to show that your story is registered with the guild. This is the quickest and easiest way to register your script. The cost is $20. Go to the WGA Web site at www.wga.org and click Online Registration Service.

If you want to copyright your screenplay through the U.S. Copyright Office (for around $30), go to www.copyright.gov.

You can also do a poor-man's copyright. Seal your script or story idea in a manila envelope, address it to yourself, and take it to the post office to be stamped for registered mail. The U.S. Postal Service is considered a legal entity and can mark your package with its USPS stamp at all the corners and sealed edges. A USPS stamp can be used in a court of law to prove you had the idea first. You don't have to mail it — unless you love getting letters. The post office can hand it right back to you. File it away in a safe place.

Easing the process with writer's software

You can find some great software programs that help you concentrate solely on the creative aspects of your screenplay (leave the formatting for later). Most of the software is very easy to use. Some of these programs offer free trial downloads so you can check them out. Most work for both PCs and Macs. Some of these programs are a little pricey, but the organization you'll gain from the software will save you time and trouble in the long run.

✓ **Story View** is a software program by Write Brothers that tracks your story with charts, cards, and color-coding, and literally creates a map of your story that you can stand back and study. Currently Story View only works with PC (a Mac version is in the planning stages). The program retails for $100, and you can find it at www.storyview.com.

✓ **Writing Partner** by Dramatica Pro helps you design your story by asking you questions, giving examples, and guiding you through the creative process of writing a screenplay. I like it because it makes you think about your story from every angle, leaving no stone unturned. It's also a lot of fun to use. Writing Partner retails for $270. Go to www.screenplay.com to order.

- **Truby's Blockbuster** software priced at $295 makes for a great writing companion. The program lets you interact with actual examples from many well-known films. It includes Truby's Story Structure Course along with a list of the 22 building blocks of every great story. Add-ons are available that help you write for specific genres such as romance, sci-fi, thriller, action, and so on. Take a look at www.truby.com.

- **Power Structure** at $179 is a powerful software program that encourages you to ask yourself questions and brainstorm ideas to develop a strong structure for your screenplay. Check it out at www.write-brain.com.

You can also find the preceding software programs and others by visiting The Writer's Store at www.writersstore.com.

Selling Your Screenplay to a Production Studio, Distributor, or Investor

When you sell your screenplay, it can mean dollars and cents or it can just make sense. You can sell your screenplay physically to a studio or distributor, and they will make the picture on their own. Or you can sell a distributor on the idea of your screenplay and story, and they could give you a written commitment to distribute the picture when it's completed. If you get a commitment from a distributor, finding investors willing to take a chance with your film, knowing it already has distribution interest, will be a lot easier.

Selling a production studio or distributor on your idea consists of setting up a meeting to verbally pitch your story. If your idea is well received, the next step is to follow up with either the story in the form of a short one- to two-page synopsis, a *treatment* (a detailed synopsis 10 to 20 pages in length), or a copy of an actual screenplay.

Getting your foot (and screenplay) in the door

You're submitting your screenplay to people who get them every day, so your screenplay ideas need to be creative and unique to stand out. You need to know the basics of proper screenplay formatting so that when your screenplay comes across the desk of an executive, buyer, or distributor, it looks like the real thing. Take a look at *Screenwriting For Dummies* by Laura Schellhardt and John Logan (published by Wiley) for the lowdown on formatting as well as writing. Also consider investing in one of the following software programs:

✔ **ScriptWerx** converts Microsoft Word into a template that formats screenplays as you write. Go to www.scriptwerx.com to order. The retail price is $130.

✔ **Screenwriter 2000** is a formatting program that also includes a setting that lets you view your scripts in outline (card) form. I especially like this software because you can export script information, such as location settings, characters, props, and scenes, so that you can begin scheduling your shoot days. I've written most of my scripts using this great software, which costs $249. Check it out at www.screenplay.com.

✔ **Final Draft** is similar to Screenwriter 2000. The software includes an "Ask the Expert" by screenwriter and author Syd Field that offers an interactive point-and-click section that helps to answer questions and guide you through the writing process. The program retails for $250. Go to www.finaldraft.com.

Some companies receive hundreds of screenplays a month, in addition to one-page summaries from eager screenwriters. The head of the studio or the producer can't possibly read every script that comes in, so the studio hires a script reader to sit all day reading and evaluating screenplays that are submitted to the company. This means you only get one chance at a good first impression — if the reader doesn't like it, your screenplay never goes any farther.

The script reader usually reads your script and then fills out an evaluation page or pages grading your screenplay — similar to what your elementary-school teacher used to do with your assignments. In addition to grading your script, the reader also writes a short synopsis of your story so that the studio executives, producer, or potential buyer can know what your script is about. It's kind of like the *CliffsNotes* of your story. These are some of the things a reader evaluates:

✔ Is it an interesting story that holds the reader's attention?

✔ Is it well written?

✔ Are the characters engaging?

✔ Does it have commercial potential?

✔ Is it a "pass" or a "consider for further evaluation"?

If your script does get a thumbs-up from a script reader, you now have to prepare for the rest of the battle. Sharpen your selling skills by warming up for your meeting with an effective pitch that you can deliver in person to close the deal on your great screenplay idea.

Penpaling

Want to use a different name on your script? Stephen King and many writers have used *pen names* for one reason or another. Maybe you're submitting the same script again with rewrites and you don't want your real name to cross-reference with the new script. Or maybe you have several projects out for consideration and you don't want them to all have your real name on them. Maybe you're not thrilled about the script and don't want to associate with it at all. Here's a suggestion for finding a pen name: Take your middle name, or your best friend's middle name, and then the street you grew up on. For example, my middle name is Michael, and I grew up on Westbrook Drive. So my pen name is Michael Westbrook.

Making a home run with your pitch

When you're trying to sell your screenplay to a studio or distributor, you need to throw a powerful *pitch*. A pitch is a verbal sales tool that explains your story and tries to convince the receiver of your pitch to accept your idea so you can land a distribution deal, a financing commitment from an investor, or a production deal with a studio to produce your film.

Who you make your pitch to is as important as the quality of your pitch. If you pitch to the wrong person, you're wasting your time (and his or hers as well). Many executives in Hollywood are hired just to say "no." You want to give your pitch to someone who can say "yes" or at least to someone who likes your screenplay and has the clout to take it to the person who says "yes." A development executive at a studio or an acquisition person at a production company is usually the person you need to get a meeting with.

The software program Power Tracker gives you a list of 5,000 potential contacts to send your script to. The program also functions as an amazing organizing program and tracks every submission with exacting detail. The software is available for $80 at www.write-brain.com.

The Hollywood Creative Directory puts out several directories, including one of producers and a separate one of distribution companies. The directories also list these companies' past and current projects, so you can decide whether your screenplay is appropriate for them. For more information on the directories, go to www.hcdonline.com.

Keep the following tips in mind as you prepare and give your pitch:

✔ **Identify your film with other successful films.** Hollywood executives need a quick reference point to decide whether your story is something they want to know more about. The quickest way to identify the genre and commercial viability of your screenplay is to cross it with at least two other well-known films.

Always cross your movie with *successful* films. If your film is the same genre as a film that just bombed at the box office, the executive you're pitching to won't want anything to do with it. My comedy parody *Miss Cast Away* crosses *Cast Away* with *Miss Congeniality,* along with the crazy humor of *Scary Movie* and *Austin Powers.* Now doesn't that paint a successful picture?

✔ **Keep pitching until you get a home run.** Babe Ruth was known for his homerun record (over 700 throughout his career), but he could have set a record for the most strikeouts, too. You have to keep swinging to get a hit. Selling your screenplay is very similar to baseball. You wind up for the pitch, you swing, and maybe you get a home run — or at least to first, second, or third base. And then again, maybe you strike out. So you wait for a new game and start all over again. Each time you strike out, go back and work on your pitch so that it's better the next time around.

✔ **Begin your pitch with a question (for example, "What would happen if the sun suddenly burned out?"), and then tell them what happens in your story.** Intrigue the listener to want to hear more.

I heard a story once about a frustrated writer who took a famous award-winning film, changed the names, updated the time and locations, and sent it out. It was turned down by every agent and studio in town. *The Wizard of Oz* was turned down by every publisher who didn't have the courage — some had no heart — but L. Frank Baum had the brain to self-publish his stories, which then attracted a publisher to pick up the sequels — and the rest is history. So use a little creativity and keep trying.

Part II

Gearing Up to Make Your Film

The 5th Wave   By Rich Tennant

"Okay, these people are financing a big part of the movie, so during the lovemaking scenes, try not to drop the snow shovels."

In this part . . .

You discover how to successfully budget and schedule your film and also find secrets for financing your film. This part guides you to the right locations for setting your story and the best cast and crew you can find.

Planning your film with a visual eye before ever stepping on set is important. In this part, I help you visualize the film through shot-by-shot sketches called *storyboards*.

Chapter 4

Scheduling and Budgeting Your Film

*B*efore you can go out and actually shoot your movie you have to budget and schedule what you're going to shoot. The schedule will help you figure out what scenes you need to shoot first and the most economical way to get your movie completed. The schedule and budget go hand in hand. Often, you don't have much choice when you have a set amount to make your movie, so you have to make your schedule fit your budget, and your budget fit your schedule.

In this chapter, you discover how to accurately budget and schedule your independent film, whether you have no budget, a low budget, or a budget in the millions.

So which do you tackle first, scheduling your film or doing the budget? Just like the chicken-and-egg debate, it depends on your situation. It would be nice if you could schedule your film and then see how much money you need, but filmmakers often have only so much money and have to make their films fit the budgets, not their budgets fit their films. It's like trying to pack too many clothes into a small suitcase — you push them in as tight as you can and hope you can still close it. If they don't fit in the suitcase, you'll have to manage without them. Scheduling your movie lets you know where the money will be directed and to which budget categories. You usually have a set amount of money, and it's the distribution of that amount that is determined by the scheduling — what will be spent where.

By breaking down your script and sorting out cast, crew, props, locations, and shooting days before doing your detailed budget, you leave nothing to chance — this at least lets you know if you have enough money to make your film. You're able to know that what you've scheduled fits within the budget, and so present a more accurate and detailed budget to satisfy your investor, if you're lucky enough to find one. This chapter helps you outline your whole shooting schedule on a production board so that you know who's shooting what, where, and when.

I also let you in on a few secrets to shooting your film on the cheap, such as deferring salaries, shooting with non-union actors, and using special guild agreements that enable you to use union actors at bargain prices.

The Art of Scheduling a Film

Even if you have a definitive budget, you need to break down all the elements of your film to determine how to distribute the money you have. These breakdowns also help you figure out how many days it will take to shoot your film. You have to make your budget fit your schedule, so be prepared to do some juggling. If you're on a tight budget, you won't have the luxury of shooting your film over a period of several months. Your budget may only allow you to schedule a 12-day shoot (every additional day is going to cost you money). Juggling includes consolidating scenes. If you can shoot the scene in the cave in two days instead of three, and the breaking-up scene in the car, instead of in the shopping mall, you'll be able to shorten your schedule — thus, saving time and money.

Scheduling a film is somewhat of an art. It's like playing with a Rubik's Cube, where you keep turning and adjusting and twisting and tweaking until the elements fall into place. And scheduling your film efficiently is essential to saving time and money.

The director and assistant director usually make the schedule together. The process includes figuring out what scenes can be shot together in the same day, scheduling actors to work consecutive days, and how to tighten the schedule so the film can be shot in fewer days. If you don't have an assistant director to help schedule and be on the set to help things stay organized, then you have to do the schedule all by yourself. Scheduling your film includes

- *Lining* the script by going through and marking items such as actors, props, wardrobe, and special effects
- Putting those items on individual *breakdown sheets,* each representing one scene from the film

- Transferring the elements on the breakdown sheets to *production board strips*
- Rearranging the order of production strips to find the best shooting schedule

A calendar is your best friend when scheduling your film. You choose the date on which to start principal photography and the date on which the shoot will wrap. By looking at a calendar, you see what days the weekends fall on and whether any statutory holidays occur that the cast and crew will have off (like Christmas and Memorial Day). I use Now-Up-To-Date from Now Software to help me design my calendar with reminders and banners. It also comes with Now Contact to organize my contact lists. It's great for scheduling appointments, too. You can download a free 30-day trial of the program at www. nowsoftware.com.

Lining your script

You break down, or *line,* your script by pulling out elements that affect your budget and schedule. With different-colored highlighters in hand, start combing through your script (or have the assistant director do it, if you have one), highlighting important items with a different color for each category. You end up with a very colorful script after the process is complete. This process is intended to flag the script so accurate breakdowns can be made. The categories to highlight include

- Actors
- Extras (background people)
- Props
- Wardrobe or special costumes
- Sets and locations
- Special effects
- Vehicles
- Animals
- Special equipment
- Special makeup
- Optical effects

Breaking into breakdown sheets

After you highlight the various categories of items, transfer the highlighted elements to individual *breakdown sheets* — one for each scene in your film. A breakdown sheet contains separate drawn category boxes to add the elements you've highlighted in the script. You enter each element in the appropriate category box, such as a hammer in the props area, either by hand or by using one of the available software programs (see the section "Making your life easier with scheduling software (and knowing where to find it)" later in this chapter).

Each breakdown sheet should be numbered so that you can go back and reference it if you need to. Every character in the script is also given a reference number, usually starting with the number 1 for your lead actor. You transfer these numbers to the breakdown sheets and eventually to the individual strips on the production board (more on this in the section "Creating production strips"). Numbering saves space so that you don't have to keep writing the characters' names (plus there wouldn't be enough space on a strip).

A breakdown sheet also has a *header* that includes the following details:

- Scene number
- Script page
- Page count (length of scene divided into eighths — 1½ pages would be 1⅛)
- Location/setting
- Synopsis of scene (one sentence)
- Exterior or interior
- Day or night
- Script day (for example, third day in the story when Mary arrives at the plantation)
- Breakdown sheet number

Figure 4-1 shows a sample breakdown sheet from my film *The Dragon's Candle*. Scene 106 has Ghandlin the wizard driving a borrowed police car and zapping traffic out of his way with his magic wand. The breakdown sheet provides separate boxes listing the elements that are needed for this scene.

Propping up your prop list

Every prop that will appear in your film must be pulled from the script and added to the props category in your breakdown sheets. A *prop* is defined as anything your characters interact with, such as guns, cell phones, brooms, and so on. On a low-budget film, try to borrow your props — especially if they're contemporary items. For hard-to-find props, you can usually rent them from a prop house or rental house listed in the Yellow Pages or the 411 directory in

New York (www.ny411.com) and Los Angeles (www.la411.com). In North Hollywood, California, 20th Century Props (www.20thcenturyprops.com) has over 100,000 square feet of storage that houses thousands of props.

Often, props are confused with set dressing, but the difference is that actors don't interact with set dressing. Set dressing includes a picture frame on a mantle or flowers in a vase on a table. The baseball bat in Mel Gibson's film *Signs* would have been categorized as set dressing, but because the actors actually interact with the bat (which is displayed on a wall), it is categorized as a prop. You address set dressing in your breakdown sheets only if it's crucial to the story.

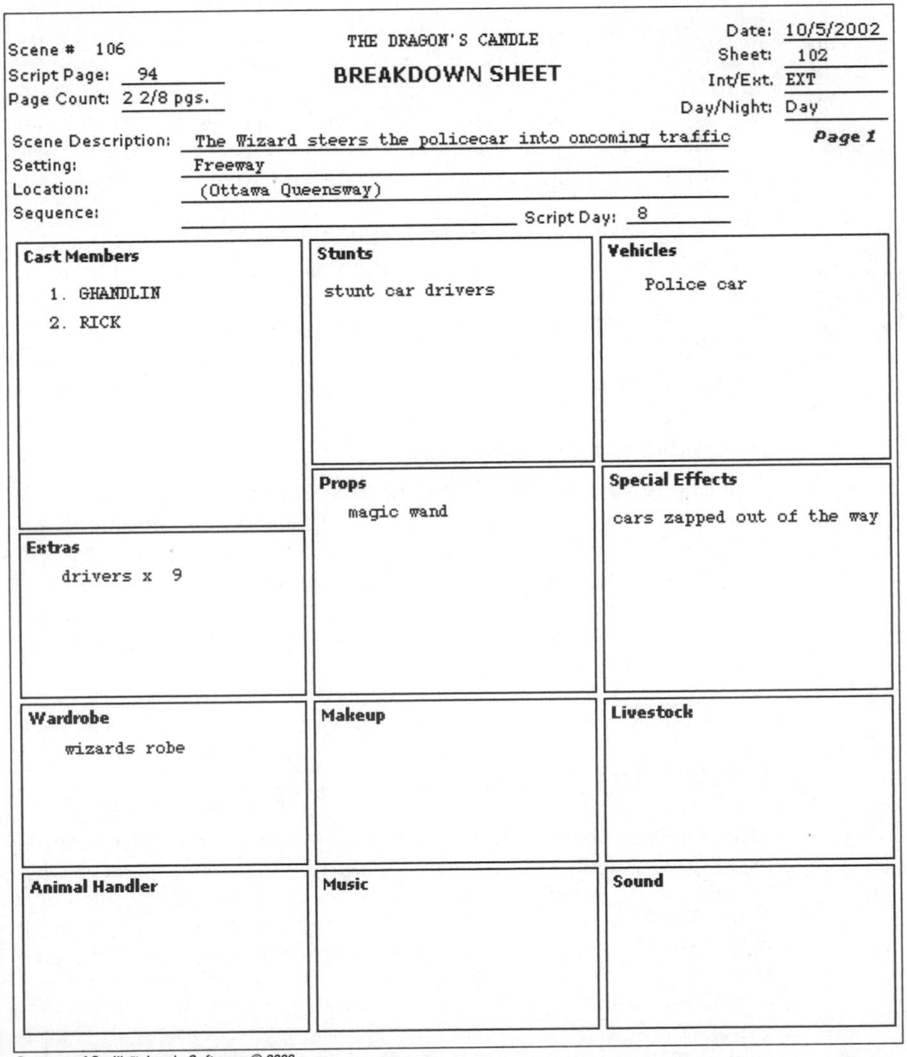

THE DRAGON'S CANDLE

BREAKDOWN SHEET

Scene # 106
Script Page: 94
Page Count: 2 2/8 pgs.

Date: 10/5/2002
Sheet: 102
Int/Ext. EXT
Day/Night: Day

Page 1

Scene Description: The Wizard steers the policecar into oncoming traffic
Setting: Freeway
Location: (Ottawa Queensway)
Sequence:
Script Day: 8

Cast Members 1. GHANDLIN 2. RICK	**Stunts** stunt car drivers	**Vehicles** Police car
Extras drivers x 9	**Props** magic wand	**Special Effects** cars zapped out of the way
Wardrobe wizards robe	**Makeup**	**Livestock**
Animal Handler	**Music**	**Sound**

Courtesy of Gorilla™ Jungle Software © 2002

Figure 4-1: A breakdown sheet created with Gorilla production software.

Dressing up your wardrobe list

You add certain wardrobe elements to your breakdown sheets, such as costumes, uniforms, or clothes that have to be sewn from scratch. A character's jeans and T-shirt don't need to be entered in the wardrobe box, but a gangster's zoot suit does. Because scenes aren't usually filmed in chronological order, each outfit is given a script day number to ensure that the actor wears the correct wardrobe in each shot. Script days (the timeline of your story) will be part of the breakdown sheets, and if the story takes place over five days, you'll sit down with the wardrobe person and decide what clothing your actors will wear each day if it's not addressed in the script.

Locating locations

You can list your location setting in the heading of each breakdown sheet. Locations dictate a lot regarding scheduling and budget. If you're using software like Movie Magic Scheduling, you can cross-reference details about the locations (Are they private or public property? Do you need to secure permits or pay location fees, and how much do they cost?). Keep your locations to a minimum; otherwise, you may end up going over budget.

You can stretch your entire budget if you decide to shoot outside the United States. Shooting in Canada, depending on the exchange rate at the time, can stretch your budget up to 45 percent or more! Don't plan to head north of the border without doing some research first, though. Many states in the United States offer incentives to encourage filmmakers to shoot in their cities. See Chapter 6 for more information about location deals and incentives.

A "special" on special effects

Scheduling special effects on your breakdown sheets helps you determine what kind of effects you can afford. Keep effects to a minimum if you're working with a lower budget. You may find that designing special effects on a computer fits within your budget better, depending on how elaborate the special effect. If you can get away without special effects and concentrate on a good story, though, I recommend that route. See Chapter 17 for much more on creating special effects for your film.

Creating production strips

After you've copied all the category elements from your screenplay onto your breakdown sheets, you're ready to start transferring these elements to the individual strips that go onto your production board. *Production strips* are about ¼ inch wide and contain the information from your breakdown sheets. Each strip represents an individual scene and contains all the elements featured in that particular scene, such as actors, props, and wardrobe. The header contains the names of your characters in the script with a number assigned to each character. These numbers are added to the strips and line up with the header, so you can see at a glance which scenes each actor appears in.

By having the scenes of your film on individual strips, you can move them around to find the most economical and effective shooting schedule. Films are rarely shot in continuity. Rather, you want to group the same locations together in your shooting schedule so that you don't have to jump back and forth. Shooting the scene at the airport, wrapping up, and then later in the story going back to the airport to shoot more scenes would be silly.

You also want to color-code your strips so that you can step back and see how many interior and exterior scenes you have, making arranging shooting times easier. If the schedule shows you there are more interior scenes, then you know you don't have to worry about weather as much. If the schedule shows you that you have a lot of daytime exterior scenes, then you know you don't have to rent movie lights and a generator — but you do have to be aware of what time the sun sets and when you'll be losing the light. You can choose the color code that works best for you. I usually color-code my strips as follows:

> Exterior Day = yellow
>
> Exterior Night = blue
>
> Interior Day = white
>
> Interior Night = green

You schedule as many scenes as you feel you can shoot in one day and group locations, rooms, and so on together. The number of days you shoot has an impact on your budget, so try to fit as much into each shooting day that you feel you can realistically cover without sacrificing the quality of your film. Always allow yourself more time than you think it will take to shoot a scene. If it's a dialogue scene, it may be quicker and easier to shoot than an action scene that needs to be choreographed and covered from several different angles. An experienced assistant director can help you determine if your shooting schedule is realistic or not.

After you've selected the scenes (strips) for each day's shoot, you separate them in your production board with a black strip and then begin the next day's schedule of scenes. You should complete your production board well in advance of shooting (during the preproduction stage) so that everyone on your crew knows ahead of time what is shooting and when.

A production board can be a heavy cardboard or plastic compartment board that allows you to fit your strips into and see your entire schedule at a glance. Boards can be purchased from Enterprise Stationers, and they come in 4, 6, 8, 10, and 12 panels, and range in price from $55 to $162. To order, contact Enterprise at 800-896-4444. If you use a program like Movie Magic Scheduling, the board is printed along with your strips onto paper and can be copied and distributed to appropriate crew members.

Stripping down your schedule

Two main factors determine the order in which you shoot your scenes: characters and locations. Start organizing your production strips by grouping the characters that appear in the same scenes together. Then arrange the strips with the same locations as close together as possible.

Actors

Try to schedule your actors so that they work as many consecutive days as possible. Otherwise, you have to drop and then pick up the actors again. In some union agreements, you still have to pay actors who are *on hold* for days they don't work. With non-union agreements, you don't have to worry about this. However, if a union actor is on hold, he or she has to be available at a moment's notice should your schedule change. If you're doing a union production with union actors, special weekly rates will save some money in the budget if you're working an actor more than two or three days at a time.

After you have your production strips in place, you can generate a *day-out-of-days* chart that shows when your actors work during the shooting schedule. You can do this by hand or generate it from the software program you use to produce your production board and strips.

Locations

Grouping the same rooms, buildings, and locations together helps the schedule. Picking up and moving your cast and crew from one location to the next takes time and money. Most films are shot out of continuity for this reason.

Schedule outdoor scenes first. That way, if it rains or the weather isn't appropriate for your shot, you can move indoors and use the time to shoot interior scenes under safe cover. If you start shooting indoors and then go outside, you aren't giving yourself a security blanket for a *cover-set* (backup location). By having a backup interior location when it rains on a day you've scheduled a sunny outdoor scene, you can go into the indoor location without shutting down production, and then go outside again when the weather has cleared up.

Making your life easier with scheduling software (and knowing where to find it)

One of the advantages of scheduling your film with a software program as opposed to taping strips of paper onto a piece of poster board is that you can easily group locations and actors and have the software present you with a series of alternative shooting sequences. The other nice thing about scheduling software is that it enables you to generate various lists and customized breakdown sheets. The software automatically transfers the items on your breakdown sheets to your production strips. The following are some great options to consider:

- **Filmmaker Software:** If you go to www.filmmakersoftware.com, you can download, absolutely free, Filmmaker Software, which provides every imaginable form and report you'll need to make your film, including breakdown sheets and strip board!

- **Gorilla Production Software:** For $199, Gorilla (www.junglesoftware.com) includes a scheduling program within its production package software (Gorilla is a full production package that includes budgeting and other reports to assist you in making your film). It's a sophisticated software package that will make the task of scheduling your movie a lot easier!

- **Movie Magic:** This scheduling software has a form of artificial intelligence. You type in what you want — for the program to group like elements together, giving you all the same sets or actors consecutively in the schedule. The software goes to work sorting and selecting and presents you with a myriad of scheduling options. It lists for $699; you can find it at www.entertainmentpartners.com. Figure 4-2 shows a production board created with Movie Magic.

Scheduling software can also be found at specialty stores that cater to filmmakers such as the following:

- **Enterprise Stationery:** Enterprise Stationery (www.enterpriseprinters.com) is the leader in entertainment reports, forms, and contracts and has more than 300 production forms, including all the materials you need for breaking down and scheduling your film. You can purchase a four-panel production board for $56.95, a bundle of 50 strips for $4.50, and a header (to list your actors and headings) for $3. It also sells the latest budget and scheduling software.

- **The Writers Store:** You can also find a selection of production board and strip products at the Writers Store (www.writersstore.com).

Header															
Sheet Number:	12	56	26		79	10	14	13	11	98	30	89	58	59	
Page Count:	1/8	3 1/8	5		1 1/8	1/8	1 6/8	1/8	2/8	2/8	1/8	1 3/8	2/8	1 4/8	
Shoot Day:	1	1	1		2	2	2	2	2	2	2	2	2	2	

'UNDERCOVER ANGEL'

Director: Bryan Michael Stoller

Producer: Bryan Michael Stoller

Asst. Director:

Script Dated: August 1998

Character	No.	EXT - COFFEE SHOP - DAY Scs. 8	EXT - COFFEE SHOP - DAY Scs. 52	EXT - COFFEE SHOP - DAY Scs. 22	— End Of Day 1 – 8/10/98 — 8 2/8 pgs.	EXT - COFFEE SHOP - DAY Scs. 75	EXT - COFFEE SHOP - DAY Scs. 6	EXT - COFFEE SHOP - DAY Scs. 10	EXT - COFFEE SHOP/STREET - DAY Scs. 9	EXT - COFFEE SHOP/STREET - DAY Scs. 7	EXT - COFFEE SHOP - DAY Scs. 94	EXT - BUSINESS STREET - DAY Scs. 26	EXT - CANTURA STREET - DAY Scs. 85	INT - FAST FOOD RESTAURANT: COUNTE Scs. 54	INT - FAST FOOD RESTAURANT: TABLE - I Scs. 55	— End Of Day 2 – 8/11/98 — 6 7/8 pgs.
HARRISON	1	1	1	1		1	1	1			1					
JENNY	2		2	2		2						2			2	
HOLLY	3		3	3		3		3	3	3			3			
MELISSA	4															
DAN	5															
JUDGE	6															
MRS. STEVENS	7															
GO-CART BOB	8															
SULLIVAN	9															
FRED	10															
BETH	11															
COURIER	12															
PASSPORT CLERK	13															
CLEANING LADY	14															
LENO	16															
1940's Woman	17															
1940's Stranger	18															
STAR GUEST	19															
Extras:							E:1				E:3				E:1	E:1

Prepared by: Bryan Michael Stoller

Scene description

Scene descriptions
Harrison mesmerized by Holly, accidentally knocks over coffee.
Jenny and Harrison having breakfast a the coffee shop. Harrison spots Holly and
Harrison and Jenny at the coffee shop getting acquainted. Harrison stares at Holly, Jenny
Harrison and Jenny at breakfast, Holly surprises them. Harrison realizes it was Holly at the track
Harrison at coffee shop, something catches his eye.
Harrison offers his newspaper to Holly.
Holly goes to newspaper vending machine, loses quarter - no newspaper.
Harrison's P.O.V. of Holly walking down the street.
Harrison sits alone at coffee shop - no Jenny, no Holly.
Harrison puts car into park outside of office building.
Holly & Jenny mail off the transcribed Dodo manuscripts.
A fast-food cashier rings up the order.
Jenny offers to adopt Harrison.

Figure 4-2:
A production board with strips from Movie Magic (with header).

Balancing Your Film Budget

If you're doing a low-budget production, you have a finite amount of money to work with. Therefore, creating a budget and sticking to it is critical; you aren't likely to have a big studio (or a filthy rich uncle) to provide you with extra cash if you overspend and come up short. Creating a budget involves allotting the proper amount to each area. Adding at least a 10-percent contingency to your budget to allow for overages is also important; otherwise, you could end up with an unfinished film.

Everything has a price. If you pay full price for everything, your independent budget could end up at $100,000. But if you're a good dealmaker, you may be able to shoot the same film for $50,000. Hollywood spends money and often doesn't have time to work the deals. You, on the other hand, probably have no choice.

If you've already found people to finance your film, they're going to want to see a detailed budget. They'll want to know how you intend to spend their money. So even if the money isn't coming out of your own pocket, you can't escape doing a budget for your film. Sorry.

Tightrope walking above the line

First, you need to determine what your *above-the-line* numbers are going to be. Above-the-line items include negotiable and influential salaries, such as those paid to the writer, director, producer, and star actors. Your cast is usually found above-the-line because they drive the commercial viability of your film, and their salaries have to be negotiated. If you're doing a studio picture, a star can demand up to $20 million or more these days. On an independent low-budget film, your actors (especially if they're union) are going to up the cost to make your film. The other above-the-line positions like the producer, director, writer (maybe they're all you) are negotiable and not controlled by a union or actor's agent wanting mucho bucks for his client.

On a non-union film, you can save a lot of money if your cast works for deferred pay, meaning that they don't receive salaries until, and if, the film makes a profit. Getting actors to work deferred is easier than getting crew members to do so, because actors often need the exposure and experience and can add the film to their acting reel and résumé.

If your cast is union, you can't defer pay, but you may qualify to do your film under a special agreement with the Screen Actors Guild (SAG) called the SAG Indie Program. This program works with independent filmmakers so that they can afford to use union actors in their films. The agreements that SAG offers to independent filmmakers include

- ✔ **Student Film Agreement:** You don't have to pay the actors to be in your film as long as your film is done under an accredited school and you are a student. The film's budget has to be less than $35,000. The film cannot be sold or distributed (you can use it to showcase your filmmaking skills and help get a paid filmmaking job in the future).

- ✔ **Experimental:** The total film budget must be under $75,000. You can mix union and non-union actors and defer salaries until and if you get a distribution deal and make profits from the film. You're allowed to showcase your film at film festivals and limited screenings (not for profit).

- ✔ **Limited Exhibition:** The total film budget must be under $200,000 to qualify for limited exhibition rules. You can mix and match union and non-union actors at reduced salary rates. Limited Exhibition is exactly what it says — limited exhibition for your film (film festivals, non-paid screenings). If your film gets distribution, you have to pay all actors SAG minimums that you originally withheld to make your film.

- ✔ **Modified Low Budget:** The budget must be under $500,000 but may be increased to $750,000 (under special casting considerations). Reduced rates apply for actors, determined by the number of days they work. You must use all union players.

- ✔ **Low Budget:** The budget for the film must be under $2 million. You pay your actors significantly reduced union rates, and you must use all union players.

These agreements pertain to the actors only, and not the filmmaker and crew members. For more details on each SAG agreement, go to `www.sagindie.org`.

Starring cameos

If you're creative, you may be able to slip a recognized actor into your film and not have to pay a $20 million salary. If you hire an actor for one day, or even a couple of hours, you can shoot several scenes and insert them throughout the film. I had Dan Aykroyd do the voice of Dexter the computer in my film *The Random Factor.* I spent a little over an hour with him and was able to use about 15 minutes of his voice-over throughout the film. James Earl Jones played a judge in two scenes for my film *Undercover Angel.* I shot with him for a whole day so I only had to pay him a one-day salary. George Carlin

performed a cameo in my American Film Institute student film many years ago. I had the camera set up and ready to go. He came in, did his scene, and we wrapped in less than 45 minutes.

The best way to approach actors is through referrals, or meeting them happenchance in a store or restaurant. (I found Yasmine Bleeth's purse after she left it in a restaurant, and then I asked her to star in my movie *Undercover Angel,* and she did!) You can also write a letter to an actor's agent or manager to see if you can convince him or her to be in your film.

Actors will work for food

Whether or not your budget allows for your actors to receive salaries, you have to budget to feed them. Feeding your actors is one of the most important things — don't skimp in this category. People can get very irritable when they haven't eaten properly, and you don't want to fill everyone up on burgers and pizza every day.

Budget for not only a great caterer, but for *craft services* (snacks) as well. Being generous when it comes to feeding your actors can make all the difference in the world. Make sure to find out if anyone requires a special diet, such as vegetarian meals or non-dairy. You don't want anyone starving on your shoot.

Hanging below the line

Below-the-line items include your more definitive numbers — flat fees and fixed salaries. These usually include your staff and crew, film stock, and other categories in which the dollar amounts aren't astronomical and in which you have choices of where to purchase or rent things to fit your budget. On a feature film for which the stars are getting paid millions, the above-the-line numbers can dwarf the below-the-line numbers.

You can find many ways to enlist staff and crew to work on your film. You can pay them something, or you can get them to work for free and defer their pay. Getting a staff member or crew person to work deferred is more difficult than getting an actor to work deferred because, unlike the actor, the crew member's work is not as visible on screen. The only advantage for a crew member to work for deferred salary is if he is new to the business and is willing to learn and even apprentice on your film. A crew member may work for less if she is looking to graduate to a higher position and receive a better credit for her résumé (for example, moving up from gaffer to cinematographer on the shoot). See also Chapter 7 for more about crew members.

You need to negotiate with each crew member and put in writing whether he or she is working by the hour or being paid a flat fee. If you're working with a non-union crew, you have a lot more flexibility in negotiating salaries. Minimum-wage laws will help you set a limited hourly payment (it starts at $5.15 an hour) for your crew so they don't feel you're taking full advantage of them. For more information, see www.dol.gov and click on Wages.

If you're doing a low-budget production, look for crew with their own equipment. You may find a cinematographer who has his own camera — especially these days, with 24progressive digital cameras coming down in price. Some cinematographers even own 16mm and 35mm cameras. Some may have lights and grip equipment, too. Your sound mixer may have her own sound equipment, including a recorder and microphones. (See Chapters 10, 11, and 12 for more on equipment.) You can make deals on renting or borrowing props, and getting locations to use in your movie through friends and family. (Other categories that you'll find below-the-line are exemplified in Figure 4-3 in the next section, "Budgeting for budget software.")

The medium on which you choose to shoot your story affects your budget, whether you shoot super-8, 16mm, 35mm, or on videotape (see Chapter 10). Your *shooting ratio,* or the number of takes in relation to the number of shots you end up using, is also going to determine what you spend on film stock and developing (or videotape if shooting video) — and ultimately your budget. Do you plan on shooting 1:1 (one take per usable shot) or 3:1 (three takes to get the shot)? Depending on whether this is your first film or last film (just kidding) will determine whether you need to do three takes to get the shot or ten takes to get the shot (even many seasoned directors like to do multiple takes). To determine the amount of video or film stock you need, multiply the number of takes times the total pages of your screenplay (one page averages one minute of screen time). If you plan on 5:1 (five takes to get one shot), multiply 5 times 100 minutes (from a 100-page script) and realize that you need 500 minutes of footage — and then budget accordingly.

Topping your budget

The budget *top sheet* is a summary of your budget that lists the main budget categories and the totals of each. You can reference each department by its budget category number assigned on the budget top sheet for a detailed breakdown in the long-form budget. (See Figure 4-3 for a sample budget top sheet created with Easy Budget software, discussed in the following section.) Usually, the top sheet is enough for an investor to see how your film breaks down in terms of cost. Eventually, an investor will want to see the detailed budget and how the categories are broken down.

Each budget item on the top sheet is assigned a category number that helps you reference the details of that category within the long-form detailed budget. It's like a table of contents. For example, Production Staff is category 200-00 and can be found on page 3 of the long-form detailed budget breakdown. On page 3 of the budget detail page, category 200-00 will be broken down listing the individual staff positions and the duration of employment and salary of each. Figure 4-3 also gives you an idea of costs associated with categories like insurance, music score, and so on, on a $214,000 budget.

ACCOUNT	DESCRIPTION	PAGE	TOTAL
	PRODUCTION BUDGET		January 1, 2003
	Your Movie Title Goes Here		
	-Above-the-Line Costs-		
110-00	STORY RIGHTS	1	$5,000.00
120-00	PRODUCER & STAFF	1	$20,000.00
130-00	DIRECTOR	1	$15,000.00
140-00	TALENT	2	$35,000.00
150-00	A-T-L FRINGE BENEFITS	3	$0.00
	Total Above-the-Line Costs:		$75,000.00
	-Production-		
200-00	PRODUCTION STAFF	3	$35,000.00
210-00	EXTRA TALENT	4	$4,000.00
220-00	ART DIRECTION	4	$3,500.00
230-00	SET CONSTRUCTION	5	$3,200.00
240-00	PROPERTY DEPARTMENT	5	$2,300.00
250-00	ANIMALS & ANIMAL HANDLERS	5	$0.00
260-00	STUNTS	6	$0.00
270-00	WARDROBE	6	$2,500.00
280-00	MAKEUP & HAIRDRESSING	6	$1,800.00
290-00	LIGHTING & ELECTRICAL	7	$4,800.00
300-00	GRIP & LABOR	7	$5,500.00
310-00	CAMERA	7	$4,500.00
320-00	PRODUCTION SOUND	8	$3,500.00
330-00	TRANSPORTATION	8	$1,500.00
340-00	LOCATIONS/SET OPERATIONS	8-9	$2,500.00
350-00	FILM & VIDEO PROCESSING	10	$3,500.00
360-00	STUDIO FEES & STAGE RENTAL	10	$0.00
370-00	TESTS & RETAKES	10	$0.00
380-00	SECOND PHOTOGRAPHIC UNIT	10	$1,500.00
	Production Sub Total:		$79,600.00
	-Post Production-		
400-00	EDITORIAL	11	$5,600.00
410-00	MUSIC SCORE	11	$10,000.00
420-00	POST PRODUCTION SOUND	11	$20,000.00
430-00	VISUAL EFFECTS and TITLES	12	$5,000.00
440-00	POST PRODUCTION LAB	12	$0.00
	Post Production Sub Total:		$40,600.00
	-Other Costs-		
500-00	INSURANCE	12	$4,500.00
510-00	B-T-L FRINGE BENEFITS	12	$0.00
520-00	ADVERTISING & PUBLICITY	13	$0.00
530-00	GENERAL OVERHEAD	13	$2,500.00
600-00	CONTINGENCY	13	$12,020.00
700-00	COMPLETION BOND	14	$0.00
	Other Costs Sub Total:		$19,020.00
	Below-The-Line Total:		$139,220.00
	GRAND TOTAL:		$214,220.00

Figure 4-3:
A sample budget top sheet from Easy Budget software.

© The Easy Budget Company

Try not to budge the budget

One concern is to make sure you don't go over budget. It happens all the time with studio pictures, but it's not as much a problem for studio pictures as it is for independent films. If a studio picture at $30 million goes over $5 million, the studio usually covers it. If your independent $50,000 movie goes over budget by $10,000, getting that additional funding and completing your movie could become a serious problem. Films often go over budget, rarely do they come in under budget. Make sure that you allow for a contingency in your budget (usually 5 to 15 percent of the total budget). This will be helpful if and when emergencies come up and things end up costing more than expected, or the schedule changes because of an actor, weather, or some unplanned event. An additional $15,000 contingency on a $150,000 movie could make the difference between having a finished or unfinished movie in the end.

Budgeting for budget software

Like scheduling software, budgeting software can take a lot of the hard work out of creating a budget for a film. The following are some of the programs available:

- ✔ **Filmmaker Software,** mentioned earlier in this chapter, has a budgeting template included in its production software. It's part of the free download at www.filmmakersoftware.com.

- ✔ **Microsoft Excel** enables you to create your own budget template.

- ✔ **BBP Software** makes a film/TV budgeting template that runs on Microsoft Excel 5.0 and up, for the Macintosh and for Windows. It has additional templates for crew and actor contact lists and sells for $99. You can download it from the Web at www.boilerplate.net.

- ✔ **Easy Budget,** which retails for $189.95 at www.easy-budget.com, really is easy to use.

- ✔ **Gorilla** has a budgeting template included in its complete production software package and is available at www.junglesoftware.com for $199.

- ✔ **Cinergy,** at $399, is available at www.mindstarprods.com.

- ✔ **Movie Magic Budgeting** by Entertainment Partners is the budget software of choice in Hollywood. At $699, it can be expensive for a low-budget filmmaker, but it's the top of the line if you can afford it. Check it out at www.entertainmentpartners.com.

The different budgeting software programs are similar, but some are easier to use than others and some have additional applications. Which program you use is usually a matter of personal preference and also depends on how much designing you want with the form. Movie Magic Scheduling has all the categories that you can use or modify. If you use Microsoft Excel, you'll have to design a budgeting template and set up the tables to give you the proper calculations. Some software like BBP Software, mentioned earlier, uses Excel and turns it into a film-budgeting program.

Insurance Is Your Best Policy

An important budget item is insurance for your cast, crew, and equipment. In the long run, insurance *saves* you money, not costs you! It's kind of like wearing your seatbelt: You may not need it, but if you do, you'll be glad that you buckled up for your journey. Better safe than sorry.

Purchasing insurance for a film production is a mix-and-match situation. You need to decide what type of coverage you need and how much of each type of coverage you want. You also need to decide how much of a deductible you're willing to pay if you ever have to activate the policy. You should consider the following types of coverage:

- **Cast insurance:** Getting cast insurance usually requires physicals for your actors to make sure that they're starting on your film in a healthy state. This coverage can be expensive and should be purchased on an independent film only if a cast member cannot be replaced.

- **General liability insurance:** This is required insurance that protects you and your production from claims against you for property damage and claims against you from the public or a third party for injury or accidents incurred on the set.

  Make sure that your general liability policy covers any interior locations you shoot at. If you're filming at the art museum and one of your film lights ignites a priceless painting and ends up burning down the museum, you don't want to be stuck without insurance to cover the disaster. No one will let you shoot on their property until you hand them a certificate of insurance, anyway. An average liability policy covers up to $1 million.

- **Film and tape coverage:** This covers damage to film or tape. A policy can also cover faulty lab work, ruined negatives, bad stock, footage lost during shipping, and so on. Also known as *negative insurance,* it pays for the cost to reshoot footage that was lost or damaged. This is not as crucial for shoots when you're using videotape. Just make sure you make backups of your video footage — just in case.

✔ **Props, wardrobe, and sets coverage:** This covers damage, loss, or theft of important props, wardrobe, and sets. If your film doesn't require expensive props and costumes, you can go without this insurance, or take out a low coverage policy (only insure for the total value of all props, wardrobe, and sets). Don't insure for more than the value — it will cost you more, and it's not necessary (you can only be reimbursed the total value of what you lost, not beyond that).

✔ **Production equipment coverage:** This covers any equipment used on the production. Many rental companies won't rent equipment to you if you don't insure their equipment under a property coverage policy. Most companies request an *insurance certificate,* which is issued from the insurance company showing proof that you have insurance and what your coverage is. On most low-budget productions, a $250,000 minimum coverage should suffice.

✔ **Errors and omissions (E&O) insurance:** Before a distributor or network will show your film, it needs to be protected with errors & omissions insurance, also referred to as E&O insurance. E&O insurance covers lawsuits resulting from copyright infringement and using products or names without permission (usually in bad taste). You can save a little on your budget by not purchasing E&O insurance until after your film is completed — and let the distributor purchase it (they'll usually deduct the cost from your sales).

✔ **Worker's compensation:** As an employer, you're required to cover your employees under worker's compensation. This protects you and the employees should they have an accident while in your employment. You can buy worker's comp coverage through an insurance agency at around 4 percent of your payroll. Worker's comp covers people who work as volunteers on your set as well as those who work for pay.

When you take out an insurance policy, you need it only for the dates of your actual production (although for cast and crew insurance, you may want to overlap the weeks or months during pre-production and right through the end of filming your movie). Taking out insurance for a period of a month instead of a year is much more affordable, especially if you're on a tight budget.

When you take out production insurance, you'll have a *deductible* (the amount you have to pay should you have damages and have to activate the policy). Depending on your coverage, a deductible is generally between $1,500 and $5,000. After you pay the deductible, your damages are covered up to the amount of the policy coverage amount. For example, if your camera and tripod fall off a cliff (it happens all the time), the price of the equipment ($30,000) that went over the cliff would be covered, minus the $1,500 deductible. If your cameraman went with the equipment, that's a more serious issue!

Finding an insurance broker

Specific insurance companies specialize in production insurance for your film. Your homeowner's or renter's policy is not appropriate for a film shoot (though it may cover some of your personal items if they're lost, damaged, or stolen while you're on a shoot). The Association of Independent Video and Filmmakers (www.aivf.org) offers insurance programs. Another great site for insurance information is www.productioninsurance.com.

Film Emporium also provides insurance to independent productions. You can fill out an insurance application form, choose the type of insurance you want, and submit for a quote. Go to the Web site at www.filmemporium.com and click on Production Insurance for more information.

You can get an immediate quote from United Agencies Insurance that covers the equipment (owned and/or rented) for a small production by going to www.gearinsurance.com/quick.asp. They gave me a very reasonable insurance production package quote of $2,200 for one of my independent films.

If you find that production insurance is too costly, see if you can go on a *rider*. A rider is what it sounds like: You ride along on someone else's insurance policy. If you're doing the film for a company, chances are you can ride on its insurance policy. Check with the insurance company to make sure that you're covered if you decide to go this route.

Be careful if you go on another company's insurance policy via a rider. The company should be legitimately affiliated with you and your production. If you end up having to make an insurance claim, the insurance company will not honor the policy if they find out another company was just letting you use their insurance and they weren't associated with your production.

Ensuring the completion of your film with a completion bond

A *completion bond* is an insurance policy that guarantees to the investor or financing source that if your film goes over budget, the completion bond company will finance the difference to complete the picture. The catch is that the completion bond company charges a percentage to do this (usually between 4 and 6 percent of the total budget), whether you need them in the end or not. And if you do go over budget and they have to step in, they can take over the film — and you're history. Usually, films with budgets of less than $1 million are not bonded, so if you're working on a low-budget production, this is not something you need to worry about.

A completion bond company conducts an extensive survey with you and all the production elements. They want to make sure that your budget is realistic. They don't want to have to finance the film — they just want their percentage fee. If you have an underwater fantasy that ends with resurrecting the *Titanic* on a $30,000 budget, they're not going to bond your film.

One of the leading completion bond companies is Film Finances. You can get more information about completion bonds and the services of Film Finances by going to www.ffi.com.

Chapter 5

Financing Your Film

· ·

In This Chapter

▶ Finding financing for your film

▶ Inviting investors to invest in your film

▶ Raising dollars through your new film company

· ·

*Y*ou can write a script with virtually no money, but to make a film you need dollars to put it all together. So how do you go about financing your film? Maxing out your credit cards or mortgaging the house is not the smartest or safest way to get the money to make your film. A better idea is to find an investor or investors who are prepared to take the risk of financing a film.

Before you even start looking for the film dollars, you need to prepare a professional presentation to show to your potential investors. After you've hooked the money people, you need to offer them a good incentive to believe in you and your project.

In this chapter, I introduce the various ways and places you can find funding for your film. And after you have the funding, I show you how to get started so you can turn the dream of making your film into a reality.

Creating an Enticing Prospectus

Making a film takes money, and that's where the almighty investor comes into the picture. An investor is your godsend — the person or group that believes in you and your film, and has faith in its commercial potential to make money for them. The investor is often referred to as your *angel* (a savior), because the investor is the one who makes it possible for you to actually produce your film. Without the investor's money, your idea would remain on paper and might never see the light of the projector.

An investor is usually someone who is used to investing and/or gambling his or her money either by playing the stock market or buying real estate. An investor's main focus is to make a good return on his or her investment, but at the same time knowing there is a risk of that potential. This is why you should concentrate on presenting to your investor the money-making possibilities should he or she invest in your project. An investor is more concerned with making a profit and looking at your production as an investment; a studio or distributor is looking at the whole picture — a film with a strong story that also has commercial potential.

I use the term *investor,* but that doesn't necessarily mean just one investor. Getting people to invest in your film is like selling stock in your film. It's easier to find ten people with $5,000 each than it is to find one with $50,000.

Before you can start looking for investors, you need some ammunition. You need to plan your work and work your plan. In order to entice investors, you need to put together a formal written presentation detailing why someone should invest in you and your project. Known as a *prospectus* or *business plan,* this presentation should be informative and entertaining. You can get software programs with specific templates to help you design an informative plan. For example, you can download PlanMagic at www.planmagic.com for $84.95, and Business Plan Maker at www.business-plan-maker.com for $49.95. Or you can write your own plan from scratch following the advice I give in this section. Putting together a prospectus not only helps get you financing for your film, but it also helps you see your goal more clearly. Keep in mind, that even though the prospectus is a written presentation, you should be prepared to verbally pitch your film idea and its commercial potential to the investor as well.

A prospectus for your film should have a table of contents page directing the investor to the appropriate sections of interest along with page numbers. Your package should contain the following information:

- ✔ **Synopsis of your film:** Most investors are only interested in knowing the gist of your story and the commercial viability of producing it into a film. Your synopsis should include references to the money-making potential of this particular type of story. A page or two is an appropriate length for a synopsis, not much longer than that. At the end of the synopsis, be sure to note that the screenplay is available upon request (be aware that an investor not familiar with screenplay formatting may find the script difficult to read).

- ✔ **Your background information and achievements:** Investors want to know your credits and experience, if any, with regards to filmmaking. If you have made other films before this, list how they faired financially. Also list related skills such as educational background and financial achievements that help support why you're capable of making this film and using the investor's money to finance your production. Be sure to include any documents, such as newspaper articles or copies of award certificates, that support your filmmaking accomplishments and educational degrees.

✔ **Cast and crew résumés:** If you don't know for sure who will sign on as members of your cast and crew, list the people you plan to approach.

✔ **Letters of interest from potential cast:** If you have interest from any actors or name stars, ask them for a *letter of interest.* A letter of interest shows that there is interest from someone who could potentially help the commercial success of your film by appearing in your production. See Chapter 8 for more on letters of interest.

✔ **The budget:** Investors obviously want to know how much the film will cost to complete. You can include a budget *top sheet,* which is a one-page summary of the entire budget broken into specific categories, or you can provide the full detailed budget with a breakdown of every category. See Chapter 4 for more on budgeting.

✔ **The profit projections:** This estimates how much your film could make in sales, based on other films and studio and/or independent productions similar to your film's budget and genre. You can find this information in the weekly box office reports in *The Hollywood Reporter* or *Daily Variety,* as well as in special marketing issues of these publications.

Investigating Investors

There's an art to finding investors. You need to know who to approach and how much to ask them for, in terms of dollars and cents. You also need to keep their interests in mind when presenting your project. Are they looking to make a lot of money? Or are they satisfied with making a small return on their investment with the association of being involved in the moviemaking business?

Identifying an investor who's got what it takes — money

Who makes a good investor? Anyone!

✔ Your parents or relatives

✔ A co-worker

✔ An acquaintance you met at a party or seminar

  ✔ Your doctor, lawyer, or dentist

  ✔ Your boyfriend or girlfriend — or their boyfriend or girlfriend

  ✔ Someone you do business with, such as the shop owner down the street

People are always looking for different ways to invest their money. Some play it safe and put it into interest-bearing accounts or long-term CDs. Others like the excitement and risk of playing the stock market, buying property, or the fun of investing in a film. Anyone who has a little (or a lot) of money to invest may be willing to take a chance and back your film; you just have to ask. (I discuss ways to successfully approach potential investors later in this chapter.)

Locating potential investors: Here money, money, money . . .

Investors are out there — you just have to find them. And remember, timing is everything. Someone may not be prepared to invest in your film today, but they might tomorrow. Don't give up — keep asking.

  ✔ **Whether you're at a cocktail party, a screening, or even at the photocopier, let everyone you come into contact with know that you're looking for investors for your film.** You never know who knows whom. Maybe Johnny's dad wants to get involved in financing a small film — you never know until you ask. Word of mouth is the best way to find financing for your film.

  ✔ **Get a mailing list of investors from a mailing list company.** Try Hugo Dunhill Mailing Lists, Inc. (www.hdml.com — look in the index under "Investors;" also try other high-income lists such as "Doctors").

Prospecting a Web site

The Internet is a great tool for promoting your film. In the past, filmmakers spent a fortune photocopying their prospectus for their film and then paying for postage or courier charges. Now all you have to do is tell your potential investors to check out your Web site. Investors across the world can check out your project in a matter of seconds, after you tell them about your Web site. (For examples, check out my Web sites at www.bryanmichaelstoller.com and www.misscastaway.com). Having a Web site gives you the ability to link to certain information and cross-reference information. If you're talking about a particular actor, you can link to the actor's Web site. Or you can create a link to a certain location or piece of equipment that takes the viewer directly to that information.

Approaching a potential investor

When you know whom to approach for financing, you need to know how to approach them. It's like going out on a date — you have to impress on the first date, or you don't get a second chance. Your first meeting with a potential investor will probably be over the phone. You need to sell him on getting involved with you and your film, so that you can move to the next step and have a face-to-face meeting. The potential investor may request a copy of your prospectus or business plan before wanting to meet in person. This should remind you how important your presentation package is — if it intrigues the investor — you'll get that in-person meeting and have a chance to close the deal.

Keep in mind the following when approaching investors:

- ✔ Be enthusiastic about your project over the phone, but don't be phony.

- ✔ Be honest and don't guarantee that they'll get rich from investing in your film.

- ✔ Prepare for your face-to-face meeting. Review all the material in your package so that the investor will know that you know what you're talking about.

- ✔ Don't come across as money hungry. Be respectful. Assure the investor that you will treat his or her money as if it's your own.

- ✔ Follow up with a thank-you note to the investor for taking the time to meet with you and for considering your proposal.

You have to look at it as a win-win situation. You could be doing the investor a favor. Don't be desperate for the money. The investor has the potential of making money with your film (also the potential to lose his pants — but you probably don't want to say that).

Be realistic. Don't ever guarantee investors that they'll recoup their investment and make a profit. Nothing in life is guaranteed, especially getting rich off making a movie. You don't want to mislead them. Treat your potential investors with respect and treat their money like it's yours. If you prove that you can be trusted, they may invest in *you* — and fund your future projects.

You don't have to find a millionaire to invest in your film. Everyday people are willing to invest their savings and extra earnings — just look at all those who go to Las Vegas to take a chance on the tables.

People get excited about the idea of getting involved in financing a film. It's a lot more exciting (and definitely more glamorous) than buying $5,000 in toilet paper stock. You can also entice your investors by offering to give them an Executive Producer credit in your film's opening credits.

Be sure to mutually agree in writing the appropriate credit that your investor will receive on the film. You can have as many Executive Producer credits as fits the number of investors.

After you've found investors, a company agreement between you and your investors must be drafted before anyone is going to hand over cash for you to make your film. When the investor agrees to participate in the financing of your film, it's time to move on to forming a company and ironing out the details of putting your project together.

Keeping the Securities and Exchange Commission in mind

Companies or individuals seeking to raise financing need to be regulated by the Securities and Exchange Commission (SEC), which is a government division created by Congress that regulates how companies can solicit for funds in order to protect investors and to ensure that all funds are reported. These regulations prevent the fund-raising company from misrepresenting the project (and committing other fraudulent acts) so that investors can make informed judgments on whether to invest and how much they want to risk.

The SEC provides bylaws that fundraisers have to follow in order to protect and properly inform potential investors. These laws include how to present your investment opportunity and how to inform the SEC of your business activities. The SEC regulates how a fundraiser identifies herself to investors and makes sure that she doesn't misrepresent her intention and that she conducts all business activities in a legal manner. The SEC reviews the registration of the fundraiser to make sure she's abiding by the rules and regulations of soliciting for funds. By not registering with the SEC, you could be fined if you don't comply with the rules and regulations of soliciting for funds.

The SEC is there to protect the investor and investments from misrepresentation or fraud. Check out the Securities and Exchange Commission Web site (www.sec.gov) for more information.

If the money is from your immediate family, friends, or a limited number of people you know, you don't need to be regulated by the SEC.

Starting a Film Company

When you find an investor who believes in you and your film project, you need to set up a production company through which to run the financing.

You often need your investors to help finance the startup of the company as well, so it's best to wait to form the company until you find an investor.

Set up some form of a production company; otherwise you're what's called a *sole proprietorship*. If you don't form a corporation or limited liability company, you have no protection from liability and are a vulnerable target for lawsuits and other headaches.

You have lots of choices when it comes to the type of company you want to form. They include

✔ General partnership

✔ Limited partnership

✔ Corporation

✔ Limited liability company (LLC)

✔ Joint venture

The different types of company formations all have their own advantages and disadvantages. You need to choose the one that best suits your situation. There are three main factors you need to consider when determining the type of company you should form:

✔ **Liability:** Who will be responsible in case of a lawsuit or bad debts? You and the company partners, or just the company?

✔ **Taxes:** What kind of tax structure does the company have? Does the company pay tax or do the taxes flow through to you and your partner's personal taxes?

✔ **Ownership:** Who owns the film and any other assets of the company?

When setting up a company, you need to consider some other items on your to-do list:

✔ **Opening a checking account (specifically for your production):** If you have a checking account specifically for your production, you can monitor the film's production expenses, and your investors can see a proper accounting of where their dollars were spent.

✔ **Creating a company logo:** A logo gives your production company a professional appearance and credibility.

✔ **Printing business cards and stationery:** Business cards and stationery add to the professional image of your new production company.

✔ **Hiring an attorney to look over all agreements:** An attorney can help to protect you from lawsuits and negligence.

Limited partnerships limit the relationship

A *limited partnership* limits one of the partner's liabilities and tax responsibilities (usually the investor in this case). The main or *general partner* is responsible for the company, while the *limited partner* remains silent and lets you do all the work. For example, an investor gives you the money to make your film, but he or she is not involved with the creative decisions or production of the film.

Only the investor's investment is at risk. Because the investor isn't responsible for any activities that are performed by the limited partnership, he or she isn't liable if there are any lawsuits against the film or the general partner.

Howdy pardner — wanna strike up a partnership?

A *partnership* is the merging of two or more people with the same goals in business who sign an agreement to achieve those goals together. Also known as a *general partnership,* this agreement gives each partner equal authority and equal liability (as opposed to limited authority in a limited partnership) for the company's activities.

Being your own boss and starting your own corporation

A *corporation* is a professional entity that is separate from you as an individual. The corporation reports to the IRS regarding taxes, and it is liable in case of lawsuits, bad debts, and so on. A corporation protects the company owners, you, the filmmaker, and your partners (to an extent), by what's called the *corporate shield.* In other words, in the event of a lawsuit, only the corporation assets are liable, not the individuals who run the company.

The costs of starting a corporation vary, depending on whether you use a corporate attorney or incorporate on your own. It can cost as little as $20 or as much as several hundred dollars, depending on where you incorporate and how. You can incorporate through an online service like www.incorporating.com, which will guide you through all the steps of incorporating.

Some people form corporations in Nevada, regardless of whether their offices are there or not, because the advantages are substantial:

- ✔ There are lower or no tax fees for running the corporation.
- ✔ There are minimal tax obligations (no state taxes).
- ✔ Owners can remain anonymous from the IRS and public records.
- ✔ There is low maintenance in running a Nevada company.
- ✔ Owners don't have to reside in Nevada.

Some people also choose to form their corporation in Delaware. Although it has a small fee to incorporate (more than Nevada, but less than any other state) and annual tax obligations, you can incorporate relatively quickly and easily in Delaware, and company owners remain anonymous. It is also a corporate-friendly state. Delaware is known to have the highest amount of corporations that are *not* physically in the state of Delaware. All paperwork, which includes setting up the corporation, filing taxes, and accounting, can all be done through the mail or online.

Let's see about an LLC: Limited liability company

A *limited liability company* (LLC) combines the best of a corporation and a limited partnership. It protects the filmmaker's assets that are separate from the LLC in case of a liability suit. An LLC is also easier and cheaper to form than a corporation. Usually the owners of the LLC are listed as members without official corporate titles. An LLC is taxed similar to a corporation, or you have the choice of directing profits and expenses through to your personal taxes.

Joined at the hip: Joint ventures

A *joint venture* is usually two companies already in business who decide to join together on one production. They can be corporations, partnerships, or LLCs. Many studios nowadays are doing joint productions because the cost of a studio film with big-name talent has skyrocketed. A joint venture is similar to the structure of a partnership (it's like a joint partnership).

Fictitiously "doing business as"

If you form a company as a division under some-one else's company, you may want to use a fictitious business name called a DBA (short for *doing business as*) or sometimes an *AKA* (short for *also known as*). A DBA or AKA is kind of like a pseudonym.

To register a DBA, go to your county clerk's office, or download the form from the Web site (check your local government Web pages for your county clerk's Web site). A DBA costs between $20 and $80 to register, depending on what city you live in, and it expires five years from the date you file it. You have to announce the name in a local newspaper to make it official and legal (you run it for four weeks in the new businesses classified section). The clerk's office will give you the information for the news-papers and periodicals that provide this service.

Going Escrow

When you've found your financing and set up your production company, you may want to consider an *escrow account.* An escrow company monitors the bank account that's been set up with the funds for your production. You don't want to be a week into filming and find out your investor hasn't sent the next installment of the budget. Having the money in an escrow account ensures that the money is indeed there and available.

The *escrow holder or agent* follows the specific conditions of a written agreement signed by you and your investors instructing what, where, when, and how the funds will be released. These instructions usually include a payment schedule for disbursement of funds with regards to the production of the film, from preproduction all the way through postproduction. An escrow account is also a security blanket for investors, ensuring them that there will be no suspicious tapping into the bank account.

Contracting Your Investor

Drawing up a formal agreement between you and your investors is the final step in securing financing. This agreement is often an adjunct to your business formation agreement (whether it be a corporation, an LLC, or a form of partnership). It spells out exactly the understanding between you and your investors with regards to the financing of your film and the participation (if any) in your company.

Every type of legal agreement has a standard contract. These agreements are called *boilerplate* agreements, meaning all you have to do is fill in the information pertaining to your specific project and budget. You can also add specific items or concerns that you or your investor want to address. Even if you do use boilerplate agreements, I recommend that you have them reviewed by an attorney to make sure you've covered yourself. You can find boilerplate agreements in Mark Litwak's book, *Contracts for Film and Television* (for more information go to www.marklitwak.com). *The Complete Film Production Handbook* also has every conceivable agreement relating to film production including a CD-ROM with printable forms, all for under $40.

You also have the choice of using an attorney to prepare your contract from scratch, but this will cost you more than starting with a boilerplate agreement.

All investor agreements should include the following information:

- ✔ **Profit:** Usually profits are shared 50/50 between the investors and you and your production company.

- ✔ **Responsibilities:** Spell out the responsibilities of you and your company and the responsibilities of the investor regarding financing.

- ✔ **Recoupment:** This is when and how long it will take before the investors will see their investment back, plus any profits, and how it will be dispersed between you and the investors. Recoupment, if any, can happen soon after the film is completed, or it may take a year or more, depending on the commercial viability of the film and the aggressiveness of your distributor.

- ✔ **Expenses:** Expenses can include your company overhead, distributor's percentage fee, distributor's advertising and marketing costs for your film, travel costs, film market costs, and any other expenses you specify in the agreement pertaining to the production.

- ✔ **Auditing:** Does the investor have the right to audit? If not, who does?

- ✔ **Bonus:** As an incentive to your investor to want to invest in your project, you may want to include a special added bonus on top of the investor's standard recoupment of his investment. A bonus can be in the form of an additional percentage on profits, or a quicker return of his investment before certain expenses are paid, and so on.

Tapping into Alternative Sources

If you aren't having much luck finding private investors, or you need supplemental funding to match funds you've already raised, you do have some additional options.

Getting a loan

One alternative to private financing is applying for a loan. Your bank may mortgage your home to give you some extra cash, or your credit-card company may increase your credit limit to give you more room for charges on your account.

Although mortgaging your home or upping your credit-card limit will help finance your project, I don't recommend going this route because the risk is too great. Think about it: If you borrow heavily on your credit card, you're going to have some astronomical monthly payments that you'll have to make until you break even on your film, which may never happen. And if you mortgage your home, the worst-case scenario is that you could lose your home — don't do it!

Pre-selling your film

You may be able to *pre-sell* your film, based on a great script or star talent. You first find a distributor, who then takes your film idea, the script, or the trailer and gets deposits upfront (usually 20 percent of the total selling price) from buyers who like the idea and who will pay the balance (the remaining 80 percent) when the film is delivered to them (see Chapter 19). By having a distributor pre-sell your film, it gives you some money to start your film, and shows that the buyers are seriously interested.

A three-minute trailer (a commercial for your film showing the highlights — see Chapter 19) or a scene from your script, can help pre-sell your film to potential investors or buyers (such as a studio or distributor). A trailer can be shot for little or no money, by getting your actors to work for deferred pay (see Chapter 4 for more on that miracle) and getting your equipment and locations donated.

Dolly Parton wrote and recorded four holiday songs for one of my films in development, *The Wishing Well*. These songs (and her name) were a great promotional tool when putting the production together. Dan Aykroyd provided the voice of Dexter the Computer in my feature film, *The Random Factor*, which gave me a bit of star power to entice a distributor to pick up the film.

Getting a grant

When I was 13 years old, I applied to a government council that financed short films. I was turned down because I was too young. I then applied to a fund that encouraged children to make their own films — they, too, turned me down, telling me I was too old. That was my first and last attempt at trying to get a grant. I don't recommend this route because it involves a lot of time, research, and paperwork — not to mention waiting (as long as two years) to know if you received the grant. But, on the other hand, you may get lucky and find it's just the thing for you.

A grant is easier to obtain if your film is about a cause or supports a charity and if it's a short film or public service announcement (PSA).

Trade you this for that: Bartering

Bartering is a form of trading. Remember the time in grade school when you traded your watch for that gnarly jaw breaker bubble gum? In bartering for a film, a company gives you the use of its product (on loan or to keep, depending on what it is), or an individual lets you use a particular element (like a location or prop) that you want to use in your film in exchange for a credit or placing the company's product on camera. Bartering is one way to bring your budget down, but it's not the way to finance your entire film.

When I was 11 years old, I used to finance my little super-8 movies by bartering. For my film stock, I contacted different camera stores that sold super-8 film. If they would donate ten rolls of film for me to make my movie, I would list them in the ending film credits. All through my teens, I bartered for on-camera products, including film stock. When I was 17, I made a film called *Superham* and raised some of the financing from a local car dealer. In exchange, the car dealer got a front presentation credit introducing the film. You can try bartering for the following products and services:

- ✔ Clothing
- ✔ Editing equipment and/or an editor
- ✔ Film stock
- ✔ Food and drinks
- ✔ Hotel accommodations
- ✔ Laboratory film developing
- ✔ Locations
- ✔ Products featured in actual scenes
- ✔ Transportation (including cars for the production and airline tickets)

Bartering in the movie business is also known as *product placement*. Product placement is when a company places its product in your film and either lends it to you, gives it to you, or pays you for featuring it in your film (especially if a major star interacts with the product). For example, while shooting my film *Miss Cast Away*, I approached The Sharper Image about featuring a remote control robot in the film. The company was excited about the product exposure and provided two robots to use in the film at no charge.

Product placement in the form of goods and services can save you hundreds, even thousands of dollars depending on what they are and what it would cost you if you had to actually pay for their use. If a food company donates sandwiches, this could save you hundreds of dollars in feeding your cast and crew.

Some companies, such as Premier Entertainment Services of North Hollywood, California, specialize in placing products in films (check it out at www.pesfilmtv.com). If you contact a product-placement company, it will request a copy of your script and comb through it, deciding where it may be able to provide on-camera product for you, based on the client products it represents.

Chapter 6

Location, Location, Location

As a filmmaker, you have the power to take your audience on a trip to exotic locales — a remote island, a picturesque small town, or deep into outer space, for example. By removing the fourth wall, you invite your audience into your story. Therefore, picking the right locations at which to shoot — or creating just the right environments on soundstages or on your computer — is very important to your film's success.

In this chapter, you find out how to discover great locations to use in your film — some of them free of charge. Depending on your budget and the setting of your film, you need to decide whether to shoot on location or on a controlled indoor soundstage, so I give you some advice about making that choice as well. Finally, to make sure that you and your film are protected, I explain the types of insurance and city permits that are usually required when filming on location. Police and firemen may be required, too, and they may show up if you *don't* hire them!

Picking Locations

After you've locked down your script — meaning there are no more changes — comb through it and determine where you want to shoot your scenes. Some software programs, like Screenwriter 2000 (www.screenplay.com), actually break down your script for you by pulling out all your scene headings and generating a list of settings from your screenplay. Of course, you can also go through the script yourself and jot down all the locations without having to use a computer. After you have a list of the settings for your film, you can start looking for the actual locations that will fit your story.

Establishing shots

As you're shooting the principal photography on your film, see whether you need to show the exterior of the setting where certain interior scenes take place. These outside shots are called *establishing shots,* and they help keep your film from having a claustrophobic feel to it.

If the film is all interiors, the audience is going to feel like they're closed in the entire time. Give them some breathing space. Establishing shots can also be part of your *second unit* shoot (see the section "Shooting Second-Unit Locations," later in this chapter for more information).

You're casting your film with actors who have a lot of character, so why not find locations with character, too? Don't list generic locations like a bookstore or a restaurant; go with specific settings that will be memorable to your audience, such as a quaint boutique bookstore or a French café with a patio overlooking a park. Does your lead character live in a small, messy apartment or a lavish house on gated grounds with an Olympic-sized swimming pool?

Managing location scouts and managers

A *location scout* searches out the perfect locations for your film — this person is your "reel" estate broker. Anyone can be a location scout, but someone who does it for a living will be familiar with every type of location, saving you weeks or even months of searching for the right place. If you can't afford a location scout, you can hire someone who's eager to drive around, make phone calls, and search the Internet — or you can do it yourself. Finding the right locations for a film takes time. Contact your local film commission (if there's one in your city) and ask if it can recommend a location scout, or call your city permit office and ask if it can refer you to a location scout. You can also go online and find a location scout at www.crewnet.com, which conveniently lets you search by state and crew position.

A *location manager* manages the locations after you've found them. He or she looks after getting the appropriate releases and permits for your locations and makes sure that the proper insurance is in place. (See the section "Securing Your Locations," later in this chapter, for more on releases, insurance, and other location-specific particulars.) Your location manager can also double as your location scout on a lower-budget production. If you go this route, make sure to find someone who is detail-oriented and persistent.

Cinema Scout (www.cinemascout.com) is a service that provides a search engine that lets you track down virtually any type of existing location in California without having to leave your desk.

Most states have guides or directories listing production services available to filmmakers interested in shooting in their cities. The guides are usually put out by the state film commissions (which you can find by calling your city hall) to encourage productions to use local businesses to help the state's economy.

Don't forget to put the word out to friends, family, and acquaintances that you're looking for locations. You never know who may have a great location that you can use for one of your scenes.

Evaluating potential locations

Filming on a soundstage or in a warehouse (discussed later in this section) is not always practical — you just may not have the budget to do it. Sometimes you can find a location at which you can film for free or for a price that's within your budget. By shooting on location, you don't have to start from scratch and construct sets for every scene in your film (not practical at all on a low budget).

Whether you're in Los Angeles, New York, or a small town in the Midwest, you're sure to find vacant buildings that can work wonders for your story and are just waiting to be razed or renovated. From an old restaurant that's been shut down to a bank that closed its doors, you can usually negotiate with the building owner or the government to film on this existing set.

When deciding on locations, make sure that they're appropriate for sound as well. You don't want a location that's too close to the freeway or a construction site. Here's a list of things to consider when scouting locations:

- Is parking available for cast, crew, and equipment vehicles?

- Is it near bathroom facilities (a public park or a local restaurant)?

- Is it in a quiet location (away from traffic, train tracks [unless out-of-service], factories, and outdoor fountains)?

- Is there available electricity to plug in your lights? (If not, you'll need a generator.)

- If you're shooting out of town, are there overnight accommodations nearby?

- Is there air-traffic noise if the site is on route to the airport?

- Do you have space to set up a picnic area to feed your cast and crew?

- Can you get permission to shoot there? Do you need a permit? Can you afford to film there?

- Does using the site require the hiring of a police officer to stop foot or street traffic?

✔ Is there a photocopy store nearby (for copying the next day's schedule)?

✔ Do cell phones work in the area? If not, are there public phones nearby?

Finding the perfect location that works both inside as an interior and outside as an exterior may be difficult. Remember that you can film the exterior of a house and then use a different house's interior, or even construct the indoor rooms on a soundstage. Doing so gives you a more controlled environment.

Taking a picture: Say "cheese" and "thank you"

With the advent of digital still cameras, you can snap some great location pictures to show your cinematographer and other crew members what locations you have to choose from. And you can download the images to a computer and e-mail them in full, crisp color to whomever needs to see them — whether they're across town or across the world! Photos are also helpful in planning your shots after you choose the locations you want to use.

I use the Kyocera FinecamS4, a 4.0-megapixel portable digital camera that takes magazine-quality photos that are breathtaking (check out www.kyocera.com). It's lightweight and small enough to fit in a handbag or jacket pocket. A digital camera like the Kyocera is an invaluable tool for any filmmaker — and not just for location scouting (I talk about other uses for a digital still camera for setting up special-effects shots in Chapter 17 and publicity pictures for your film in Chapter 19).

Sounding off about soundstages

Soundstages are a convenient way to shoot interior scenes mainly because you don't have to worry about unplanned sounds interrupting your takes. A soundstage is basically a soundproofed room. All exterior sounds are blocked out of an industrial soundstage after the doors are closed. A soundstage is an acoustic environment that has padded walls that absorb sound to prevent an echo or reverb in your dialogue, as would happen if you filmed in an uncarpeted room.

Another advantage of shooting on a soundstage is that you can set up several interior sets for different locations in your script without having to move your whole production team. You can have a courtroom, a cell block, an apartment, a coffee shop, and an interior fast-food restaurant all on the same soundstage.

20th Century Props (www.20thcenturyprops.com) has pre-built sets like a full-scale submarine in its parking lot.

When you see an airport and airplane scene in a film, chances are it was shot on a controlled soundstage. Air Hollywood in Los Angeles (www. airhollywood.com) houses several airplane bodies that have removable walls and seats for convenient filming. Air Hollywood also has a full airport terminal that includes X-ray machines, a magazine store, and a bar. I like shooting at Air Hollywood because I've never experienced a flight delay, and I've never had to use the air-sickness bag. You do have to bring your own peanuts, though.

A soundstage can also be a warehouse, a school gym, or a vacant apartment — any place where you can build sets and hold a decent-size crew. Remember that you have to deal with outside noises if the room or building is not sound-proofed. I once shot an office scene in an IKEA store where mock-up rooms are exemplified for customers. Many furniture stores use these type of displays, which make perfect sets — if you can get permission from the store and keep the customers quiet (and don't forget to hide the price tags!).

You can make your own soundproofed room, or at least cut down on the reverb, by putting up *foam sheets* on the walls, or on stands (outside of the camera's view) close to the actors performing their dialogue. These foam sheets will absorb reverb and prevent sounds from bouncing back. You can also rent *sound blankets* (the kind used by moving companies). Sound blankets also help to prevent echo and reverb by absorbing sound the way carpeting does. You can hang them outside of the shot or lay them on bare floors (when you're not showing the floor in your shot).

Putting up walls around you: Using flats

If you're going to shoot on a soundstage or in a warehouse, you have to construct your sets from scratch. You may need to hire carpenters or people with construction knowledge, or you can do the building yourself and with the assistance of volunteers. If your budget allows, you could bring in a *production designer* (sort of like an interior designer) and maybe even a person versed in architectural design.

Soundstage sets usually involve *flats,* which are separate moveable walls constructed of wooden frames with support stands to keep them upright. When you go to a theater to see a stage play, you often see sets created with flats. Putting together a simple room, such as an apartment, by using flats is fairly easy. Flats can also simulate exterior walls made of brick, logs, concrete, or stucco. Of course, if you have an elaborate set, like the interior of a dry cleaner or an ancient church, using the actual location is easier and cheaper.

The advantage of filming on a soundstage using a set constructed with flats is that you can remove the fourth wall where the camera is, which allows more room for your crew and equipment to comfortably shoot the film. The problem with flats is that they're big and bulky; you need a truck to transport them and several helpers to carry and set them up.

You can build your own flats or find them at your local theater company. If you're in Los Angeles or New York, try one of the movie studios for renting flats, or you can find scenery houses and set-design companies listed in the Yellow Pages or an entertainment directory like the Los Angeles 411 (www.la411.com) or the New York 411 (www.newyork411.com).

You can make your own flats by building a wood frame out of light plywood. Then you paint or wallpaper it, set it up, and bring in some furniture and set decoration — sort of like home decorating. If you're looking to create an exterior scene, you can attach paneling that resembles brick, log, concrete, or some other surface. You can cut out your own windows and put a scenic background outside the window to simulate an outside setting (or put some branches outside the window to suggest a tree). You can see how to construct sturdy flats in the *Stock Scenery Construction Handbook* by Bill Raoul. Also check out www.thestagecrew.com and click on "Flats" for a complete lesson on building your own walls.

Figure 6-1 shows a basic example of a flat and how it should be supported.

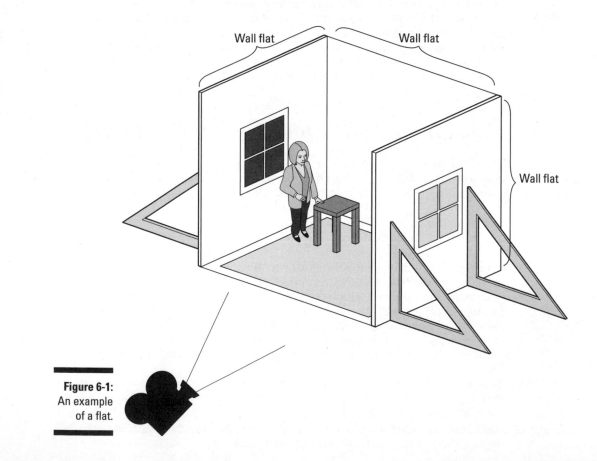

Wall flat

Wall flat

Wall flat

Figure 6-1:
An example
of a flat.

Deciding Whether to Shoot in the United States or Head North of the Border

You may not have the luxury of deciding where to shoot your film: Your hometown may be all that you can afford. However, you may face the decision whether to film on locations in the United States or take your production to Canada, where prices can be much cheaper. You may even be able to consider going somewhere else in the world (if the cost of transportation and accommodations is still less than shooting in your hometown). This section examines the pros and cons of both options.

Researching U.S. government incentives

Shooting outside the United States — often in Canada — has become much more common because the incentives (tax and labor rebates, along with the stretching of the value of the dollar) are usually much cheaper. This phenomenon, known as *runaway production*, has become a concern for cast and crew who lose work to foreign workers. Runaway production is also a government concern, and local agencies are interested in keeping the film industry within the United States by sponsoring incentives to encourage filmmakers to shoot locally. Making films is good for the economy; businesses, including restaurants, hotels, and parks, benefit from it. If you aren't located in a major city that has a film commission set up by the government, you can contact your local city hall.

Many states offer tax rebates to filmmakers who shoot locally. A tax rebate reimburses the sales tax you paid for expenses related to your production. Usually, you're reimbursed after submitting receipts and proof of sales tax payment. In Canada, two taxes, PST (Provincial Sales Tax) and GST (General Sales Tax), are eligible for reimbursement.

AFCI.org

The Association of Film Commissioners International (AFCI) can help you find answers to important location questions and even put you in contact with worldwide government contacts for on-location shooting. AFCI also puts on location trade shows; check its Web site at www.afci.org for dates and locations. At the Locations Trade Show, you can meet state and worldwide film commissions all under one roof. The trade show takes place annually in Los Angeles (usually in April). AFCI also publishes an informative magazine called *Locations Magazine,* which you can subscribe to by going to the Web site.

Shooting outdoors

Weather is the number-one concern when shooting outdoors (unless you live in California, where it never rains). Your favorite cable network becomes the Weather Channel. Rain, snow, hail, and wind can ruin any shoot, or at least make it extremely difficult. Hot or cold environments can also affect your camera's performance. Condensation can form on the camera's lens when moving from a cool outside environment to a heated interior. Be prepared to shoot indoors at the last minute if you do get rained out, or be prepared to shoot your scene and have your actors acknowledge the weather in the scene if it is windy or storming.

An incentive program offered by the California Film Commission is the State Theatrical Arts Resources (STAR) program, which provides unoccupied state-owned properties at no charge or a nominal charge to filmmakers. Currently, three dozen such properties are available under the STAR program.

Traveling to Canada

Sometimes shooting a film in Canada, as many U.S. studio movies and television shows are doing, is easier. Some of the advantages include

- More dollars — the value of the U.S. dollar stretches because of currency exchange (40 percent or more)
- Rebates on federal and provincial sales tax
- Lower rental costs on locations
- Government rebates on labor (up to 22 percent)
- Rebates on labs and computer animation

The downfall of shooting in Canada is the added expense of having to fly your cast and crew there (unless you hire them locally) and put everyone up in a hotel. You need to decide whether it's more economical to shoot in Canada or stay at home.

Locating Stock Footage

Want an aerial shot of a city lit up at night? An explosion over the ocean? Chances are you can find the perfect footage already shot and just insert it into your film. That's what *stock footage libraries* are all about. Just like locating a sound effect from a sound effects library or a piece of music from a music library (see Chapter 16 for more on sound and music libraries), you can license existing footage (usually without actors in the shot) that integrates perfectly into your film. A *license* gives you permission to feature particular footage from a film library in your film for a specific fee.

I've used stock footage from the Artbeats Digital Film Library (www. artbeats.com) in many of my projects. They have every piece of footage imaginable, from old black-and-white vintage scenes to astronauts and outer-space footage. You can view its entire digital library online and even purchase and download the footage on your computer. I recommend ordering its free demo CD-ROM or DVD. A starter package gives you six stock footage shots for only $39. Library packages start at $399. After you license the footage, you have nonexclusive rights to use it in your film. Following is a list of footage from the Artbeats stock footage library that I've used in some of my projects:

- Flying through fluffy white clouds
- Skydivers jumping from a plane
- Icebergs floating in the ocean
- An airplane's landing gear pulling up as it leaves the runway

Stock footage can raise the production value of your film and make it look like a much higher budget. If you have an aerial opening shot, the audience isn't going to know that you didn't shoot it, or that you paid less than $400 for the footage from a stock footage library.

Some footage from a stock library has been shot on film, and other footage on video. If you're shooting on film or with a digital 24p camera and you buy footage on video, you can use software like Bullet, available at www.redgiantsoftware.com, to make the video footage look more like it was shot on film. This helps disguise the fact that you have intercut stock footage into your production. (See Chapter 10 for more on choosing a medium in which to shoot your film.)

Stock footage libraries don't just license their footage; they're always looking to buy footage to add to their extensive libraries. Have you shot anything that may work for a stock footage library? You can earn a little money back to cover the expense of shooting the footage, and possibly make a little profit, too — every bit helps.

Virtual Locations: Creating New Worlds on a Computer

Need to shoot on another planet? Traveling to the moon isn't economical, and besides, you get motion sickness in outer space. Does the location you need exist only in your mind? Try creating it on your computer.

Bryce, a great software program by Corel (www.corel.com), enables you to create realistic-looking scenic backgrounds, from tree-topped mountains and rolling hills to sandy beaches next to flowing waterfalls. You can create your virtual locations in Bryce and then superimpose your actors onto the background using a blue- or green-screen process (see Chapter 17 for more information about blue-screen). I was able to use this software to create a desert location and add my dog to the scene (see Figure 6-2) even before reading the Bryce manual — in other words, it's simple to use.

Figure 6-2:
A virtual location created with Corel's Bryce software.

Securing Your Locations

After you find the ideal locations for your film, you need to have a formal agreement in writing between you and the property owners granting you permission to film at the location and outlining the specifics (for how long, how much, and any restrictions). You need to be guaranteed the use of the property and make sure that no surprises await you when you show up to start filming. There are services that can assist you in securing locations, either through the cities' permit offices, a location service, or your local film commission (which you can find by contacting your local city hall office).

Make sure that the person who signs the agreement to let you use the location has the full authority to do so. There should be a clause in the agreement that clarifies the person signing is an authorized signatory, so he's held responsible if it turns out he misled you.

You can have an attorney draft a one-page location contract. You can also use Enterprise Stationers, which has location agreements in addition to more than 400 other entertainment forms, including contracts and releases. For more information, go to www.enterpriseprinters.com.

Acquiring permits

Most public locations require a permit from the city or state (this is separate from the agreement with the location owner), whether you're filming outside or inside. You don't want to be filming with cast and crew and have a police officer show up asking for a permit. If this happens, you could be asked to leave, and you and your cast and crew will be virtually left out in the cold. Permits are usually inexpensive, averaging a few hundred dollars; many cities' film commissions encourage filming and waive the fee. Check with the city or state permit office to find out if the fee can be waived. If you can't find a permit office, start by calling city hall.

TIP

If you're in Los Angeles and having problems finding the permit office, it's because it's listed under Entertainment Industry Development Office. The official Web site is www.eidc.com. For New York City, go to www.nyc.gov and in the City Agencies drop-down list, select "Film/Theatre."

WARNING!

Under no circumstances should you ever sneak onto private property. Trespassing is illegal, and you could be arrested and thrown in jail. Your cinematographer can roll the camera documenting you being hauled off to prison. Won't that be fun?

Lining up the proper insurance

What if someone trips and knocks over a light stand, causing the hot light to ignite the drapes and burn down the location? This is when you'll be glad you bought location insurance under general liability coverage. If people know better, they won't let you film on their property until you present them with a certificate of insurance. This certificate is issued by an insurance carrier under a general liability policy, proving that the location you're using is covered in case you or your production company cause damage. General liability insurance doesn't really cost you money — it saves you money in the long run. See Chapter 4 for more information about all the insurance you should consider purchasing for your film.

Bartering for credit

You may be able to get a location for free if you can offer something in exchange. If you're filming away from home and you give a hotel a credit or even feature the hotel on camera, you could get free accommodations or at least a discount for your cast and crew to stay there. Lodging can be expensive, and many independent films can't afford to put up cast and crew. So writing in a scene where you actually see the hotel, or adding a big thank you in the end credits, may be worth it.

Movie trailers (not the coming-attraction kind)

A movie trailer can be a midsized RV or an oversized Winnebago. A trailer is a luxury not always available to the low-budget filmmaker. On studio pictures, the stars always have their own private trailers with all the comforts of home: a kitchen, a bathroom with shower, and a bed. But even on a low-budget production, trying to get even a small RV to use as a production trailer when you're on location isn't a bad idea. The trailer can be a sheltered place to take meetings, a place for actors to have some private space or even take a nap between takes if they don't have their own trailers. Also, a trailer can be a place of refuge when the weather is bad or a good place to retreat when you need to get your bearings for the next shot.

Mapping out your locations

When your locations are set, you need to make sure that your cast and crew can find them. Usually the first or second assistant director supplies location maps to the cast and crew. Photocopy a local city guide and write down the directions. Internet mapping sites such as www.mapquest.com and www.maps.com are also handy — but always double-check Internet directions.

Policing your locations

If you need to stop cars or direct traffic around the area you're filming, police may be required. Police are usually required when you're shooting on city or state properties as well (be careful when using the word *shooting* around police officers). Some states offer discounts and rebates on police officers' salaries when filming on government property.

Always have the police direct or stop traffic. You have no authority to do so, and you will either get arrested or some angry commuter will jump out of his vehicle and a foot chase will ensue. Also, my mom taught me that playing in traffic is dangerous.

Fire!

If you're dealing with explosions, firearms, or any potential fire hazard, you're required to have a firefighter on the set (and, of course, a pyrotechnician who is skilled with explosives and gunpowder). Depending on which city you film in, you may get a reimbursement or rebate on the salary you pay to a firefighter.

Shooting Second-Unit Locations

Second-unit photography is footage that is not filmed at the same time as your principal photography and usually doesn't require your main actors (or allows you to use doubles for a distant shot). Second unit is often filmed after your main shoot, when you've had a chance to make a list of additional shots to weave into your main shots, such as establishing exterior shots of certain locations.

If your story is supposed to take place in New York, but you live in a small town in the Midwest and you're on a tiny budget, you can't afford to take your whole cast and crew to New York to film. Instead, buy yourself one plane ticket. Pack your digital video camera and shoot some establishing shots that you can cut into your film.

For my film *Miss Cast Away,* we shot most of the footage along the beaches of California to save money but went to Hawaii for second-unit footage. We used helicopter footage of the islands and establishing shots of the ocean waves hitting the tropical shores.

Chapter 7

Crewing Up: Hiring Your Crew

As a filmmaker, you may be the driving force and creative fount, but you can't make a film all by yourself. Whether you have a 2-person crew or 30 people assisting you in your vision, you need to find people who are as passionate about your film as you are. Chances are if it's a low-budget film, your crew members aren't doing it for the money. You may be paying something up front, or deferring their entire salary. So either they're your dear friends and family (and you hope they'll continue to be after your film shoot) or they're enthusiastic students or crew people who love making movies.

In this chapter, I list the necessary positions required on an independent production along with a description of each crew position and what traits, skills, and knowledge are required. You discover the advantages and disadvantages of hiring an independent contractor versus an employee, along with great tips regarding crew members who may take a pay cut if they get other perks. You can be the producer, director, cinematographer, writer, editor, and even the star of your film — but you need a crew to help with lighting, grip equipment, props, wardrobe, sound, and so on. You can't go it alone like a writer or painter can. However, you can double up positions on a small production. For example, your prop person can also do wardrobe and maybe even help out in one of the grip positions.

Something to Crew About

An independent production, especially one that's shooting with a digital video camera, doesn't require as large a crew as you do with film. When shooting video, you have sound and picture together and may not need a separate sound mixer. With video you also don't need a second assistant cameraperson because there are no film reels to load or film reports to send to a lab. Video also requires less lighting, which will help cut down on lighting and grip equipment. If you love overworking yourself, you can even operate the camera and sound yourself, as well as position the lights and move the equipment around. You can still get away with a small crew if you're shooting film. But here is a list of the main production team you should try to assemble, whether you're shooting film or video.

Producing the producer

A *producer* is responsible for putting the project together and finding the financing. Without the right producer, the film may never come to fruition. (My mother requested a special credit on the last film I directed — she was the *producer of the director.*) Another good definition of a producer, who is often the filmmaker (the person responsible for the project being produced in the first place), is the first one on the project and the last one to leave. If the director is not also the producer, the director usually shows up after the producer is on set, and leaves before the producer leaves, because the director has a lot of homework (planning) to do off set, to be ready the next time he or she is on set.

An *associate producer* is usually a glorified title reserved for someone who contributes an important element to the production — such as finding the financing or the name stars. Agents and managers often get an associate producer credit for bringing a star or major element to a project.

Directing the direction

Everyone wants to direct, don't they? Even my dog has a T-shirt that says, "What I really want to do is direct." A *director* has to be a multitalented individual who handles multiple tasks. The director is captain of the ship, the leader of the pack, and he or she has many responsibilities to make all the creative elements come together (see Chapters 13 and 14 for more on what a director does). Many first-time filmmakers can take on the job of directing, and if you do your homework (like reading this book) and are passionate about making your film, you'll find it a rewarding experience. If you'd rather hire someone else to direct, start collecting demo reels — whether they're short films, features, or commercials — from prospective directors.

When searching for a director, look for these attributes:

✔ **Are they good with telling a story?** After viewing their work, is the film they made logical in its sequence of events? Did they tell an intriguing story?

✔ **Are the actors' performances believable?** Do they come across sincere? Do you care about the characters in the film?

✔ **Are camera shots and movement effective?** Does the director use effective angles? Are the shots interesting but not distracting to the story? Does the camera movement enhance the shots?

✔ **If the film's a comedy, is it funny?** Does the director have a good sense of comedic timing? Is the comedy funny or too silly?

✔ **Is the direction consistent?** Do the shots have a certain style? Do all the elements, shots, dialogue, setting, and so on have consistency, or does their work seem all over the place?

Assistant director

Many people have a misconception of what an assistant director does. He or she does *not* assist in directing the film. An *assistant director* (also known as the A.D.) is more of an assistant *to* the director. The assistant director keeps the set moving and the film on schedule. The assistant director's duties include

✔ Breaking down the script with the director (to schedule the shoot days).

✔ Relaying the director's technical instructions to the cast and crew.

✔ Getting the shots ready by making sure that all production personnel and actors are in place and ready to do their job when the director needs them.

✔ Working with the extras on a small budget, and relaying instructions for the extras to the second assistant director on a bigger production.

✔ Making up the *call sheets* (lists of which cast members work the next day and any special equipment or elements needed for the shooting). On bigger productions this is usually handed off by the first assistant director to the unit production manager.

✔ Calling the actors who need to work the next day on a small production. On a larger production where you can afford a unit production manager, he or she contacts the actors.

✔ Getting the set settled to start filming (asking if sound and camera are ready and then calling to the mixer to roll sound and the camera operator to roll camera). Sound and camera need to be rolling before the director cues the actors or action begins.

The director — never the assistant director — calls "action" and "cut." The assistant director's authority ends when the director calls for *Action!*

Second assistant director

The *second assistant director* (the second A.D.) is an assistant to the assistant director and is also responsible for a fair amount of paperwork — especially if it's a union shoot, because there are strict rules and regulations, and everything has to be documented properly. I liken a second A.D. to an executive assistant — this person does paperwork, works on the computer, and helps to make the boss's job easier.

The filmmaker's apprentice

An *apprentice* is usually someone new to the world of filmmaking but who wants to be a successful filmmaker one day. He or she is usually willing to work for free in exchange for learning everything possible on the set and being mentored by the director or producer. An apprentice's tasks usually include running errands, making phone calls, and just being by the producer or director's side.

Some of the second A.D.'s paperwork includes handling call sheets, collecting from the camera department the *camera reports* (shots and footage for the day's shoot), collecting talent releases for background players, and so on. The second assistant checks everyone in at the beginning of each day's shoot, calls the actors for camera when they're needed on the set, and then checks everyone out at the end of the shoot.

My sister Nancy was the second A.D for my film *Undercover Angel,* and her job was crowd control. For the final dramatic scene in the film, Nancy rounded up almost 1,000 extras, which was no small task.

Stepping over the line producer

The *line producer's* job is to work with the budget and line up, and keep tabs on the items in the budget categories that make up make your film. The line producer works with the producer in getting good deals on equipment, props, locations, and other elements that make up the budget. On a small production, the line producer can often have the job of producer and even unit production manager. On bigger-budget projects, each is a separate position. When interviewing potential line producers, find out what budget amounts they've worked with on past productions. Have they worked on budgets similar to yours? Chances are, you're shooting a low-budget film, so you need to hire someone who's had the experience of line producing an independent film before. A line producer who has worked on a multimillion-dollar budget may have difficulty relating to a small budget.

Line producing an independent low-budget film is actually an art form; it requires great skill, because you have to work with what you have and can afford. Make sure you get references from a producer or director whom your prospective line producer worked with in the past.

You can find a qualified line producer (and many other crew and staff positions) by checking out the Los Angeles 411 (www.la411.com) or the New York 411 (www.newyork411.com). These are industry directories that have produced some of the finest resources for productions in the film and television industry.

Uniting with a production manager

The *unit production manager,* also known as the UPM, works closely with the line producer and assists in getting good deals on equipment and other elements for the shoot. The UPM also ensures that all equipment is on set, on time. A UPM is kind of a co-line producer. Most low-budget productions have no UPM, only a line producer. A UPM on a low-budget production will often take a lower salary to get a better credit as a line producer.

Supervising the script

Someone with a good eye, a decent memory, a knack for recalling details, and a keen sense of observation, is the kind of person you need for *script supervising.* Also known as the *continuity person,* a script supervisor must know the script inside and out.

Wardrobe, props, and hair must match from shot to shot. Without the script supervisor, cups of coffee may leap into actors' hands, props may simply disappear mid-scene, and chairs may rearrange themselves. Preventing this from happening is the job of the script supervisor. That's why she takes those Polaroid pictures (many now use digital still cameras) to remember what the set was like the last time the camera rolled.

Some of the script supervisor's duties include making sure

- Action matches from shot to shot.
- Screen direction is correct (see Chapter 14), meaning when one actor is supposed to be looking at another actor, they're facing the right direction.
- Wardrobe, props, hair, and make-up match from shot to shot (still photos help match actors' appearance from shot to shot). This is known as *continuity.*
- The director has shot enough coverage for each scene (for example, that appropriate close-ups were shot for important emotions, or certain angles were shot to show the full impact of the action).

✔ Actors say their lines verbatim from the script and are corrected if they change a line or assisted if they forget a line or two (or three).

✔ Lenses and frame sizes used for each shot are noted so the director will know whether he has shot enough coverage. This is also helpful to the editor when cutting the picture together and knowing what coverage there was for the scene (giving the editor more cutting options).

✔ The editor receives assistance with scene notes and other details to help edit the picture together in a coherent fashion.

Ask to see a candidate's script-continuity notes to see whether they're organized and legible. Getting referrals and talking to a director who's previously worked with this script supervisor is always a good idea.

Directing photography with a cinematographer

The *director of photography* sees the world through the single eye of the camera and helps you envision your film from script to screen. On low-budget productions, *you* may even be the director of photography.

The director of photography is often referred to as the D.P. (or the D.O.P. in Canada) and is also called the *cinematographer*. If you're interviewing potential cinematographers, the first thing to request is a *demo reel* (a VHS videotape or DVD that features samples of the cinematographer's work). Usually, a reel will have short samples of the D.P.'s work from different projects, preferably showing a diverse style from film to film. Every cinematographer has a demo reel — if the one you're talking to doesn't, beware. That's like a screenwriter without a script.

If you're shooting a low-budget production, your cinematographer will often be the camera operator, as well. Only on bigger-budget productions does the cinematographer have someone else operate the camera.

Your cinematographer is one of the most important players on your team. After all, the audience doesn't care how much work went into getting each shot; all they see is the final product. So look for the following attributes when choosing a director of photography:

✔ Does their demo reel reflect a style that you like?

✔ Are they pleasant and personable? Will they be easy to work with?

✔ Are they knowledgeable about the technicalities of the camera?

✔ Can they work quickly without compromising quality?

✔ Do they have a gaffer and other crew members they like to work with?

✔ Are they willing to work long hours with low pay?

✔ Will they work on deferment (meaning some of their salary is deferred)?

✔ Do they have references from other filmmakers?

✔ Do they own a film or video camera to use on your production?

Nowadays, many cinematographers have their own 35mm or 16mm motion-picture cameras. Some own video cameras, and a few have the new digital video 24p cinema camcorders. You may be able to get both a camera and a cinematographer for the price of one — definitely a plus on a low budget. (For more on motion-picture and digital video cameras, see Chapter 10.)

First assistant camera

The *first assistant cameraperson,* or first A.C., works alongside the camera operator or director of photography — whoever is operating the camera — and changes camera lenses, inserts camera filters, cleans the shutter gate for dust and particles (if it's a film camera), and adjusts the focus. This position is also referred to as the *focus-puller,* because that's the most important duty of the first A.C.: to make sure everything that's supposed to be in focus is in focus.

An assistant cameraperson on a film camera will use a tape measure and a precision focus knob on the camera to ensure that all images that are supposed to be in focus are. They should be prepared to *rack-focus,* meaning focus from one element in the same shot to another, with precise timing and accuracy. An assistant cameraperson on a video production will often take measurements using the camera's focus through the lens by using a video monitor to see what the camera sees. Many new digital camcorders have visual focus numbers in the frame (that are not recorded on tape), which the A.C. can dial in after rehearsing a focus point before the camera starts taping.

Second assistant camera

The *second assistant cameraperson,* also known as the second A.C., is required to load and unload the film magazines (if you're shooting film as opposed to video, see Chapter 10). You need someone who is extremely careful not to expose your precious film to the light as he or she unloads your footage and readies it for development at the film lab.

If you're shooting digital video with a small crew, you usually don't need a second assistant cameraperson. The second A.C. is also responsible for slating the clapboard for syncing sound to picture when shooting film (see Chapter 12 for more on syncing sound). The second A.C. also records camera reports, detailing what shot was recorded on what film roll (or video cassette, if you're shooting video). When shooting film, camera reports are crucial because they accompany the exposed film to the lab, and provide instructions if any special developing and/or printing is required.

Going with your gaffer

Your *gaffer* works closely with your cinematographer to make sure the mood and lighting of each scene works effectively. Ask your cinematographer if he or she has enjoyed working with a certain gaffer in the past. This saves you a lot of time and trouble. You want to have people who are familiar and comfortable working with each other.

Best boy is a good boy

The *best boy* works closely with the gaffer, dealing with electricity and powering the lights. He or she (yes, a best boy can be a woman) also runs the extension cords and checks that everything is plugged in correctly. The gaffer sometimes can recommend a best boy he or she has worked with. If not, ask the cinematographer or another crew person.

Electrician is electric

On a smaller shoot, you can hire an electrician from the Yellow Pages and pay him or her for an hour or two of work at each new location. An *electrician's* main job is tying your lights directly into the electrical circuit box to avoid a power overload. If you're doing a video shoot in a small location and only using two or three lights, you may be able to plug directly into the wall plugs and not need an electrician to monitor the set. Checking with an electrician first isn't a bad idea, though. You don't want to blow a fuse or, even worse, start a fire.

Getting a grip

Grips are the film set's manpower: They move equipment and help position lights according to the gaffer and cinematographer's instructions. Having a few grips on hand speeds up your setup and saves time and money.

My friend Peter Emslie wanted to work on a project I was developing for Dolly Parton — and he eagerly volunteered to be the dolly grip! A *dolly grip* is in charge of setting up the *dolly* (which is used to move the camera during shots) and the tracks the dolly moves on; he or she skillfully pushes the dolly while filming.

Sounding like your sound mixer

Next to what the audience sees, sound is very important in any film. I've worked with *sound mixers* like Al Samuels, who did the film *Swingers*. Al's production sound was so good that little or no re-dubbing of dialogue was required by the actors in postproduction. I've also worked with other sound mixers who recorded unusable sound on set because they didn't know how to mix correctly. They also didn't have the *boom* person (see the following section) position the microphone correctly, and most of the dialogue had to be re-recorded during postproduction (see Chapter 16 for more on this process).

The sound mixer is responsible for recording the actors' dialogue on set and ensuring that it's clear and comprehensible. The sound mixer on a film will have a separate sound machine, either a Dat recorder or a Nagra (see Chapter 12). Along with their sound recorder, the sound mixer will also have a mixing board that allows them to input several microphones (for several microphone placements within the scene) and mix them into the recorder to get the appropriate balance of all mics. They also make sure that there is no interference in the recording, whether it be background noise that interrupts the dialogue (like a plane overhead or an air-conditioner buzzing) or hissing or electrical interference on the actual line.

Booming the sound

Because the boom person and the sound mixer must communicate clearly with each other, your sound mixer often recommends or brings his own boom person — someone he has worked with before. The boom held by the boom person is a long pole (sometimes called a *fishpole*) with the microphone positioned on the end. A *boom person* anticipates the actor's performance on set in order to position the microphone at the right distance and angle to get clear, crisp dialogue — and at the same time avoid letting the mic and boom creep into the shot. The job requires skill, and without the right operator, the recording will suffer.

Propping up the prop master

The *prop master* is in charge of any object that an actor interacts with — such as a telephone, a lamp, a gun, or a glass of champagne. On smaller productions, the prop person can also be the *set dresser* (the person responsible for items the actors don't interact with, such as flowers on a shelf, placemats on a table, picture frames on a mantle). The prop master can also double as the *greensman,* in charge of plants, flowers, even trees — anything that requires a hand with a green thumb.

When interviewing people for the position of prop master, you want to know whether the person has access to *prop houses* (like 20th Century Props, www.20thcenturyprops.com) or other places that can provide props for free or at a low rental cost. A prop person also needs to be organized, reliable, and detail oriented. If you're not close to any major production centers, you can check into local theater groups where you'll likely find a candidate to provide you with props for your film.

Dressing up the wardrobe department

Your *wardrobe person* should have the skill to sew from scratch — on an independent budget you can't always afford to purchase or rent certain wardrobe or costumes. It's also helpful if this person has contacts for inexpensive clothing rentals. The wardrobe person is also in charge of making sure the actors are wearing the appropriate wardrobe in each scene to match continuity. They number the wardrobe or outfits for each scene and keep track of what the actors were wearing in the last scene and whether there are any wardrobe changes for the next scene.

On low-budget productions, the actors usually wear their own clothes, which the wardrobe person has selected by looking through their closets (with their permission, of course). Wardrobe has to be checked out each day and checked in at the end of each day — even something as simple as boots (if the actor takes them home and forgets them the next day, continuity won't match). The wardrobe person keeps clothes hanging on a wheeled rack like the ones you see in a department store. Each piece of wardrobe is tagged and marked for which scenes they are to be worn in. The wardrobe person also makes sure the actor's wardrobe is kept clean (or dirty) depending on what the scene requires.

Making up your mind

Make-up is often overlooked on low-budget productions and should never be filled by an inexperienced make-up person. The wrong make-up or coloring can cause disastrous results on film or video. A make-up artist knows how to work with different skin tones and make them look even under different lighting conditions. Make-up can make circles under the eyes vanish, blotchiness on the skin disappear, blemishes go away, or bruises appear.

You also need to allow for a make-up kit rental fee in the budget for make-up supplies including sponges, powder, puffs, and tissues.

With special effects make-up, your make-up artist can create a deformed character, age an actor, and make creatures come to life with the aid of *prosthetics* (latex appliances attached to the face — see Chapter 17).

Gopher this, gopher that

A *gopher,* professionally called a *production assistant* (also known as a *runner*), is usually a student or eager beaver who wants to get on a film set. They go-pher this and go-pher that. The position doesn't require skill as much as it does eagerness to work on a film set. Reliability and hard work are the main prerequisites of a good gopher. The difference between a gopher and an apprentice is that the gopher is hired to work on the set, and often an apprentice is working for free to gain the experience and to learn about the filmmaking process hands-on.

Gophers are easy to find. Post ads at the local colleges and in trade magazines and flyers.

Keeping your composer

The *composer* scores music to accompany the images of your film and to help set a mood. Finding a composer is a lot like finding your cinematographer (see the "Directing photography with a cinematographer" section earlier in this chapter). As soon as you hear a sample of a composer's sound, you'll know immediately whether you like what you hear. Collect CD samples from composers to hear their work. You can find composers through the various music organizations — BMI, ASCAP, and SOCAN (see Chapter 16). If you go to www.crewnet.com, you can click on "Composers" and find a list of potential people who could score your film.

The composer sets the mood of your film, so liking his or her style and sound is very important. You want to make sure you both have the same vision for the film. After you select someone, sit down and discuss the type of music you hear in your head for certain scenes. I often give my composer a rough tape or CD of songs and movie soundtracks I like, and tell him or her to compose in that style. For my film *Turn of the Blade,* I told my composer, Greg Edmonson, that I liked the sexy sound of the saxophone used in the *Lethal Weapon* soundtrack. This gave him an idea of the style I wanted, and he was able to give me a similar feel for my film.

Never use copyrighted music without permission. If you want to use a commercial song or soundtrack, you need to license it (see Chapter 16). You can be inspired by music that's out there, but don't copy it or even get too close to it — you don't want any legal problems.

Edit this!

When interviewing a potential *picture editor,* a person who is experienced at cutting film or video images together to form a visual story, ask to see a sample of something he or she has cut together — either a short film or a feature-length film.

Here's a list of things to look for when interviewing a potential picture editor for your film:

- ✔ Technical knowledge of non-linear editing and equipment. Non-linear is the technique of having your individual shots as separate entities and available to be assembled in any order.

- ✔ A non-linear editing system. (Many picture editors own their equipment nowadays.)

- ✔ Good pacing (timing) to their cutting (with no lags or slow spots in the action).

- ✔ Effective use of cutaways (reaction shots, parallel scenes happening at the same time).

- ✔ Seamless cuts (no jarring cuts or jump-cuts that look like frames are missing).

- ✔ Tight scenes (no laborious entering and exiting of actors).

- ✔ Effective transitions from one scene to another.

And the rest . . .

Depending on the size of your budget, there are other positions that you may need to fill. On a low-budget production, many of the following could be you or someone filling one of the positions mentioned earlier in this chapter.

- ✔ **Casting director:** Often, in a low-budget production, the filmmaker is also the casting director.

- ✔ **Location scout:** The filmmaker can also be the location scout. I've driven around town many times looking for the perfect place to shoot.

- ✔ **Transportation person:** A person solely dedicated to driving the crew and cast around from hotel to set, or parking area to set. If it's a small production, everyone usually drives his or her own car, or sometimes you have another crew member pick you up, and you carpool!

- ✔ **Production designer:** Most small-budget films don't have the luxury of having a production designer. A production designer designs the overall look of a film. Some films (for example, *Batman,* where a whole world had to be created from scratch) depend on a production designer.

- ✔ **Stunt coordinator:** If you have stunts in your film, don't try to save money here. Always hire a professional stunt person who is skilled in even the most basic of stunts. Try to avoid stunts on a low-budget film, it can be expensive and risky, as well as raise your insurance package.

- ✔ **Postproduction coordinator:** Usually, the filmmaker is the postproduction coordinator. This is a luxury on a low-budget film. The postproduction coordinator coordinates the completion of the film, schedules when the picture editing and sound elements are to be done, and sets a finishing date for the final production so distribution plans can begin (see Chapter 19).

✔ **Still photographer:** You need to think ahead and hire an on-set still photographer to take photos that can be used for publicity. When you find a distributor (Chapter 19), they will request production stills to use in a poster and in *one-sheets* (flyers advertising your film). You'll also need photos for film festivals and newspaper and magazine articles.

Finding Your Crew

You're ready to make your film and you know the positions you want to fill. Now how are you going to find the people to help you put it all together?

✔ **Run an ad requesting that people submit themselves for crewing your film.** You can run an ad in one of the trade publications, like *The Hollywood Reporter, Daily Variety,* or *Backstage West* (if you live in Los Angeles or New York). If you live outside of the Hollywood environment, run an ad in your local newspaper or neighborhood flyer. Go on a local TV show or news program and get the word out that you're looking for crew. Post ads at local schools and colleges.

✔ **Get a hold of the Los Angeles 411 or New York 411 directory.** In addition to crew listings these are also great directories for other production resources. Check out www.la411.com or www.newyork411.com.

✔ **You can do some re-crew-ting at** www.crewnet.com **via the Internet and find crew all over the United States and Canada.** You can also try www.media-match.com. You can even post a free ad on the sites and request resumes via e-mail or fax.

Interrogation Time: Interviewing Your Potential Crew

After you start getting résumés from potential crew members, you're ready for the interview process. You're not just looking for skills, but also for personality and temperament.

Get references from all potential crew members, even if you don't plan on contacting their references. If they have nothing to hide, they'll gladly volunteer letters of reference or contact names. If they say they have no references, beware!

Looking at Creative Ways to Pay Your Crew

Now that you've found your crew, you have to figure out how to pay them. When you're shooting a low- or no-budget film, you don't have a lot of money to throw around, if any. No one is being forced to work on your production, especially if there is low or no pay. But you can save on hiring your crew and still have a win-win situation for both parties.

Paying later: Deferments to cast and crew

One of the ways to save money on cast and crew is to *defer* their salaries. Deferments work by paying your crew if and when you start seeing a profit from your film's sales. But profit isn't guaranteed, and many crew members prefer to get something up front, knowing that they may not see anything more in the back end. If they do, it's a bonus.

Offering points (they can be sharp)

Another way to save money is to offer your crew *points* on the back end (if and when the film starts to make profits). This way you can save money up front and put it up on the screen (into the actual production) and enhance the production values of your film. *Points* are similar to deferments, except that instead of a deferred salary of a specific amount, you reward the crew with one or more points: One *point* may be 1 percent of the profits of the film. If the film makes a lot of money, points continue to add up and continue to be paid as long as the film makes money. Deferments are usually a specific dollar amount; when that amount is reached, the crew member doesn't receive any more. Deferments or points are a good incentive to offer crew when you don't have the money to pay them what they're worth up front. I recommend deferments over points, because points obligate you to pay out points every time money comes in from the picture, which can be a lot of extra paperwork and expense to keep track of.

Giving 'em credit

Your potential crew may not be excited about the pay, if there is any, but you may get them excited about working on your film by giving them a credit that they haven't been able to earn yet.

Let's make contact

Now Software makes a program called Now Contact, which I use to compile all my contact information, including information for crew members. It's an address program that goes further, allowing you to attach letters, contract files, and résumés to the contact. An information window lists details on meetings, contract terms, and special notes about that crew member. My favorite part of the program is a drop-down menu on your desktop, so it's always available. You can download a free trial version of Now Contact at www.nowsoftware.com.

Another great program called Gorilla includes a template for crew (and cast) contact information (plus a complete production-management program for scheduling and budgeting for the independent filmmaker — see Chapter 4).

Getting a credit with more prestige on your film can help your crew get better positions on the next film they work. For example, a gaffer who has studied to be a cinematographer may take a cut in pay, or no pay, if he or she gets a chance to be the director of photography on your film (make sure he or she is qualified though). An art director may be excited to get a production designer credit.

Hiring student bodies

Another way to save on your budget is to go to school. Many students still in or fresh out of college would love to work on a production to gain experience and get their first film credit on their résumé. Some colleges will even let their students earn a school credit if your film meets their educational requirements. If you're making a low- or no-budget film, a student assistant in each department can be an asset to your production.

Paying a kit fee

Another way to save a little bit of money is to split up the salary you pay your crew member by paying him a kit fee. A *kit fee* is like a rental fee for the equipment that the crew member brings to your production. What's great about a kit fee is that it can save crew members on taxes that would otherwise be taken out of their salary, because rental fees don't count as crew labor — and so they may agree to give you a discount on their salary for paying them this way. You can pay kit fees for:

✔ Your make-up artist's kit with make-up supplies
✔ Camera equipment from your cinematographer

✔ Lighting equipment from your cinematographer or gaffer

✔ Props provided by your prop master

✔ Your sound mixer's own equipment

Hiring crew as independent contractors

You can save yourself and crew members a little money and extra paperwork if you're able to hire each crew member as an *independent contractor*. This way you don't have to withhold any taxes on crew members' salaries, and you don't have to pay social security and benefits since they're operating as freelance workers. An *independent contractor* works independently without an employer constantly looking over his or her shoulder. Location scouts, wardrobe designers, freelance writers, and storyboard artists can all easily be independent contractors. You have to send each independent contractor a 1099 tax form at the end of each year in which they worked for any payment over $600. You can get standard 1099 tax forms at any stationery or office store.

When crew have to work specific hours on set, as opposed to working on their own time, you may have to hire them as employees. At that point, you're required to issue W2 forms, which then requires either hiring a payroll company or enlisting a bookkeeper or accountant to do all the payments and tax withholding, including workman's compensation and so on. Check with your accountant who will advise you which crew members can be hired as independent contractors and which ones should be hired as employees.

Putting a Contract Out on Your Crew

You should always have a signed agreement between you and each crew member. Whether the crew member is an independent contractor or an employee, a written agreement prevents any misunderstandings and clearly spells out exactly what's expected of the crew member, including the following:

✔ **Position and title:** Define the title they get in the production credits.

✔ **Salary:** Specify what they are getting paid (if anything) or getting in deferred pay or points (if any).

Note that you may be able to pay non-union employees a flat fee, whereas union employees usually require hourly pay. See the "Union or non-union — that's the question" sidebar in this chapter for more on union employees.

- ✔ **Employment status:** Specify whether they are working as independent contractors or employees.

- ✔ **Work hours and work week:** Set out how many hours a day (8 to 12) and how many days a week (5 to 6) are required during production.

Specify *turnaround* time (time off between shoots) in the crew contracts — and make sure it's enough. Turnaround time usually means at least ten hours before the crew member has to return to the set. You need to respect your crew and show you appreciate their dedication to your film, especially if they're working hard for little money.

- ✔ **Copy of completed project on VHS:** Promise the crew member a copy of the film on videotape when it's completed.

Boilerplates are hot: Don't get burned

Boilerplates are preexisting contracts that have already been drawn up by an attorney or used for previous productions. All you have to do is fill in the blanks with the crew person's name and other relevant information. The best scenario is to use boilerplates as a guide and then consult an entertainment attorney who can review them and add or subtract where necessary.

One book that I find very informative is *Contracts for the Film & Television Industry* by Mark Litwak (published by Silman-James Press). Mark is a prominent entertainment attorney in Los Angeles who works very closely with independent filmmakers. In addition to his series of legal books, check out his Web site at www.marklitwak.com. Mark's industry book contains 40 contracts that are useful for TV and film production, including a 3-page crew deal memo (again, I recommend consulting a lawyer to review any boilerplate contract before using it — doing so protects all parties).

Union or non-union — that's the question

If you're doing an independent low-budget film, you may not want to deal with the additional expense and paperwork involved with hiring a union crew. Unions are very strict, and if you default on any of their regulations, it could slow down, or shut down, your production. Plus, unions require you to pay minimum salaries, which may not be in your budget.

Many crew people may be union, but they can decide whether they want to work on a non-union production. A lot of independent films can't afford to shoot with union employees and have to pass up experienced union crew, unless that union member wants to work on the production and take a pay cut in doing so.

If you do a union production, you have to follow all union rules to a T. And be prepared for penalties, including paying for overtime, and so on. You don't need that headache on an independent production — and most of the time you can't afford it anyway.

"I'm calling my lawyer!"

Contracts need to be specifically tailored to your production. If you're in a town that doesn't have an entertainment attorney, you can always find an attorney who is familiar with the film industry via the Internet in Los Angeles, New York, or Toronto. You don't even have to meet face to face. You can send forms and contracts via e-mail and fax machines. I'm in Los Angeles and so is my entertainment attorney — and in a year's time I've only seen him in person twice (and one of those times was when I ran into him at a department store).

Chapter 8

Assembling Your Cast of Characters

....

In This Chapter

▶ Reeling in your cast

▶ Conducting auditions

▶ Casting correctly

▶ Contracting your actors

....

The time has come to breathe life into your screenplay's characters and have them jump off the page. In this chapter, you discover how to find the perfect cast for your film and how to talk to agents, managers, and casting directors. You find out what to look for in actors (and their résumés), what to expect when you meet actors, and how to read them for the part. I also give you some important tips to relay to your actors so that you get the best audition from them. You may just discover the next Al Pacino or Meryl Streep. You may also want to pick up a copy of *Breaking Into Acting For Dummies* by Larry Garrison and Wallace Wang (published by Wiley) for more tips on the auditioning and casting process.

Spreading the Word: Finding Your Cast and Reeling Them In

Casting is one of the most important decisions you make when putting your film together — it's half the game. So how do you go about finding your cast of characters? There's no shortage of actors (or wannabes), and there's no shortage of places to find them. You can discover your leading lady or leading man on the street, through a mutual friend, at a talent showcase, online, or even at your family reunion (who knew Cousin Benny had that star quality you were looking for all along?). Actors can also be found by:

> ✔ Contacting agents, managers, and casting directors
>
> ✔ Placing casting ads in newspapers and trade papers
>
> ✔ Calling casting services
>
> ✔ Scouring actor directories

Talking to agents 'cause they talk back

Just because an actor has an agent doesn't mean the actor is working a lot. An agent is more of a legal representative for actors — someone to protect them from being taken advantage of on the set and to make sure they receive payment for services rendered. An agent usually does all the contractual work with you for the actor he or she represents, whether it be a detailed agreement or a simple one-page *deal memo* (see "Handling Actors' Agreements" later in this chapter).

An agent usually collects the actor's payment and takes a 10 percent agent commission fee before paying the performer. A manager can charge up to 15 percent as a commission fee. This is important for you to know, because sometimes an agent and/or manager will ask for the actor's fee, plus the agent and manager fees on top.

Most agents will not consider a project for their client until they have received and read the screenplay. If they don't like the script, or think their client isn't appropriate for the project or part, they will decline. For my film *Undercover Angel,* I asked the agent who represented Yasmine Bleeth (who played the lead in my film) who he could recommend to play the male lead opposite his client. This is how I ended up casting Dean Winters (of HBO's *OZ*).

Casting through casting directors

Casting directors are always on the lookout for new talent to feed the myriad productions being produced. In Hollywood, the casting director has a lot of power because if an actor doesn't get past her, he'll never have a chance to meet the filmmakers. A casting director not only filters the piles of pictures and résumés that are submitted, but also schedules auditions with the chosen ones. This saves the filmmaker from having to see everyone who walks through the door — even the ones who can't act their way out of a paper bag (which by the way my dog can do very well). A casting director also builds relationships with talented actors whom he's seen perform in the past, and he keeps a roster of these talented individuals should an appropriate part come along for them to try out for.

The casting director is only the guard at the gate — the bouncer outside the club — that the actor needs to get past in order to get to you, the filmmaker. The casting director does not make the final decision; she only filters the talent or suggest name actors by giving you a list of names they can approach for your film. The film director or producer makes the final decision on cast.

Placing casting ads

One way to find talent for your film is to place casting ads. A *casting ad* is similar to a job classified ad, but instead of seeking someone for an office position with the proper qualifications, you're seeking an actor with acting experience who qualifies for a very specific acting role. You can place an ad on a job board at a theater company or at local colleges and high schools. Some larger cities even have periodicals devoted to scouting talent. For example, if you're in a major city like Los Angeles, you can place an ad in *Backstage West,* a weekly periodical for actors and industry professionals. The magazine is predominately for Los Angeles and New York casting, but anybody can subscribe to it, and you can place a casting ad no matter where you reside. *Backstage West* also has an online service where you post your casting ads immediately, making them available to online subscribers (www.backstagewest.com).

When you post an ad looking for actors for your film, you should list the following information:

- ✔ Log line of your film (one- or two-line synopsis of the story)
- ✔ Character's name
- ✔ Character's age range (such as 24 to 29)
- ✔ Character's body type (balding, skinny, chesty — preferably not all three)
- ✔ Character's idiosyncrasies (knowing that the character has a lisp, a twitch, or a type of attitude is helpful to the actor in the audition)
- ✔ Character role (lead, supporting, or day player)
- ✔ Acting experience (required or not)
- ✔ Seeking union or non-union actors (many independent low-budget films can't afford to hire union actors and follow union regulations under the restraints of a small production — see Chapter 4)
- ✔ Pay or no pay (important to mention)
- ✔ Benefits such as a copy of the film and meals on set (important, especially if no or low pay is offered)

Your ad should have contact information for actors to send their picture and résumé.

Cattle calling

Round 'em up! A *cattle call,* not unlike rounding up a herd of cattle, is a casting call where anyone can show up and be seen by the producers. Lines usually wind around the block depending on what the role and film are. You can place a cattle call casting ad in your local newspaper, in an entertainment trade magazine, or through a casting service. If you're offering generic parts that can be filled by almost anyone, your cattle call could cause a stampede!

With the advent of the Internet, picture and résumé submissions can be delivered in seconds instead of hours or days. Nowadays, an attached e-mail photo can be viewed immediately and in high photo quality.

Utilizing casting services

A casting service is a service that hooks the filmmaker up with the actor — a win-win situation. A filmmaker puts out a call for a particular type of acting role, and a casting service gets that call out to the agents, managers, and actors who could fill that role. Nowadays, many casting services use the Internet, because it's faster than using snail mail, using courier services, or sending faxes one at a time.

Many cities have casting services, and the best way to find out is to talk to agents in your area. If any type of casting service is available, they'll be using it. If you're in the Los Angeles, New York, or Vancouver areas, I suggest contacting Breakdown Services (see the "Breaking into Breakdown Services" sidebar in this chapter).

Looking through actor directories

Just like browsing through a rental directory with photos when looking for an apartment, or a real-estate guide when shopping to buy a new home, actors have their own directory. You can flip through pages of a directory that features actors and their contact information, all at your fingertips.

The Academy of Television Arts and Sciences puts out the *Players Directory,* a series of books categorized by leading, ingenue (roles played by young women), and character actors. You can also access it online at www.playersdirectory.com. The books and Internet access cost $75 per set. Most actors in the directory are located in or near the Los Angeles or New York areas (but most are willing to travel for that great role).

Evaluating an Actor's Information

After you've received an actor's submission, you need to evaluate whether this actor is a potential candidate for one of the roles in your film. Some of the things you'll consider from reviewing their picture and résumé:

- Do they look the part?

- Do they have the qualifications (acting experience)?

- Do they have some professional training?

- Do they have any special skills listed that may help add believability to playing that part? (Can they roller-skate? Juggle? Do accents?)

- If they submitted a demo reel, is their performance believable?

- Are they a union or non-union actor? If an actor is union, you have to follow union rules and pay the actor appropriately (see Chapter 4). Many low-budget films can't afford to hire union actors. Some union actors are willing to work non-union (which the unions don't encourage).

Headshots and résumés

You can tell how serious actors are by how they submit their picture (called a *headshot*) and résumé. I've received folded photocopies of pictures in letter-size envelopes (saving the sender on postage). If an actor doesn't take him- or herself seriously enough to submit professional materials, you can't take him or her seriously either. The only actors who probably don't need a professional headshot are those auditioning for the role of the headless horseman in *Sleepy Hollow!*

When you receive pictures and résumés from actors, especially if you receive them in the mail, make sure all pertinent information is on the résumé, including a contact number for the agent, manager, or actor. I have received résumés where the actor didn't include any contact information on his or her résumé (not even a phone number!) and I was unable to call the actor in for an audition — I had to cast him or her into a trash bag instead.

Also, make sure the pictures and résumés you receive in the mail are stapled together so that you don't lose track of what résumé belongs with which picture. Otherwise, you may want to staple them yourself (and deduct the staple from their salary if they get the job).

Reading and reviewing résumés

Here are things you should find on an actor's résumé that will help determine if he or she is qualified for one of the roles in your film:

- ✔ **Height, weight, hair and eye color.** Since the photo doesn't say, "actual size," there should be a height on the résumé, along with hair and eye color, as most photos are in black and white.

- ✔ **Union affiliations if any.** Just because an actor may not be in a union, doesn't mean he isn't a good actor. Every successful actor at one time was not in a union.

- ✔ **List of credits.** See what experience the actor has. Just as important as acting experience is the experience of being on a set and knowing the rituals.

- ✔ **Commercial credits.** Usually a résumé says, "Commercial credits upon request." You are welcome to request them.

- ✔ **Stage work.** Lets you know if they have any live-performance experience (just keep in mind that stage acting is quite different from film acting).

- ✔ **Training and special skills.** Anything that may enhance the character you're considering them for.

- ✔ **Contact information (agent, manager, sometimes cell phone, and e-mail address).**

Sometimes you can find an actor with little experience, and he or she ends up being perfect for the part. I never judge an actor by a lack of credits on his or her résumé. Call them in — you can't tell personality from a résumé.

Heading toward headshots

An actor's *headshot* is usually an 8-x-10-inch black-and-white photo with a résumé stapled to the back. Rarely does an actor need a color picture — you expect the actors themselves to be in color. Redheads tend to send color pictures because they feel they are a minority (everyone else is blonde in Hollywood), and their hair color may help them land a part.

Zed cards are a series of different shots on one card. Even though they're submitted more for modeling work, I like to see several shots of an actor (if available), just to get a better idea of what they look like.

I've rarely met an actor who looks exactly like his or her photo. Don't hire an actor based solely on the headshot — always meet him or her in person! I've made this mistake and regretted it.

When you look at an actor's photo, do you see some personality? Is there a gleam in their eye? I've received headshots where the actor looks like he's a frightened deer in a tractor-trailer's headlights, or she's putting on a goofy face that immediately warns me she may be an over-actor.

Taping their act

An actor may submit a *demo reel* with his résumé and headshot. A demo reel is usually a videotape (VHS) or DVD that features a selection of acting scenes that the actor appears in (usually between 3 and 5 minutes in length).

Spinning an actor's Web site

Not only do the actor's tools include a headshot, résumé, and a demo reel, but also either a personal Web page or a Web site where he or she posts a résumé and headshot. Many actors' Internet sites put up pictures and résumés for filmmakers to reference. One such service is www.hollywoodsuccess. com, which posts actors' pictures and résumés from all over the country.

A filmmaker will know an actor is serious and professional about her career if she also has an electronic résumé on a personal Web page with the following:

- ✔ Several photos to give you an idea of her look
- ✔ An updated list of credits and skills to get an idea of her experience in front of the camera
- ✔ An e-mail address for her and her agent so that you can easily make contact
- ✔ A streaming demo reel (not mandatory, but effective) to give you an idea immediately of her on-camera persona

Auditioning Your Potential Cast

The audition is the first face-to-face meeting between you and the actor. First impressions are always the most important — especially in the casting process. The audition not only gives you a chance to "test" the actor, but it also lets you see if he really does resemble his photo — minus the magic of a professional photographer and airbrush artist. This audition session will also give you an idea of whether this person can take direction. Have him read some lines from the script, and then tell him to try it a different way — with an accent or using a different tone or attitude.

Fostering a friendly environment

If you're personable with the actors, they'll be much more comfortable talking with you and more likely to be themselves. People tend to mirror people —

so if you're uptight, they'll be uptight or uncomfortable. Be professional, but be respectful and friendly; not only will the casting process be easier for the people you're auditioning, but it will also be more effective for you.

Always conduct auditions in a place of business — never in your home, no matter how small your production. Having people come to your home is a bit suspicious and, besides, it's not professional. Why would you want every Tom, Dick, and Harriet coming to your private residence anyway? You can find an office, conference room, dance studio, or rehearsal hall to rent for a few hours at a reasonable price ($10 to $40 per hour), or borrow an office space through a friend.

Evaluating an actor's etiquette

When you meet an actor for the first time, he or she should make an impression on you. Is this someone you would like to work with? There are several things you should look for in an actor:

- Are they punctual? Does the actor show up on time for the audition? If not, this could be an indication that he's not reliable or at least not punctual.

- The number-one most important trait of an actor is personality. Without personality, no one is going to care about any of the characters that your actor portrays. A strong personality in general helps infuse personality into the character the actor is playing.

- How an actor acts before and after the reading often impresses me more than the reading itself. It gives you a chance to see if that person has a sense of humor, funny quirks, or interesting mannerisms.

- An actor should dress appropriately for an audition and not wear unlaundered clothes or a baseball cap, or look like he stopped in for the audition on his way to the gym (unless the part requires that look).

Breaking into Breakdown Services

Breakdown Services, with offices in Los Angeles, New York, and Vancouver, enables casting directors, producers, and directors to send out a call for a certain type of character or characters that they need for a film or TV production, with regards to physical description and acting abilities. You submit a breakdown of your cast, and Breakdown Services posts it on its service that is seen by the many agents and managers who subscribe to the breakdowns. Breakdown Services also has a service called Actor Access that allows actors to see certain casting notices on the Breakdown Services Web site (www.breakdownservices.com). Placing a breakdown ad is free if your production is union; it's $50 if non-union.

> ✔ An actor should be polite, cordial, and pleasant at an audition.
>
> ✔ Actors who send a thank-you note (or postcard with their photo on it) after you've met always stand out. Less than 10 percent of actors have sent me thank-you notes over the past 20 years, but I've actually singled out actors who do and hired them because they reminded me of our meeting. It tells me they're thoughtful, probably reliable, and they take their acting career seriously. This is someone I want to have on my set.

Slating on video

You may want to videotape the auditions so that you have a video reference of all the people you audition. When you videotape auditions, always have the actor start by *slating*. *Slating* means that the actor introduces him or herself on camera and then gives a contact number (cell phone, voice-mail, or agent or manager numbers). This saves you the time and trouble of tracking down pictures and résumés.

Avoiding bitter-cold readings

Some directors have actors do a cold reading of *sides* (two or three pages from the script) without any study time on a first audition. This is effective when you want to see how the actors work with no preparation. If you want to get a better idea of their performance abilities, then you may want to give them at least ten minutes with the material before they attempt to perform it for you.

To help calm the actors' nerves and bring out their personality, talk to them for a few minutes before they read; doing so helps you see whether they're personable and have a quality that the audience will be attracted to. Then have them read to see whether they can inject their personality into their reading. I often tell actors it's okay if they miss or add some words if it keeps them from staring at the script pages. I'm not looking to see how well they can read words; I'm looking for a natural performance that impresses me during the audition phase.

Monologues leave you all by yourself

Actors have been conditioned to bring *monologues* to perform at auditions for the casting director, producer, or director. I'm not a fan of monologues because rarely do you have a film where the actor is talking for three minutes straight with no interaction from other characters. Monologues are more suited in auditioning for stage plays, as they tend to make the actor *project* (reach and speak louder).

When an actor prefers to do a monologue, I have him pick an actual person in the room to talk to, and I have that person sit or stand at the distance he would if he were in the actual scene. This helps the actor to target his voice level and emotions much better. I also have the other person silently react, so the performing actor has some interaction with a live person. Also, many actors who perform monologues make the mistake of talking to the casting director or person conducting the auditions (the director or producer). This is like looking straight into the camera, which is a no-no! And it makes you very uncomfortable if you're conducting the auditions. You want to observe the performance, not feel like you're part of it.

Making the Cut: Picking Your Cast

Choosing your final cast is not always the easiest job for the filmmaker. The actors you finally decide on will have the responsibility of carrying your film. They will be the blood that will keep your film alive.

Calling back

When you like an actor who has come in for an audition, you call her back for a more personal meeting. This is appropriately called a *call back*. The call back gives you and the actor a second chance to become familiar with each other and for you to see whether she's appropriate for the role you're considering her for. You usually have more time to sit down and talk to the actor and get a better feel of her personality. You can take some time to have her read some pages from the script as well.

Screen testing

A *screen test* is an actual dialogue scene from your film that you have the actor perform so that you can see how he comes across on camera. Screen testing is usually only done when you're seriously considering a particular actor, but you're not sure whether he can effectively play the role. Screen testing also lets you see how comfortable the actor is in front of the camera, and how well he takes direction.

You can shoot an inexpensive screen test with a video camcorder. The picture quality and lighting are not important. You are looking only at performance here.

And the winners are . . .

Now it's time to make the final decision. You've searched high and low for the perfect actor to play the role and you've finally found the needle in the haystack. This is the actor who's going to breathe life into the character.

The first thing you have to do is call the actor's agent (if he is represented by one) and tell her you're interested in casting her client. It's then the agent's job to contact the actor and tell him the good news. If an actor doesn't have representation, you can call him directly and personally tell him that you're looking forward to working with him.

Don't turn down second choices until your first-choice actor has agreed to do the film. You still have to deal with egos, agents, and managers, and your first-choice actor may suddenly not be available. Some agents want their actor clients to get parts and build up a reel, and they're glad to negotiate a deal that you can afford.

Make sure that the actor or the actor's representatives understand all the details of the job. Be up front. If there's low pay or no pay, let them know this right away. Let them know that you will give them a video copy of their scene, and that you'll feed them on the set. After you do decide on hiring an actor, you need to contract that person, which means arranging a legal agreement between you or your company and the actor. Read on for more information about agreements.

Handling Actors' Agreements

Once you cast an actor to be in your film, it's important to get a written agreement between you and the actor, and/or her representative (agent). The agreement not only protects the actor, but you, the filmmaker as well. An agreement spells out the terms of what is expected of both parties. It is a binding agreement, signed by you and the actor with responsibilities to each other. The actor plays the assigned role, for a certain period of time, and gets paid (or sometimes doesn't). An agreement also contractually obligates the actor to your film, and she cannot take another project unless you don't fulfill your end of the agreement.

If you're hiring union actors with the Screen Actors Guild (SAG), you'll have to use its contractual agreements. SAG's contracts lay out strict rules and regulations that you have to abide by, including minimum salaries (close to $700 a day) to its union members. (This is why the first-time filmmaker should try to avoid doing a union production.) There are special SAG agreements for independent productions that may fit into your budget (you can read about these in Chapter 4).

Contracting the primary players

A non-union actor's agreement can be issued in two phases. The first phase involves a *deal memo,* which is a short, preliminary contract or agreement usually made up of a few sentences stating that you're interested in hiring the actor for your film and that a more formal agreement will be drawn up in the near future. The main purpose of a deal memo is to come to an agreement on the main points for your deal without having to wait for the attorneys to do their thing. Why even waste money on an attorney if you aren't able to agree on the initial deal memo points?

Then, when contract points are negotiated in detail, a formal agreement, usually called the *long-form agreement,* is drawn up by your attorney. You may be able to find an appropriate agreement from an entertainment book, such as Mark Litwak's *Contracts for the Film & Television Industry* (see his Web site, www.marklitwak.com). Regardless of where you get your contracts, always have an attorney review them before sending them out to be signed.

If you're doing a union production utilizing SAG (www.sag.org), the American Federation of Television and Radio Artists (AFTRA, www.aftra.org), or the Alliance of Canadian Cinema, Television & Radio Artists (ACTRA, www.actra.ca), then you'll have contractual stipulations to abide by. You can get details on the various contract agreements on their Web sites. If you're shooting a very low-budget production, you may want to avoid the paperwork hassles and extra costs of becoming a signatory to one of the unions. The Screen Actors Guild has several special contracts for lower-budget productions (see Chapter 4); check out its Web site for details.

In addition to a deal memo, you may want to give the actor a monetary *retainer* to show that you're serious about hiring him. The retainer can be $1, $100, or a $1,000 — depending on how badly you want that particular actor for the part. (If you're contracting your younger brother, you may want to ask him to pay you!) The retainer legally attaches the actor to your project so you can start planning your shooting schedule or concentrate on casting the other roles. If the actor has name value, then having him committed to your film may be of interest to potential distributors and/or investors.

If you're lucky enough to interest a big-name actor in your film, ask her for a *letter of interest,* which is a letter from the talent saying that she is aware of the project and is interested in being a part of your production contingent on salary requirements and schedule. (Usually, you write the letter, and the actor signs it.) Often, the first thing a distributor or studio asks is not "What's the story about?" but "Who's in it?" A letter of interest from a recognized actor could help get you financing and distribution.

An actor's formal long-form agreement should include the following points:

- ✔ Name of the character role the actor will play
- ✔ The number of shooting days involved
- ✔ Salary
- ✔ *Per diem* (pocket money if on location)
- ✔ Perks (such as a trailer, a manicurist, a masseuse, or candy!)
- ✔ Automatic Dialogue Replacement (ADR) availability (for re-recording additional actor's dialogue in postproduction over the picture)
- ✔ How the actor will be billed on the film and poster

In addition, the contract could specify that the actor will receive a DVD or VHS copy of the project when it is completed.

Make sure that your agreements let you use the actors' *likeness* in *perpetuity*, which means forever. You don't want to have to track them down ten years later to renew.

Securing releases from extras

In addition to written agreements with your main talent, you also need to have releases signed by *extras* (any other individuals appearing on camera). Yes, everyone. Even if people are walking by in the background or sitting at a bar, you need to have them sign a release. Just ask my sister, Nancy. In my film *Undercover Angel,* the dramatic final scene had over 1,000 extras. My sister, working as the second assistant director, made sure every single person signed a release. And now whenever I see my sister Nancy, she starts singing, "Please release me, let me go. . . ."

If the person is a minor (and I don't mean a coal miner), a guardian over the age of 18 must sign on his or her behalf.

A release can be a simple one-paragraph letter giving you permission to use the actor's likeness in your film. (Don't forget: As with lead roles, an extra's release should allow you to use his or her likeness *in perpetuity* so you don't have to track him or her down years later to renew your rights.) A studio or distributor releasing your film will require that you have these releases.

Union actors working in non-union productions

A union actor may decide to do your film even if it's non-union — always a controversial topic. *Financial core* was established by the Supreme Court to protect union members from coming under fire from their own union if they take non-union jobs. Financial core encompasses all U.S. unions, not just the ones related to entertainment. Search the Internet for "financial core" to get the latest updates on this controversial topic.

Many times low-budget productions only go union if they have name actors (who can make your film more commercial to distributors). Many actors will work non-union to get a good part (though the unions definitely discourage it). The Screen Actors Guild puts out some low-budget agreements to help independent filmmakers cast union members in low-budget productions (see the guild's Web site, www.sag.org). Also see Chapter 4 for more information on low-budget agreements.

A short release can read as follows:

> For value received, I, [PERSON'S NAME] hereby consent that all photographs and/or images of me and/or voice recordings in whole or in part for [YOU THE FILMMAKER], may be used by [YOU THE FILMMAKER] and/or others with its consent for the purposes of illustration, advertising, broadcast or publication in any manner in perpetuity.

Make sure to include the date and have both parties sign the agreement. Having an attorney review this and any other agreements with regards to your production is always smart.

If you feature people in your film who didn't sign a release, they can legally keep you from showing the footage that they appear in. So don't forget, always get a signed release — even from your mother, if she's in the film!

Chapter 9

Storyboarding Your Film

· ·

· ·

*I*f you've ever read the Sunday comics, you're already familiar with story-boards. If a picture is worth a thousand words, then a storyboard literally speaks volumes about your film.

This chapter shows you the advantages of storyboarding and how to break your script down into separate shots that become illustrated panels. You find out about the elements that make up a storyboard panel and the different sizes they come in and why. You see how a professional presentation of your film in the visual form of a storyboard helps to sell your concept to an investor or studio. Don't think you can draw well enough? I provide suggestions for making your own storyboards with the help of some great software products. If you don't want to draw or use software products, I tell you how to find the right artist for your project and what you should expect to pay.

Understanding the Basics and Benefits of Storyboarding

Storyboards provide an illustrated version of your screenplay — they tell your story with pictures. By storyboarding your film, you, the cast, and the crew can visualize what the film is going to look like before you even start shooting.

Storyboards serve as a visual reference and are helpful in the following situations:

- ✔ Making a presentation to a client, such as an investor or a studio

- ✔ Helping your cast and crew see your vision of the film so that they're on board with you

- ✔ Showing your cameraman (director of photography) exactly what type of framing you want for each shot (more on framing later in this chapter)

- ✔ Scheduling your shots for each day

- ✔ Determining whether you have any unique shots that require action or special effects

- ✔ Budgeting (planning ahead with storyboards saves you time and money)

Storyboards consist of a series of separate *panels* or *frames,* each one representing individual shots in your film. If you look at the DVD menu section of your favorite film, it probably gives you a choice of chapters and shows you the still frame that begins each scene or chapter. The same idea of frames is used in storyboarding, only the storyboard frame or panel represents the first frame of each individual, continuous shot.

These individual shots then make up scenes, and scenes make up the whole film. You can have a few dozen storyboards, or 1,200 designed for your film — it all depends on the type of material you're storyboarding. For example, an action picture requires more precise planning; storyboarding is helpful because it's easier to see and coordinate the shots. You may also want to cover the action from numerous angles and preplan those angles to heighten the excitement, along with storyboarding any stunts, so the crew can see exactly what's going to happen on set. Steven Spielberg storyboarded almost 70 percent of his shots for *Indiana Jones and the Temple of Doom.* (He had help — although Spielberg draws initial concepts for his storyboards, he usually enlists the skills of a seasoned storyboard artist to realize his vision even further. I discuss the benefits of hiring a storyboard artist later in this chapter.)

On the other hand, not every filmmaker relies on storyboards. Sometimes the story is so simple that it doesn't require the details of each shot to be illustrated. A love story, such as the romantic comedy *When Harry Met Sally . . .,* may not demand hundreds of complex storyboards because the shots are basic, although some simple storyboards showing angles and types of shots are always helpful.

Each panel of a storyboard shows you exactly what's needed for that particular shot, eliminating the guesswork for you and your crew. For example, storyboards let you know how big your set needs to be. If you plan to have aliens exit a spaceship, storyboards give you and your crew an idea about whether you need to build the whole ship or just the door area. Another example, does your storyboard show a crowd in the stands watching a football game? From your storyboard panel, you know that you only need a small crowd and not a whole stadium full!

You don't need to have storyboards rendered in full color unless you use them to impress a client or investor when selling your idea. Often, completed panels are acceptable in pencil, ink, or even charcoal — as long as they depict your vision as the director accurately.

Suiting Up to Storyboard

Before you create your storyboards, you have to perform certain tasks and make certain decisions. First, begin by evaluating your screenplay and picturing it in terms of separate shots that can be visually translated into individual storyboard panels. Then you determine what makes up each shot and also which images need to be storyboarded and which ones don't. After you start storyboarding, you'll need to determine whether you're shooting for a TV movie or a theatrical release, which will ultimately affect the frame dimensions of your panels. Read on for the details!

Breaking down your script

The task of turning your screenplay into a film can be very overwhelming. But remember, a long journey begins with a single step, so begin by breaking the screenplay down into small steps, or shots. A *shot* is defined from the time the camera turns on to cover the action to the time it's turned off; in other words, continuous footage with no cuts. Figure out what you want these shots to entail and then transform those ideas into a series of storyboard panels. Stepping back and seeing your film in individual panels makes the project much less overwhelming.

Evaluating each shot

You have several elements to consider when preparing your storyboards. You first need to evaluate your script and break it down into shots. Then, as you plan each shot panel, ask yourself the following questions:

✔ What is the location setting?

✔ How many actors are needed in the shot?

✔ Do you need any important props or vehicles in the shot?

✔ What type of shot (close-up, wide-shot, establishing shot, and so on) do you need? (See Chapter 14 for specific information about shots.)

✔ What is the shot's *angle* (where the camera is shooting from)? Is it a high angle? A low angle? (See Chapter 14 for more on angles.)

✔ Do any actors or vehicles need to move within a frame, and what is the direction of that action?

✔ Do you need any camera movement to add motion to this shot? In other words, does the camera follow the actor or vehicles in the shot, and in what direction?

✔ Do you need any special lighting? The lighting depends on what type of mood you're trying to convey (for example, you may need candlelight, moonlight, a dark alley, or a bright sunny day).

✔ Do you need any special effects? Illustrating special effects is important to deciding whether you have to hire a special-effects person. Special effects can include gunfire, explosions, and computer-generated effects.

Creating a shot list

After you determine what makes up each shot, decide whether you want to storyboard every shot or just the ones that require special planning, like action or special effects. If you want to keep a certain style throughout the film — like low angles, special lenses, or a certain lighting style (for example, shadows) — then you may want to storyboard every shot. If you only want to storyboard certain scenes that may require special planning, keep a *shot list* of all the events or scenes that jump out at you so that you can translate them into separate storyboard panels.

Even if you've already created your shot list, you aren't locked into it. Inspiration for a new shot often hits while you're on set and your creative juices are flowing. If you have time and money, and the schedule and budget allow, try out that inspiration!

Constructing storyboard panels

Before you actually draw your storyboards, you need to create a space for them to call home. The shape and dimensions of your storyboard panels will be determined by whether your film is going to the TV screen or the theatrical screen. These two different dimensions affect how much information is drawn into your storyboards and what will ultimately be seen on the appropriate screen.

A storyboard panel is basically just a box containing the illustration of the shot you envision for your film. You can purchase pads of storyboard panels in different format sizes at many art and business stores. If you don't want to spend extra dollars on a pad of professional storyboard paper, you can draw your own panels — four to six on a regular 8½-x-11-inch piece of paper (keeping them at a legible size), or you can even print blank storyboard panels using your desktop computer. Here are some quick steps to design your own storyboard panels:

1. **Decide which shape and size of panel to use.**

   A television storyboard panel, like the screen on your television set, resembles a square, only slightly wider. Theatrical feature-film storyboards are rectangular in shape, almost twice as wide as a television screen (see Figure 9-1). Many filmmakers hope for a theatrical release and also like the picture information available with the larger, rectangular storyboard panel, but shooting a happy medium between the two is safer. You're more likely to end up on TV and you don't want a lot of your picture information lost on both sides of the image.

2. **Draw the shape of the panel and add a thick black border (approximately ½ inch in width) around the square or rectangle.**

   Placing a border around each panel helps you to see each panel as a definitive separate shot, and subliminally creates the illusion of a TV or darkened theater around your shot, giving you an idea of what that individual image will look like. With theatrical panels you may want to avoid the thick border to save on page space (and black ink!).

3. **Create a *description panel* by drawing a 1-inch empty box just below the bottom of the frame panel (as shown in Figure 9-1).**

   Use this box to write down important information that describes in detail what the illustration doesn't show or enhances what is drawn in the frame above. For example, include any important dialogue, camera directions, scene numbers, or special-effects instructions.

Figure 9-1:
A storyboard TV panel from *The Frog Prince,* and a theatrical panel from *Miss Cast Away.*

©Stellar Entertainment (Artist: Tom Decker)
©Stellar Entertainment (Artist: Cuong Huynh)

Storyboards are just like comic books

When I was a kid growing up in the '60s, I was an avid reader and collector of comic books. I spent endless hours absorbed in my Spiderman, Batman, Richie Rich, and Archie comics. Little did I know that years later I would work with comic panels, or storyboards, to map out my shots for a film. Reading comic books at a young age taught me how to break a story into shots and angles — and I was learning about movement within a single shot or panel that I would one day apply to my filmmaking ventures. Now you'll never look at the Sunday comics the same way again!

Putting Pencil to Paper: Deciding What to Include in Each Panel

After you create your storyboard panels, you need to decide exactly what you want your shots to look like. First, determine what the best angle is to capture the drama in a particular shot and whether you're going to move the camera. Also, think about lighting effects (shadows, special lighting, and so on) and other special effects that can be clearly exemplified in your boards. You should also draw any physical elements that will be inside the frame, including special props and, of course, your actors.

Distinguishing and choosing the right angles

You need to decide where you want to position the camera for the best *coverage* (the best angle to see the action). Angles have a subliminal effect on your audience. A low angle, in which the camera is positioned on the floor looking up at the actor, can make an actor appear bigger and more menacing. So in your storyboard panel, you draw the low angle looking up at the actor with the ceiling behind him. A high angle that looks down on an actor can make the character appear innocent, small, or weak. The storyboard sketch must make it clear that you need to have the camera up high. (See Chapter 14 for examples of what the various camera angles look like in the frame and what effects they have.) Make a note if you will require special equipment, such as a high tripod or a crane to get your high-angle shot (check out Chapter 14 for more information about types of dollies and cranes).

Considering camera and actor movement

Camera movement emphasizes a feeling or mood in a scene, and your storyboard panels need to depict any such movement in each shot. (Check out Chapter 13 for additional tips on camera movement.) This is also a good time to decide if your actors are going to move within the frame as well. You can plan basic actor movement in the storyboards and save detailed movement of your actors, called *blocking* (see Chapter 13), for when you're actually on the set.

Three-dimensional arrows usually show movement within a panel. The arrows point in the direction of your camera movement, whether it pans up, down, left, or right. They also convey the camera moving in or out of the shot or leading or following an actor or vehicle. They can even show the camera in a spin when you want to create a dizzying effect. Figure 9-2 illustrates the use of arrows in a storyboard panel from my sci-fi fantasy *Light Years Away*. Notice that the larger arrow shows the direction the character is moving within the shot, and the smaller arrow shows the movement of the camera following the action.

Figure 9-2: The use of arrows for movement.

David sees Misty in the beam of light from the heavens.

(as David approaches, Camera moves around Misty in the light)

©Stellar Entertainment (Artist: Tom Decker)

Animating animatics

Animatics is a new form of storyboarding that incorporates your individual panels and turns them into a moving picture show. Animatics can be as simple as a video presentation with zooms and pans of the storyboard frames. On a more sophisticated level, you can animate your storyboard panels, with your characters and vehicles moving within the panels, and add in narration or dialogue.

The DVD of Pixar's *Monster's, Inc.* shows the actual animatics for the film. Many animated films use animatics because the character styles already exist (although cruder and simpler

drawings are used to illustrate the characters' movements within the shots). TV commercials also rely heavily on animatics because it's easier to convince a client with a moving visual presentation that resembles the final product than with some still sketches. Of course, it's also easier to do an animatic for a 30-second commercial than a 2-hour film.

StageTools makes two popular software programs that can help you design animatics for your film. Check out www.stagetools.com for MovingPicture and MovingPicture Producer for free software demo downloads.

Planning your special effects

Special effects can be costly if they aren't planned properly. By storyboarding your special effects, you see exactly what they entail. For example, if a giant dinosaur looms up into the frame, you know the shot requires at least the head of the creature and some blue sky behind it. You and your special-effects team know exactly the elements you need for the shot (and the creature knows he doesn't have to worry about what shoes to wear that day). Now, if in the next frame you have the monster from head to toe, chasing the villagers, your special-effects team has a lot more work to do.

Storyboarding is also important to see how the camera needs to move during the effect, which can be tricky when the frame has computer-generated images. If the shot consists of an explosion with an actor in the same shot, then you can see by this panel that either you have to have the actor as far away from the explosion as possible (unless you don't plan on using the actor in any more shots — just kidding!) or you need to add the actor to the shot during postproduction. By illustrating these effects or stunts in a storyboard panel, you have a better opportunity to actually see what elements are in the shot and what safety precautions may be required.

Use the *description panel* (the little box below the panel frame) to detail exactly what is required for a shot. In the previous example, the description panel notes that explosives are set in the alley behind the dumpster, and that you will superimpose the actor into the shot during postproduction. Additional information may mention that the dumpster lid is made of light plastic, and it isn't hinged to the bin, so it can fly into the air on detonation (that reminds me, I forgot to take out the garbage).

Figuring out the actors, props, and vehicles you need

As you inspect each shot, you see what actors, props, and vehicles are required. If you decide that one storyboard panel is a close-up of an actor, you sketch that one actor, and only that actor, in the panel. You may decide that you want a two-shot (see Chapter 14 for more information on different types of shots), so you need to frame two actors in this panel somehow.

Deciding on lighting and location

Lighting can emphasize a certain mood or tone in a shot and so you want to point out any special lighting techniques when drawing your panels. If it's a dark chase through an alley, cryptic shadows and darkness add to the suspense and need to be illustrated in your storyboards. You can give more detail in the accompanying text box below each storyboard panel about what you're trying to show in the illustration.

You don't need to draw actual locations in detail unless something in the setting is crucial to the shot, or a character interacts with it somehow. If a car is driving down the road, you only need to draw the road and not the surrounding trees and buildings. If an actor enters a room, you only need to draw the door from which the actor enters. Some scribbles or lines on the walls can show that the scene is taking place inside. If you're using a software program to design your storyboards, the program can repeat a background location so that you don't have to draw it by hand every time (see "Working with storyboard software" later in this chapter for more information).

I Can't Draw, Even If My Life Depended on It

Many people are not trained artists, and some of us can only draw stick people (who look like skinny actors who don't eat — I know a few of those). But never fear, in the following sections I outline a few solutions for the artistically inept, such as storyboard software and hiring an artist.

Working with storyboard software

If you're not satisfied with drawing happy faces on stick people, but you still want to create the storyboards yourself, try using some storyboard software.

Utilizing a storyboard program gives you a library of pre-drawn generic characters (male, female, children) that you can choose, click on, and drop right into your storyboard frames. You can manipulate the size and shape of each character, and even rotate each character's position. Along with a cast of characters, there is usually a library of common props and generic locations to place in your frames as well. A few different software programs are available to help you out:

- ✔ **Atomic Storyboard** is a free software program that you can download at www.atomiclearning.com/storyboard. The price is right!

- ✔ **ShotMaster** is available for $99.95 at www.badhamcompany.com from director John Badham *(Saturday Night Fever, War Games)*.

- ✔ **Boardmaster** software can be bought for $180 at www.boardmastersoftware.com. This is a unique storyboard program that actually lets you create camera movement (panning and zooming) and timing of shots while viewing the storyboards on your computer.

- ✔ **Storyboard Quick** from PowerProduction is at www.powerproduction.com for $280. This is a great program that's easy to use and makes for quick storyboarding (see the nearby sidebar, "More on storyboarding with Storyboard Quick").

- ✔ **Storyboard Lite** is a cool software program (costing a cool $500) that allows you to create realistic three-dimensional characters and objects within your storyboards. It's available at www.zebradevelopment.com.

Seeking the help of a professional artist

You've been reading this chapter and thinking to yourself, "I can't draw well enough to put my shots into storyboards" or, "I'm not computer literate; I won't be able to run the storyboard software programs." Don't panic! If you aren't happy with your stick characters in your frames, and you can afford it, you can always hire a professional storyboard artist.

Knowing what to expect from an artist

A storyboard artist is very much like a crime sketch artist. You describe in detail what your shot looks like, and the artist does his best to put your vision on the page. The artist starts by sketching very rough pencil drawings and making any special notes during your meeting — with you looking over his shoulder to see that he's on the right track. He then goes home (or wherever he feels most comfortable drawing) and returns later with the completed panels. A storyboard artist can ink in the pencil drawings or leave them a little rough, depending on your taste.

Photogenic frames

Another way to create storyboards if you're not an artist is to take photographs! Get several of your friends together and have them act out your screenplay in pictures. The most economical way to do this is to get your hands on a digital still camera (I use the Kyocera Finecam S4, `www.kyocera.com`). Have no friends? Use dolls, toy soldiers, or puppets — whoever your real friends are. George Lucas shoots amusing low-budget video storyboards with dolls of his Star Wars characters for his sci-fi *Star Wars* epics.

If you ask a storyboard artist to *conceptualize* (meaning to design the look of a piece of equipment, a wardrobe, or a vehicle, like a spaceship), you want him to render it in full detail and color for optimum presentation.

Finding an artist

Lots of talented artists are out there who would be glad to storyboard your film. Even an artist who has never done storyboards can still sketch some great panels after getting a basic understanding of camera shots and lenses. If you decide to hire a professional artist, there are several ways to find one:

- ✔ Art schools are a good place to find budding talent.

- ✔ Cartoonists who work for a local newspaper may enjoy a change of pace.

- ✔ *Picture Book* is an annual reference guide packed with hundreds of artists' samples and contact information. You can check it out at `www.picture-book.com` or call 888-490-0100.

- ✔ *RSVP: The Directory of Illustration and Design* is similar to *Picture Book* and also features hundreds of artists' sample work. You can find out more information at the Web site at `www.rsvpdirectory.com` or send an e-mail to `info@rsvpdirectory.com`.

- ✔ Famous Frames, Inc. is a company that specializes in providing storyboard artists for independent and studio feature films. Find the company at `www.famousframes.com`.

- ✔ *Animation Magazine* features interviews and articles on cartoonists and also has helpful ads and classified sections that list artists available for freelance work. For subscription information, call 818-991-2884 or go to `www.animationmagazine.net`.

- ✔ An Internet search for "Artists" and "Cartoonists" can also turn up some valuable contacts.

More on storyboarding with Storyboard Quick

My favorite storyboard software program is Storyboard Quick by PowerProduction Software. A great feature of Storyboard Quick is that you can input your entire screenplay so that every piece of dialogue has its own storyboard panel. It's a great way to break down your script. Storyboard Quick works for both PCs and Macs.

After storyboarding every shot, Storyboard Quick then lets you choose what elements you want in your separate panels. You can drag and drop illustrations of different characters and put

them anywhere within the frame. You can resize your characters to any size and turn and flip them in any direction. Storyboard Quick comes with libraries of images that include characters, props, and locations (such as various rooms, beaches, mountains, deserts, and even interiors of vehicles). You can also buy add-on libraries for additional prop, character, and location images. You can get more information on Storyboard Quick and buy a copy at www. powerproduction.com.

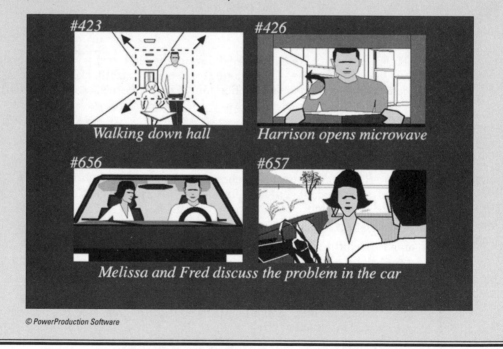

#423 Walking down hall

#426 Harrison opens microwave

#656 #657 Melissa and Fred discuss the problem in the car

© PowerProduction Software

Assessing the artist's qualifications

You need to do and discuss several things when interviewing professional artists to storyboard your film:

✔ **Be sure to ask if he or she has ever drawn storyboards before.**
Working with a storyboard artist who is versed in camera angles and lenses and has a basic knowledge of cinematic language is best.

- ✔ **Make sure the artist draws in a style that works aesthetically for the style of your film.** If the film is a comedy, the style should be light and even have a slight cartoonish feel to it. If it's a serious drama, the illustrations should depict a more formal style with shadows and more serious undertones.

  Request samples from other films the artist has storyboarded to see not only whether you like her style but also whether she has an understanding of the process. Her current work should speak for itself.

- ✔ **Assess your compatibility.** It's very important that you get along as a team so that the artist can translate your shots more accurately and effectively into the storyboard panels. Keep in mind that even though you call the shots, you may get some great ideas from the artist.

- ✔ **Negotiate a fair price.** You want an artist who will work at a reasonable rate that fits within your budget. Often on independent films, storyboards are a luxury, so you want to make sure you have enough money to pay for a storyboard artist. Sketches per panel can range from $5 for a rough thumbnail pencil sketch to $50 for a detailed black-and-white ink rendering. Remember, though, the price is completely negotiable between you and the artist.

- ✔ Make sure that the artist's turnaround time works for your schedule. (*Turnaround* means the time it takes from working on the rough sketches with the artist until the artist comes back to you with the final rendered storyboard panels.)

You can even work with your artist via e-mail and have him scan his rendered storyboards and send them to you as an attachment. However, sit down with the artist first and make sure his rough sketches match up to your expectations — he can then e-mail you what he's working on to see whether he's on the right track (tell him you'll e-mail his check, too — it's worth a shot).

Part III

Ready to Roll: Starting Production on Your Film

The 5th Wave   By Rich Tennant

TROUBLE ON THE SET

All the software in the world won't make this a great film. Only you can, Rusty. Only you and the guts and determination to be the finest Frisbee catching dog in this dirty little town. Now come on Rusty—it's magic time.

We're losing the light, Dad.

In this part . . .

*H*old onto your director's cap because you're going to discover some pretty amazing stuff in this part. What was once unattainable to the independent low-budget or no-budget filmmaker is now attainable. Welcome to the future!

In this part, you see that the creative elements to making film are the same, whether you shoot with a traditional film camera, a basic camcorder, or one of the new digital 24-frame progressive camcorders that emulate the look of film.

This part takes you behind the scenes and shows you the meaning of "Lights, camera, action!" You're sure to find the chapter on lighting illuminating and I'll have you tuned in on the sound production chapter. I give you the right directions in Chapter 13 on directing your actors and then direct you onto your film set in Chapter 14.

Chapter 10

Filming through the Looking Glass

. . . .

In This Chapter

▶ Comparing film cameras and camcorders

▶ Looking at lenses

▶ Filtering your motion pictures

▶ Finding your focus

. . . .

With the magical box called the movie camera, you can capture your story, turn it into pictures, and show it to audiences all over the world. In this chapter, you see the difference between motion-picture film cameras and video camcorders, including advanced digital cinema camcorders. This chapter also explains how the single eye of the camera sees and how you can harness that single eye to get the best picture possible. I help you choose the correct lenses to capture your shots and use them to their full benefit. Finally, you find out how to add filters and other accessories to your filmmaking toolbox.

The 21st century has brought some amazing technological advances to mankind, including digital filmmaking. All the filmmaking techniques and creative skills described throughout this book can also be applied to digital filmmaking. The only difference is in the type of equipment and the technical means of getting a finished product.

Finding the Right Camera

Before shooting your film, you need to decide whether you want to use a traditional film camera (that uses film *celluloid*), an analog consumer video camcorder (the type you use to record family events), or the emerging technology of digital camcorders including the digital 24 progressive cinema camcorders (that use digital videotape and emulate the look of shooting with a film camera).

Staying up to standards with ASA and ISO

You can buy film for your camera in a variety of speeds. *Film speed,* in relation to American Standards Association (ASA) and International Standards Organization (ISO), refers to how quickly the film responds to light. The higher the ASA or ISO rating, the more sensitive the film stock is to light. Some films can actually "see in the dark." An ASA of 800 is more light sensitive and can expose darker images than, say, a film speed of 200 ASA. (When you buy film for your 35mm still camera, you have the same choices of ASAs as well.) In the past, higher ASA films that worked well in shooting low-light situations often had a grainy picture quality. Kodak has made some amazing developments over the years, producing high-speed films such as Vision2 color negative 5218/7218 with much less grain and very sharp, crisp picture quality.

In terms of digital camcorders, light sensitivity is determined by the camera's CCD and Lux capability and not by the videotape stock (see Chapter 11 for more information on Lux).

Rolling with film cameras

The *film camera* (also referred to as the *motion-picture film camera*) has been around since the late 1800s. Because the film camera runs film stock through its housing, it's a much bigger and heavier piece of equipment than a video camcorder. Film cameras also rely on manual focus, exposure, and settings.

Film has a nostalgic feel to it, creating the illusion of something that's happened in the past — the feeling of reflecting on a cherished memory. Film photographs a softer, more surreal image than the sharp, sometimes harsh and unflattering picture that video camcorders present.

Film cameras come in various formats that utilize different film stock sizes depending on which camera you choose to shoot with:

- **Super 8:** Film stock that's 8mm in width; small format usually used for home movies and documentaries (has a flatter image than other film types). It's the least expensive route when shooting with film and costs approximately $10 per minute of film, including developing.

- **16mm:** Film stock that's 16mm in width, allowing for more depth in picture quality than Super 8. Often used for TV, low-budget features, student films, and documentaries. The cost is approximately $20 per minute of film, including developing.

- **35mm:** Film stock that's 35mm in width. Used for TV and feature films. The most commonly used stock by motion-picture studios and considered a professional format. The cost is approximately $55 per minute of film, including developing.

You can cut your film costs by buying 16mm or 35mm *recans,* which are rolls of film that have been put back in the film can by a production company that ended up not using all the film stock it purchased. You can buy recans or film ends (under 400-foot reels) at prices much cheaper than the cost of new film stock. Film Emporium (`www.filmemporium.com`) and SHORTenz (`www.shortenz.com`) are two reliable companies that guarantee their short ends and recans.

Reading the camera magazine

You can't read a camera magazine because it's not the type of magazine you may be thinking of. Instead, a *camera magazine* is a housing that looks like Mickey Mouse ears on the top of the motion-picture film camera; it holds the raw (undeveloped) film that winds off the reels into the camera and past the exposure gate. The magazine is sealed tight and perfectly light-proof (so the film isn't accidentally exposed and ruined by the light). After the film winds up on the back magazine during shooting, it can be detached easily from the camera and downloaded by the assistant cameraperson (see Chapter 7 for details on crew responsibilities). The exposed film is then sealed in a film can and sent to the lab for developing.

Video tapping

With a film camera you have the capability of recording the image at the same time onto videotape with the use of a *video tap* also known as *video assist.* Nowadays, most film cameras come with a video tap that enables a video signal to record exactly what the film camera is seeing through the lens (see the "Video assisting Jerry Lewis" sidebar in this chapter, for the history of video assist). Video assist can save time and money on the set, by allowing the director to see the actual camera movement and framing by the cinematographer on a TV monitor. A shot can also be played back on the monitor so you can decide if it has to be reshot or if the crew can move on to the next setup.

One of the advantages of shooting your film with a video camcorder is you automatically have your video assist!

Digital camcorders in motion

Video images are captured by a video camera that's connected to a recording deck or a camcorder that houses both the camera and recorder (that's why it's called a cam-corder) in one unit and records images in an electronic digital environment. When using a digital camera, you also have the option of two types of digital formats in terms of how the final image will look:

- ✔ **Digital camcorders:** These cameras are better quality than analog video camcorders because they use digital technology that records a sharper picture image that doesn't lose quality when making copies to other digital tapes. Digital camcorders have exceptional image quality and can be used in most professional applications that are appropriate for video recording, such as news footage, documentaries, and entertainment programming.

- ✔ **Digital 24progressive cinema camcorder:** This is also a digital camcorder but can emulate the look of a film camera without the expense of film stock, lab and printing costs, or *telecine* (transferring-to-video) costs. This type of camera utilizes the new technology of making video resemble more of the soft and pleasing look of film.

Going over the advantages of video camcorders

Shooting your film with a video camcorder has many advantages:

- ✔ **A camcorder is lighter and smaller (and more portable) than a film camera.**

- ✔ **You don't have to reload every ten minutes as you have to with film magazines.** For digital camcorders, each mini-DV tape is one hour, and it's easy to pop in and out, just like with a VCR. Plus, tape is cheaper than film. Edgewise Media (www.edgewisemedia.com) sells mini-DV tapes for around $3 each. Analog video camcorders use either VHS or Beta tapes.

- ✔ **You can save tape and rerecord over it if you don't like the take, or you can reuse older tapes that you're finished with and want to erase.**

- ✔ **You see the image instantly on the camcorder's LCD built-in screen, so you don't need a video assist tap** (see the "Video assisting Jerry Lewis" sidebar in this chapter).

Century Optics makes an LCD Magnifier that works on specific camcorders, enlarging the image and shading it from the sun so you can see the image and be able to better determine if your exposure and focus are correct. Check it out at www.centuryoptics.com. You may want to connect a small television monitor to your camera to get a better idea of what your final picture will look like. Make sure your TV monitor has been set correctly for proper skin tones and other coloration.

- ✔ **You can plug in a microphone and use the digital sound from the camera.** If using a digital camcorder, your sound will be professional digital quality!

Make sure the camera has an input for a separate microphone (most do). You rarely want to use the microphone that comes attached to the camera because you'll hear everything in front of and behind the camera (this is called an *omni-directional microphone*). See Chapter 12 for more on microphones.

✔ **You don't have to take the footage into a lab and have it developed.**

✔ **You can import the footage directly into your editing system.** You don't have to transfer it to tape from film — it's already on tape and you can start editing!

✔ **Software programs can make your analog or digital video footage look more like you shot it on film (if you aren't using a digital 24progressive camcorder).** There are also new digital camcorders that simulate film cameras and 24-frame motion (see the following section).

Taking a peek at digital cinema camcorders (24p)

Panasonic has come out with a 24p (24-frame progressive) camera called the AG-DVX100 Cinema Camera (see Figure 10-1). At the price of a consumer camcorder (around $3,700), this camera can give you a traditional video look or, at the switch of a button, emulate very closely the texture of a celluloid film image. The camera uses technology similar to the digital cameras George Lucas used in his *Star Wars* films *The Phantom Menace* and *Attack of the Clones,* in which Lucas proved that the picture quality of digital cinema camcorders can emulate closely the look of film. Robert Rodriguez shot *Spy Kids 2* entirely with digital video cameras and has said that he'll never use film again.

Figure 10-1:
The new
Panasonic
AG- DVX100
Digital
Cinema
Camera,
which
shoots video
and also
emulates the
look of film.

Courtesy of Panasonic Broadcast

Shooting on video with a digital cinema camera saves you a lot of money over shooting on film. If you can't afford to buy a digital cinema camera like the AG-DVX100, you may need to rent one from a camera rental house or your local TV station. Or better yet, find a cinematographer who owns one of these cameras. This camera takes regular mini digital tapes that also work in the regular digital camcorders that don't do 24 progressive film style.

Video assisting Jerry Lewis

Jerry Lewis directed and starred in many of his films, but he had difficulty gauging his performance while doing double-duty as director. He needed to find a way to see what he shot, while he was shooting it and not be surprised a day later when the footage came back from being developed at the lab.

In 1956, Jerry attached a video camera to the film camera so that he could capture his scenes on video at the same time the film camera was rolling. This is how *video assist* was born. Jerry Lewis created a new technique that virtually every filmmaker shooting with a film camera uses to this day.

With the new age of digital video technology utilizing 24 progressive to emulate a film look (without having to use film), more and more productions are being produced on video. However, all these productions have to be transferred to film for theatrical release, unless they're projected by video projectors, which only a minority of theaters and auditoriums can do. Many productions will never make it to a movie screen, however, and if shot in digital video with the 24 progressive cinema look, they'll be fine for a television screen.

Most digital camcorders (including the 24p cinema versions) allow you to emulate a wide-screen image similar to the shape of the screen in a movie theater (this is also helpful if you're planning on blowing your 24 progressive digital video to 35mm film to show in movie theaters). The camcorder puts a black border at the top and bottom of the screen and creates a rectangular shaped frame, rather than the squarish shape of a TV set (see Figure 10-2). Many films on DVD give you the option to view the film in the wide-screen format, also referred to as *letterbox*. Chapter 9 shows you the various screen shapes.

Figure 10-2:
A cam-corder image with the wide-screen (letterbox) frame turned on.

Do You Need Glasses? Types of Lenses and What They Do

Camera lenses are sized in millimeters, which represent the circumference of the lens or the ring size that attaches to the camera housing, in order to control the size of your shots. (Note that camera formats are also referred to in millimeters, as in 35mm, 16mm, and Super-8mm — here, millimeters refer to the width of the film stock the camera uses.) The assortment of lens sizes needed depends on the camera format being used. For 35mm film cameras, a set of standard lenses for picture area consists of the following: 18mm, 25mm, 35mm, 40mm, 50mm, 75mm, and 100mm (see Figure 10-3 for examples).

Figure 10-3: A wide, medium, and telephoto lens for an older model 35mm Arri camera.

Each lens serves a purpose and gives a different image size when attached to the camera. A lens can also change the characteristics of the image. For example, a wide lens like the 18mm makes things appear more spacious by slightly bending the image (squeezing more information into the shot). A wide lens is effective for shooting establishing shots to make rooms and areas look roomier than they really are. A telephoto lens tends to flatten and compress images and make things appear closer together. Telephoto lenses are good for bringing distant objects closer to the camera (using magnification).

Lower-priced video camcorders come with a fixed lens that is a permanent part of the camcorder and can't be detached (unless you take a hacksaw and cut it off — but you don't want to do that now, do you?). Professional-model and higher-priced camcorders, like the Canon XL-1, use *interchangeable*

lenses, which allow you to detach the existing lens and screw on different-sized lenses (telephoto, wide-angle, zoom, and so on). In most digital video camcorders, the lens functions are similar to a film camera's lenses (if the camera accepts interchangeable lenses), but they are measured differently. The measurement used to determine a digital video camera lens for image size can be eight times less than a film camera lens measurement (depending on the make and model of the camcorder). Therefore, a 4.5mm wide-angle lens on a digital camcorder is equivalent to a 32.5mm lens on a 35mm film camera.

The normal lens

A 50mm lens on a 35mm film camera or 35mm still camera is known as the *normal lens.* It's equivalent to what your eye sees (look through the lens and open your other eye, and you will be seeing about the same size image). This normal lens does not create any distortion and presents the most realistic image to what you see without the camera. Many filmmakers prefer this lens when shooting actors. Depending on your subject, a normal 50mm lens can be more complimentary to your actor's features (a wide lens may make your actor look heavier or distorted, a telephoto lens may flatten your actor's features).

For cameras other than 35mm film cameras, the size of the normal (50mm) lens is smaller. Table 10-1 shows the measurement of normal, wide-angle, and telephoto lenses for various types of cameras.

Table 10-1   Normal Lens (50mm) Measurements for the Various Camera Formats

Camera	*Type of Lens*	*Measurement*
35mm	Normal lens	50mm
	Wide-angle lens	18mm
	Telephoto lens	100mm
16mm	Normal lens	25mm
	Wide-angle lens	9mm
	Telephoto lens	50mm
Super 8mm	Normal lens	15mm
	Wide-angle lens	7.5mm
	Telephoto lens	30mm

Camera	Type of Lens	Measurement
Digital video	Normal lens	5.5mm
	Wide-angle lens	3.4mm
	Telephoto lens	20mm

Digital video lenses vary in sizes depending on the particular make and type of video camera, so check the manual that comes with the camera.

Short or wide-angle lens

A *wide-angle lens,* also called a *short lens,* consists of a curved glass that bends the light coming into the camera and pushes the picture back to create a wider frame than what you see with the naked eye.

When using a 35mm camera, a wide-angle lens is lower in number than the 50mm normal lens. (For other type of cameras, the numbers for a wide-angle lens are much lower — refer to Table 10-1.) Therefore, a 40mm or 25mm lens (on a 35mm film camera) pushes the image farther back to appear as if you're farther away than you really are. The image is reduced so that more of your subject or scenery can fit into the frame. Wide-angle lenses make locations and sets appear more expansive (more picture information is squeezed into the frame). However, wide-angle lenses can create some distortion, so the closer you are to the subject, the more noticeable the distortion will be.

A *super wide-angle lens* is sometimes referred to as a *fisheye* lens because it resembles a bulbous fish eye. Often these lenses are 18mm or lower for a 35mm camera. This type of lens (see Figure 10-4) distorts the picture and makes everything look rounder. Usually you only want to use a really wide lens when you want to create an effect like someone looking through a peephole in a door, or for comic effect when you want a character's nose to be bigger and his or her face distorted.

Figure 10-4: A super wide-angle lens (left), and a super wide-angle lens in action (right).

Super wide angle lens

Super wide angle lens in action

You can add a wide-angle lens to your camcorder by screwing a *converter lens* (with threads) onto your existing camera lens so that you can go even wider than the permanent lens on your camera allows.

Going long with telephoto

A *telephoto lens* (also called a *long lens*) is higher in number than 50mm for 35mm film cameras. Therefore, a 75mm lens gives you an image that appears to be closer than the normal lens (50mm) does. If you look through the camera with a 75mm lens and open your other eye, you'll see the image closer in the viewfinder than it really is in person.

A telephoto lens is often used for close-up shots, throwing the background out of focus. An out-of-focus background lets the audience concentrate on an actor or object in the frame without being distracted by the surroundings. A telephoto lens is also used to capture close-ups of buildings or objects that are at a fair distance from the camera. A pair of binoculars works similar to a telephoto lens by bringing the subject closer. Explosions, car stunts, and other dangerous situations can be safely captured on film from a distance using a long lens.

Zooming in on zoom lenses

A *zoom lens* does the work of several lenses in one. You can frame a wide-angle shot, a medium shot (usually framing your subject just above the waist to slightly above his or her head), and also a telephoto close-up shot by using a single zoom lens. Most video camcorders come with a zoom lens that's permanently attached to the camera. A zoom lens saves the time of removing and attaching different lenses and of having to make sure no dust gets in the camera while changing lenses.

Clearing the Air about Filters

You've heard the term, "seeing life through rose-colored glasses." Well, in a nutshell, that's what *lens filters* are all about. They're like sunglasses for your camera. But each sunglass serves a different purpose: You can change colors, set moods, and correct the picture. By placing a filter in front of your camera lens, you can magically change or enhance an image by:

- Removing annoying glare
- Changing the color of the sky
- Softening the subject through the lens

✔ Adjusting the exposure (darker)

✔ Correcting the image color

✔ Making colors pop (stand out)

The Tiffen Company (www.tiffen.com), one of the largest and most recognized filter companies, puts out a line of quality filters. Table 10-2 gives you some examples of what Tiffen filters can do.

Table 10-2	Tiffen Company Filters
Filter	*Effect*
Pro-mist	Softens the image
Polarizer	Reduces or eliminates glare
Star	Causes light sources to sparkle
Neutral Density (ND)	Lowers the exposure, making the picture darker
85 and 80	Color-corrects the image
Sunrise (half)	Adds warm sunrise degradation to the sky (the bottom part of the filter is clear, and a warm color — orange or yellow — gradually gets deeper toward the top of the filter)
Blue Sky (half)	Adds richer blue to the sky (the bottom half of the filter is clear, and the upper half gradually becomes a deep sky blue)
Full Orange	Warms the entire image
Full Blue	Cools the entire image (also emulates nighttime)

Lee Filters (www.leefilters.com) is a company that offers similar filters, as does Schneider Optics (www.schneideroptics.com). Samy's Camera (www.samys.com) also carries a wide variety of filters and camera accessories.

Filters come in two format types and can be used on both film cameras and video camcorders:

✔ **Screw-on filter:** This type of filter can be screwed directly onto the camera lens (you need to match the lens circumference millimeter size to fit your specific camera). Screw-on lenses don't require a bulky *matte box* (see the following section), which keeps the camera portable and lightweight.

✔ **Slide-in filter:** This requires a matte box into which the filter slides, in front of the camera (see following section). The advantage of a slide-in filter is that it works with any camera, because it doesn't depend on having to screw a fitted sized lens directly onto the camera. Instead a standard 4-x-4-inch filter slides into the matte box. Also, using multiple filters in a matte box is easier.

Whenever you put a filter or additional lens over your camera lens, you need to adjust the exposure because the camera is now working through more levels of lenses to give you a good picture (see the "Exposing Yourself to Exposures" section later in this chapter).

Welcome matte (box)

A *matte box* is an optional device that you mount in front of your camera lens. The filters, which are approximately ¼-inch thick and 4 x 4 inches in size, conveniently slide in and out of the matte box. The Tiffen Company, in addition to making screw-on filters, also makes slide-in filters, which can be used with its FilterFlex matte box (see Figure 10-5). A matte box can also be used for inserting effects masks, which suggest looking through keyholes, binoculars, or a telescope view.

Figure 10-5:
A matte box with slide-in filters, and an example of visual effects masks to suggest looking through binoculars, a keyhole, or a telescope.

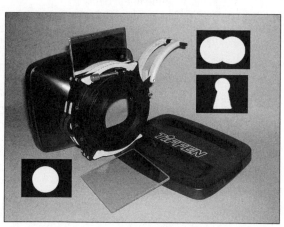

Courtesy of Tiffen

Slide-in filters for the matte box are quicker and more convenient than screw-on filters — you just drop the filter in the slot. Slide-in filters can also be turned sideways, something you can't do with screw-on filters. Both types, however, allow you to use multiple filters at the same time if you want to use a combination of filter effects like a warm color filter, plus a filter that softens the picture image.

Color filters

The main purpose of color filters is to correct the film or video image so that the colors resemble what the human eye sees, whether you're shooting indoors or outdoors. Without proper color balance, your picture will have a slight off-colored tint to it.

On a film camera, the color filters you use depend on the film stock you're using and the color temperature of your lighting source (see Chapter 11 for details on color temperature). For example, a number *85 filter* color balances *tungsten* (film stock designed to be used indoors) for outdoor filming so that your scenes don't have a blue hue to them. A number *80 filter* color-corrects daylight film being used indoors so you don't have a yellow, red, or orange tint to your picture. Chapter 11 also discusses color corrections and effects using *gels,* which can be placed in front of your film lights. In addition, your film footage is color-corrected or adjusted by the timer in the lab or while transferring your film footage to video via telecine (see Chapter 15).

If you're using a digital camcorder, you can manually set the color balance by pointing the camera at a white card or object to establish a point of reference for your camera. Or you can use the automatic white balance that sets the correct color balance for you (but the exposure can fluctuate if you move the camera within different lighting conditions). After establishing what the color "white" should look like, your camcorder then recognizes the correct colors of other objects.

One of the advantages that digital video has over film is that you immediately see on your LCD or TV monitor the results of the color correction. You don't have to wait for the film to come back from the lab to see whether you got it right.

Get a color chart from Kodak (it resembles a colored checkerboard) or the *Macbeth* color chart (you can purchase this chart at Samy's Camera, www.samys.com, for under $60). You can photograph the chart at the beginning of each film roll or videotape to use as a color reference when color-correcting in postproduction.

Day for night and night for day

Sometimes you can't conveniently shoot a night scene at night or a day scene during the day. By putting on a blue filter during an overcast day (and avoiding showing the sky in the scene), you can fool your audience into believing that the blue cast is night.

To create the look of daytime after the sun has gone down, you use large lights called *HMIs,* which simulate sunlight and also use a warm-colored filter to enhance the effect. By keeping your shots fairly close on your subjects and avoiding the horizon in the frame (such as keeping the actor against a building), your audience will think the scenes were shot during daylight hours.

Neutral density filters

A *neutral density filter,* also known as an ND filter, is used to reduce the amount of light coming into the camera lens — much like a pair of sunglasses cuts down on the amount of light hitting your eyes. In bright-light situations, an ND filter helps to avoid an overexposed picture. These filters come in various degradations, each one darker than the next. You screw on, or slide in (if using a matte box), a neutral density filter in front of the film camera lens. If you're shooting with a digital camcorder, you can turn on the neutral density filter electronically by flipping a switch.

Polarizers

Certain surfaces, like a metallic robot, a shiny car, or sparkling windows, can cause distracting reflections. *Polarizers* usually take care of this problem. If you're filming someone through a car windshield, for example, you often get a glare, making the driver difficult to see in the car (see Figure 10-6). A polarizing filter can be adjusted until the glare is minimal or completely eliminated.

Figure 10-6:
Without
polarizer
(left) and
with
polarizer
(right).

Exposing Yourself to Exposures

Exposures control the amount of light entering the *iris* (also called the *aperture*) of the camera lens, which reacts to light entering the lens and opens and closes to allow more or less light into the camera. The human eye iris works similarly, but the response is automatic. The film camera's eye needs human assistance to adjust the settings for focus, exposures, and so on. Most digital camcorders have advanced circuitry and do a lot of this for you (when set on automatic).

When you look outside on a bright day, the iris of your eye shrinks to a smaller circle because the eye has plenty of light to see. The iris of the camera works the same way where concentrated light is directed through the tiny aperture of the camera causing objects to appear in sharp focus (this is also why people who don't have 20/20 vision see better during daylight hours than at night). Have you ever noticed that when you turn off the lights in a room, your eyes take a moment to adjust? That's because your brain is telling your iris that it needs to open wider to compensate for the lack of light. The iris of the camera works the same way and has to be opened up wider to allow for more light to enter the lens to be able to expose an image with enough light.

F-stopping to a "t"

The various sizes of the iris as it opens and closes to light are measured in f-stops. These settings need to be manually set to get a proper exposure (allowing enough light to enter the lens to record a proper image — not too dark, not too light). Or you can use the automatic setting on your camera. The disadvantage to using the automatic setting is that the lighting will fluctuate as you move the camera within different lighting conditions. Figure 10-7 illustrates the *aperture* opening of different exposures. The higher the number, the smaller the opening of the iris. F-stops are also measured in t-stops, which are more accurate. Most film cameras are marked with both f- and t-stops on the side of the lens.

If you take a film lens and adjust the f-stops while looking into the lens, you can actually see the iris adjusting in size, similar to the iris of your eye as it adjusts to light.

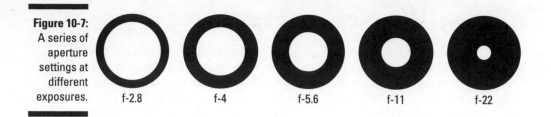

Figure 10-7:
A series of aperture settings at different exposures.

f-2.8   f-4   f-5.6   f-11   f-22

Shuttering to think

Shutter speed affects how the motion of an image is captured on film celluloid or recorded on videotape (on an analog or digital camcorder). High shutter speeds are appropriate for shooting fast-moving subjects, such as a car chase or a competitive sporting event. By setting your camera for a higher shutter speed, you avoid having your subject blur or smear in the frame. For example, if you pause the footage on your VCR, the subject looks like a clear still photograph, rather than a blurred image moving across the frame. Slower shutter speeds are best for low-light situations where the image needs adequate light to get a properly exposed picture.

On a film camera, the standard shutter speed at 24 frames per second is $\frac{1}{50}$ of a second. The film camera shutter can be adjusted up to $\frac{1}{1,700}$ of a second. On a camcorder, the standard shutter is $\frac{1}{60}$ of a second (equivalent to a video camera shooting 30 frames per second), and the shutter speed can be adjusted on some cameras, like the Canon GL-1, as fast as $\frac{1}{15,000}$ of a second.

Depth of Field: Focusing a Sharper Image

Depth of field deals with the depth of focus in your shot. In other words, what distance in front of and behind your subject are in acceptable focus? Knowing how depth of field works helps you to compose more interesting shots. The left shot in Figure 10-8 was taken with a 50mm lens set at 8 feet (with a small aperture setting of f-16) resulting in the actress and background both being in focus. The right shot was taken with a 100mm lens (with an f-stop of f-4) with the actress 25 feet from the camera. Notice that the actress is in focus, but the background is now out of focus.

Make sure the eyepiece on your camera is focused to your eye. Otherwise, you can't tell if your subject is in proper focus.

Figure 10-8:
With a medium (50mm) lens, everything is in focus (left). With a telephoto (100mm long lens), the background is out of focus (right).

The type of lens, shutter speed, and f-stop all affect the area in the frame that will be in focus. Table 10-3 shows the range of focus (what will be in focus at different exposure f-stop settings) within the frame, using a 50mm lens (normal lens) on a 35mm film.

Table 10-3	The Distance Range in Focus at Different F-Stops			
Lens Setting	*F-4*	*F-5.6*	*F-11*	*F-22*
15 ft.	11 ft. to 23 ft. 8 in	9 ft. 11 in. to 30 ft. 9 in.	7 ft. 6 in. to 20 ft. 8 in.	5 ft. to infinity
8 ft.	6 ft. 8in. to 9 ft. 11 in.	6 ft. 4 in. to 11 ft.	5 ft. 3 in. to 16 ft. 11in.	3 ft. 11in. to infinity
5 ft.	4 ft. 6 in. to 5 ft. 8 in.	4 ft. 3 in. to 6 ft.	3 ft. 9 in. to 7 ft. 5 in.	3 ft. to 14 ft. 1 in.
2 ft.	1 ft. 11 in. to 2 ft. 1 in.	1 ft. 11 in. to 2 ft. 2 in.	1 ft. 9 in. to 2 ft. 3 in.	1 ft. 7 in. to 2 ft. 8 in.

The higher the f-stop, the larger the area that the camera sees in sharp focus. You can find myriad cinematography books at your library or local bookstore that contain every conceivable depth-of-field chart for film and video cameras and the various lens and exposure settings. *The American Cinematographer Manual,* edited by Rod Ryan (published by A.S.C. Holding Corporation), makes a great reference book as well.

Most video camcorders give you the option to focus manually, and this is your best bet. Zoom in as close as you can to the object you want to concentrate on, focus as clearly and precisely as you can, then zoom out and frame your image. Now you know your subject is in focus, regardless of objects or things moving behind or in front.

You have to be careful if you use the automatic focus because certain situations can fool it:

✔ **Shooting through a cage or a fence:** The camera doesn't know whether to focus on the bars or the object behind it.

✔ **Images that aren't centered in the frame:** The camera may try to focus on an image that's in the foreground or background but not the main subject.

✔ **Fast-moving objects:** These can trick your auto focus into trying to follow-focus the image.

Chapter 11

Let There Be Lighting!

*L*ittle did Thomas Edison know that the simple light bulb he invented in 1879 would take on so many shapes and color temperatures and be instrumental in controlling the look of every image captured on film. Without the proper lighting and exposure, your actors will be sitting (or standing) in the dark.

Lighting, the focus of this chapter, is the technique of creating a mood. Here, you develop a feel for composition, color temperatures, and the distribution of light and dark. You also get a short primer on lighting safety.

Lighting Up Your Life

Lighting brings life to your shots. Light lets your audience "see" where your actors are and where they're going. Instead of just flipping on a light switch in a room with one overhead light, you have the power to control the lighting in your shots by positioning a myriad of lights (on stands) virtually anywhere to illuminate your scene. Lighting can bring aesthetic beauty to your shots, or true ugliness, depending on the final results you're looking to achieve. When lit correctly, your lighting will pull your actors away from the walls and furniture. Creative lighting can reach behind your actors and separate them from the background. You can create depth and perspective with proper lighting and control the mood of the scene by coloring your lights.

Don't be afraid to experiment with light. Pick up your lights on their stands and move them around your subjects. Watch what light does to your actors as you lower, raise, and tilt your film lights at different angles toward your subjects. See how you can create a mood with shadows and make your actors look more pleasing by bouncing light off the ceiling or using other lighting tricks and tools, like scrims and glass diffusion, discussed later in this chapter.

Shedding Some Light on Lighting Jargon

Before delving deeply into this chapter, take a minute to review two important lighting terms.

Foot-candles: Lighting for film cameras

The illumination of light falling on a subject is measured in *foot-candles*. One foot-candle is the amount of illumination produced by a single candle at a distance of 1 foot away from the subject. For example, if your light meter (see the "Lighting with light meters" section later in this chapter) reads 200 foot-candles, that means that your light source is equivalent to the illumination of 200 candles falling on your subject from 1 foot away. The exposure is also determined by the speed of the film, which in turn controls your exposure (see Chapter 10 for information on stops and exposures). Motion-picture film cameras measure light in foot-candles.

Lux (and cream cheese): Lighting for digital

A *lux* is the European equivalent of a foot-candle, but instead of being the equivalent of a single candle at a distance of 1 foot, one lux is the illumination of 1 square meter (European measurement) per single candle. Digital cameras measure light in lux.

Digital camcorders are much more sensitive to light than motion-picture film cameras are, so you can more easily shoot in low-light situations. Lux allows the camera to dig into the darkness and gives you an acceptable image that's not grainy or muddy in appearance. This is similar to the newer fast-speed films, with less grain, which have been developed for motion-picture cameras (see Chapter 10).

Digital cameras contain chips — not potato chips, but digital chips known as *CCDs*. CCD stands for *charge-coupled device* and is a circuit that stores data and converts what the camera records into an electrical image. CCDs are also light sensitive, allowing the camera to "see" into dimmer environments and produce acceptable images. A one-chip camera lends itself to home movies and non-broadcast projects, while a three-chip camera is suitable for professional broadcast with colors and a digital image that is cleaner and sharper than one-chip cameras. Three-chip cameras are more expensive, so if you decide you want one, you have to dip deeper into your wallet (chip and dip).

A standard lux rating averages around three lux and is affected by the CCD and the lens speed. CCDs are light sensitive and determine the lux in a video camera. A 60-watt light bulb is equivalent to 10 lux, so a 3-lux camera is extremely sensitive to light when recording.

Taking your color temperature

Different types of light radiate different color intensities, called *color temperatures,* which affect how the light is recorded by the camera. The color temperature of the lighting affects the final colors in your film. Color temperature is determined by the intensity of light that radiates from your film lights and is not to be confused with thermal temperature that measures hot and cold.

When you're imagining how color temperature works, think of a blacksmith heating up and shaping a horseshoe in a forge. As the black mass heats up, it turns different colors. This is how color temperature works.

Our eyes adjust to the colors of light, but the camera does not have that capability without some assistance. That's why gels, white balance, and filters (see Chapter 10) are used to get the film or video camera to see what the human eye sees. The camera has a mechanical eye (with film cameras) or an electronic eye (with video cameras) that has to be programmed so that lighting will look natural to what the human eye sees. Many video camcorders do emulate the human eye when you set them on automatic.

Every color has a temperature that's measured in *Kelvins* (named after Lord Kelvin, who discovered the system). Kelvin is a rate of measurement in degrees, similar to Fahrenheit and Celsius, and it's usually shortened to °K. Warmer colors like red and amber have lower Kelvin ratings. For example, sunlight is yellow, orange, and red — a lower Kelvin rating than the blue Kelvin rating of the moonlight. Film is a sensitive material that lets light burn its color into it. The higher the temperature in °K, the cooler the color. In other words, the hotter the temperature, the bluer the hue; the lower the temperature, the warmer the hue (reds, oranges, yellows). Table 11-1 shows standard Kelvin ratings.

Table 11-1	Kelvin Ratings
Light Source	*Average Color Temperature (in °K)*
Candle	1,600
Sunrise/sunset	2,000
3,200 Tungsten lights	3,200
Early-morning/late-afternoon sunlight	4,200
Midday sunlight (hottest)	6,000
Light shade/overcast	7,200
Full shade/hazy day	8,000
Dusk	9,500
Early evening	13,000

The average indoor color temperature of your lights is 3,200°K, and the average lighting provided by the sun during daylight hours is about 6,000°K.

Soft lighting versus hard lighting

Soft light is any light source bounced off a reflective surface and then onto your actors in order to create a softer effect. You can create soft light by simply bouncing light off a ceiling or a white card or by using a portable lighting device that has the bulb facing into a reflective lighting housing that bounces the light back out. You can also soften light by placing a translucent cloth-like material in front of the bulb to filter any hard direct light from falling on your subject — this is called *diffusion*. (The company Rosco, www.rosco. com, makes a line of light control filters called Cinegels, which includes cloth diffusers.) A lampshade is a perfect example of softening light; rarely does a room have exposed light bulbs (naked bulbs should not be seen in public!). Photoflex (www.photoflex.com) makes a soft-light fixture that houses a 1,000-watt bulb in a soft covering to diffuse and soften the illumination of the subject (see Figure 11-1).

Hard light creates a harsh, bright look on your subject and should be avoided — it's not flattering to most subjects. An example of hard light is the intense rays of the sun. Most professional cinematographers prefer filming outside on cloudy days (rather than sunny days), because the clouds diffuse the sunlight and add softness to everything. On larger productions, the lighting crew actually stretches a large white translucent tarp on a metal frame over the scene to diffuse the harsh rays of the sun falling on the actors. On close-up shots, you can easily hold a translucent cloth in the path of the sun above the actor to diffuse the harsh sunlight and create a soft light on your actor's face.

Figure 11-1:
Starlite soft
light by
Photoflex.

Painting with Light

Lighting your film is similar to a painter painting a picture with brush strokes onto a blank canvas. An artist brushes on light to create a mood and cast light on the subject or objects in the painting. It's similar to how you set up and position your film lights. You throw light onto your set and subjects. In order to create a three-dimensional look to your shots, you need to understand the basic lighting setup that helps pull your subjects away from the background that could otherwise cause a flat-looking image (see Figure 11-2):

- ✔ **Key light:** The main light (and often the brighter source than your other lights) that is set up first and then supplemented with two or more other types of lights.

- ✔ **Back light:** Also used as a *hairlight,* the back light is directed at the back of your actors to pull them out of the background. It can also create a soft halo around your subjects.

- ✔ **Fill light:** The fill light is used to fill in or supplement the other lights for a more natural look. It also helps soften shadows.

- ✔ **Background light:** As its name implies, the background light lights your background to separate it from your actors and to create more depth in the shot.

- ✔ **Eye light:** This is usually a small light attached to the camera. It's used to bring out the sparkle and life in an actor's eyes when shooting close-ups.

Figure 11-2:
A basic
lighting
setup using
a key light,
a fill light,
a back
light, and a
background
light.

Equipping Yourself for the Best Light

You can light a scene in many ways. Turn on a corner lamp. See the light find your subject. Now turn on an overhead light. Each lighting source enhances and sets a mood for your shot. A candlelit dinner wouldn't be half as romantic if the room were bathed in bright light. A haunted house wouldn't be nearly as scary if it were as bright as day inside.

Lowel, a popular lighting company, makes some great portable kits that include accessories like reflectors, scrims, and barn doors with its lights (all of these are discussed in this section). You can view the company's catalog at www.lowel.com. Samy's Cameras (www.samys.com) also carries a wide variety of lighting equipment.

Getting to know halogen lights, incandescents, and HMIs

A *halogen* bulb (also called *halogen quartz*) is used in most film lights and is usually at a color balance of 3,200°K (see the section "Taking your color temperature" earlier in this chapter). Inside each bulb is a *tungsten coil* that heats up the halogen gas in the bulb to create a steady, consistent light, giving an even color temperature — thus, ensuring a consistent color balance for the scene.

Incandescent light is a source that you probably use every day in the form of your household light bulb. An incandescent also contains a tungsten wire filament that heats up, but unlike the halogen lamp, the bulb doesn't contain halogen gas and so isn't as energy-efficient as halogen bulbs. Household incandescent lamps have color temperatures of around 3,000°K, depending on the wattage.

Halogen bulbs last two to three times longer than a regular incandescent light bulb and burn at higher temperatures.

Don't ever touch a halogen bulb with your bare hands — even if the bulb is cool. The oil on your fingers creates a spot on the surface of the bulb that eventually weakens the glass and causes the light to explode.

An *HMI* (short for *halogen metal iodide*) is a powerful, expensive, bulky light used to emulate sunlight (it has the same color temperature as sunlight.) It can supplement real sunlight when the sun is setting or on overcast days. You can also shine an HMI through the windows on your indoor set to create the appearance of bright sunshine beaming in, or you can place it outside a window at night to simulate daylight outside. An HMI can also be used to fill in shadows on an actor's face caused by the sun.

When you're working on smaller interior sets, like an office or bedroom, a portable lighting kit usually suffices. A *lighting kit* usually consists of three to four small halogen lights with collapsible stands that you can adjust to whatever height you need (see the "Seeing C-stands and lighting stands" section later in this chapter). I have several great lighting kits that I ordered off the Internet from Lowel Lighting (www.lowel.com) and PhotoFlex (www.photoflex.com). Lighting kits usually come neatly encased in a sturdy case or canvas bag that you can carry conveniently (see Figure 11-3).

Figure 11-3:
A portable
lighting kit
that comes
with a
reflective
umbrella
and a
convenient
carrying
case.

Pick up a couple of halogen lamps for under $60 from your local hardware store; they're cheaper than renting professional studio lights or a complete lighting kit. Often called *work-lamps,* they come with sturdy stands, and the lights are bright enough to light a small outdoor parking lot.

Choosing between indoor and outdoor film

If you're shooting with a motion-picture film camera, you need to make sure the color temperature of the film stock matches the color temperature of the light you're filming under. *Daylight* film is color balanced for the Kelvin temperatures radiated by the sun.

Indoor film is balanced for tungsten lights. Tungsten halogen lights are usually rated at 3,200 Kelvin (color temperature) and are consistent in the color temperature they radiate. Household incandescent lamps will have a color temperature of around 3,000°K, depending on the wattage.

If you're using indoor film and you have sunlight coming through the windows, you need to use an 85 (amber-colored) filter (see Chapter 10) to color-correct the daylight. If you're using outdoor film indoors, you use an 80 (blue-colored) filter to color-correct your halogen indoor lights for the outdoor (daylight) film stock.

You're on a roll with gels

Instead of using filters over the camera lens (see Chapter 10), you can change the color on the set by placing rolls of colored *gels* over the lights (or in the case of sunlight, over windows). You can mix and match different colored gels with different lights and pinpoint certain colors on certain objects or people in the scene. For example:

✔ A blue gel on a light creates a blue hue to simulate a moonlit night.

✔ A warm yellow/orange gel can add to the warmth of a romantic scene in front of the fireplace.

Gels are often used to color-correct light sources in order to balance the film stock. An 85 amber gel converts incoming sunlight to indoor color balance to give you correct coloring with your tungsten lamps for your indoor scene.

Gels create artistic hues on set, diffusing and controlling the lighting environment designed by the cinematographer and the gaffer. The company Rosco puts out a free color-swatch booklet that has close to 300 gels, called Cinegels, with diffusion samples in a little flip book — visit Rosco's Web site at www.rosco.com to request the free swatch book.

Gels come in rolls for a reason: You may need to use a lot of them. For example, if you're filming indoors and have a big bright window in the shot, you're going to get a blast of overexposed light if you don't do something. You can put a gel over the window to color correct and also cut down the light.

Reflecting on reflector boards

You can't control the sun when you're filming outside, other than knowing what position it will be at any given time of day. But you can control the direction of the sun with a little portable shiny device called a *reflector*. If your subject can't face the sun, you use a reflector board to catch the sun's rays and bounce the light back onto your subject (see Figure 11-4).

Photoflex makes a portable pop-open reflector disc called the MultiDisc that collapses to the size of a steering wheel, and comes in three sizes: 22-inch, 32-inch, and 42-inch. It also includes additional white, gold, silver, and translucent reflective surfaces. You can also diffuse the sun's harshness by placing the translucent MultiDisc between the sun's rays and your subject. Check out the MultiDisc at www.photoflex.com (click on "Products" and then "Reflectors").

You don't need to run out and buy a professional reflector board if it's not in your budget. Instead, you can use a white foam card or flexible piece of shiny aluminum. Mother Nature makes a great reflector in the wintertime — it's called snow. (Even Mother Nature is into snowbusiness.) The white snow helps to reflect sunlight off the ground and upward to get rid of shadows under an actor's eyes, nose, and chin.

Figure 11-4:
An otherwise dark subject receives a boost of reflected illumination from the sun with the help of a reflector.

If the sun is behind your actor and you don't use a reflector board, you'll most often end up with a silhouette of your actor (referred to as *backlit*) because the light of the sun behind the actor is brighter than the light in front of your actor. The camera exposes for the brighter image and leaves your subject in the dark. Silhouette shots can be effective for scenes where you have an actor on a camel crossing the hilltops against the sun.

Using barn doors: No cows here

You may need to control the spread of light falling on your subject from a lamp with *barn doors*. Barn doors resemble miniature black flags and shade the light as it beams out of its housing. A typical barn door has between two and four metal, hinged doors that open up like — you guessed it! — barn doors.

Cooking with cookies, scrims, and diffused glass

When using film lights, sometimes the light is too bright and you want to control the intensity. There are many ways to do that, using cookies, scrims, and diffused glass placed over the lights to soften or create a lighting effect:

✔ **Cookies:** These *cookies* aren't edible — but they are kind of like a cookie cutter. Cookies are used to break up light or simulate the shadow of tree branches, window blinds, and so on. They come in a variety of shapes, and you can easily make your own.

For an inexpensive cookie, take a small branch off a tree (the one the gardener was going to trim anyway) and clamp it to a stand, putting it in the path of your light. The branch casts an abstract shadow, simulating a tree outside a window.

✔ **Scrims:** *Scrims* resemble the screen in a screen door or window. They cut down on the intensity from hot set lights and are placed in a holder or on a stand in front of the lamp.

For an inexpensive scrim, go to your local hardware store and buy some black mesh used for patio screen doors or windows. Cut it to fit in front of your lights, and clamp it in place with a black binding clamp from an office-supply store.

✔ **Diffused glass:** A *diffused glass* diffuses the light source when you place it in front of your light. This creates a softer light on your subjects that makes them look better than under a harsh light with no diffusion.

Waving flags and snoots

If the first thing you think of when you hear the word *snoot* is an elephant or an anteater, you're not far off. A *snoot* directs light through its trunk-shaped funnel and produces a concentrated beam of light similar to a spotlight. It is used a lot in shooting miniatures, because the light can be pinpointed on small areas.

A *flag,* on the other hand, probably makes you think of the country's flag flapping in the wind with the sun shining brightly behind it. In filmmaking, however, the sun can be flagged by a flag. A flag is usually a black opaque piece of material stretched over a wire frame that's placed to block light from a film light or the sun that may be glaring into the camera lens — just like you use your hand to flag the sun's glare out of your eyes (or like your car visor flipped down to keep the sun out of your eyes while you're driving).

Lighting with light meters

To accurately record an image on film, you need to use a light meter. A *light meter* resembles a battery tester, only you dial the film stock you're using into the meter, and then take a light-meter reading of the lighting on your set. The meter will tell you the correct exposure to set your camera at.

Light meters read the intensity of the light on the subject in foot-candles, letting the cinematographer know what his *f-stop* or *t-stop* setting should be (more on *f-* and *t-stops* in Chapter 10).

Some light meters give you both *reflective* and *incidental* readings (see Figure 11-5):

- ✓ **Incidental light meter:** An *incidental light meter* reads direct light shining into the meter from the actual light source. These meters are quite accurate and are not misled by large areas of light and dark in the same shot.

- ✓ **Reflective light meter:** A *reflective light meter* measures the reflected light off the subject and back into the meter. A *spot meter* is a reflective meter that reads the light in a particular spot so that you know how light falls in different places over your subject and can choose an average reading — even if you have large light and dark areas that normally confuse a meter. A video camera works similarly to a spot meter. It allows you to zoom in on a particular spot and get an accurate reading that way.

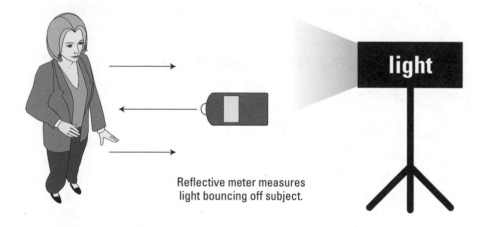

Reflective meter measures
light bouncing off subject.

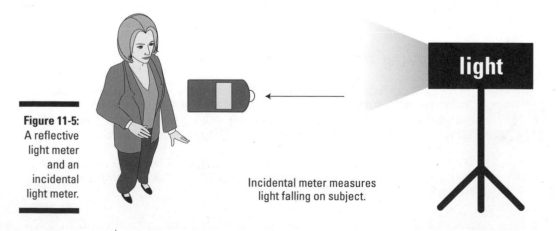

Figure 11-5:
A reflective
light meter
and an
incidental
light meter.

Incidental meter measures
light falling on subject.

When you're using a digital video camera, take a light reading and then set your exposure manually. This way, if the camera follows a subject or a brighter or darker object enters the frame, the camera won't try to automatically adjust the exposure and cause the picture to flutter lighter and darker.

Collecting Your Lighting Accessories

In addition to all the complex, technical lighting tools detailed in the preceding section, you also need to think about a few low-cost accessories, including clamps, clothespins, C-stands, lighting stands, and gaffer's tape. These may seem like simple items, but they're a necessity on the set.

An *expendable* refers to an element that can be used up and is replaceable. Light bulbs (halogen, fluorescent, incandescent) eventually burn out, break, or just plain don't work. They are expendable and have to be replaced. Tape, glue, batteries, and even gels (which eventually fade, melt, or wear out) fall into the expendable category, as well.

Clamping down on clamps and clothespins

Clamps and clothespins are used to hold diffusion cloths or scrims over your lights, as well as clamp things to your C-stands. Clothespins can be helpful to clip light things together, attach or hang props, and so on.

Seeing C-stands and lighting stands

C-stands can be lifesavers. These stands can be adjusted to varying heights, and the extended folding arm post can be adjusted into many positions for holding flags, cookies, *scenic backdrops* (see Chapter 17), or props.

Do you have a decent broad?

A *broad* refers to a film light that has an open-faced reflector housing and can illuminate a wide area. The light from a broad has little control, unless you use barn doors, or flags, to help direct the light, because the lamp doesn't have an adjustment to focus the intensity of its beam.

Generate power with generators

You're not always going to be near an electrical outlet, and if you're shooting outdoors as night is falling, you may need to supplement your lighting. Even if you're shooting a night scene, you still need lights to get a properly exposed image. Some indoor locations may not let you use the electricity, or you may be filming in an older house or building that can't take the voltage required by your lights. These are times when you need a portable generator. Generators run on gasoline. Don't forget to have a can of gas ready to refill the generator.

Light stands are adjustable in height and usually have three extended legs that spread out to help balance the weight of the light securely so it doesn't topple over.

Meeting Mr. Sandman and his bag

Sandbags may not seem important — after all, they just lie there like a lump and don't look very impressive. But when you have light stands and other pieces of equipment tipping over, you may wonder how you ever survived without them. A sandbag is simply a filmmaker's paperweight. A standard sandbag weighs about 15 pounds and resembles a saddlebag.

Sandbags can be rented or bought for about a dollar a pound, or you can make your own. You can buy empty plastic sandbags at most hardware stores for under $1 each and 50 pounds of play sand for around $4.

Going with gaffer's tapes

Your *gaffer* works closely with you or your cinematographer to perfect the lighting of your scenes (see Chapter 7 for details on the gaffer's job). Included in the gaffer's arsenal of tapes are masking tape, Scotch tape, double-sided tape, and spray-on glue.

Don't Blow a Fuse: Taking Safety Precautions

Gaffers and electricians (see Chapter 7) are trained to not overload the electrical circuits. Lights use a lot of voltage and need to be distributed properly.

You don't want the fire department showing up after you've blown the fuse for your entire neighborhood.

 Plug in your lights using several different circuits. Don't plug them in using the wall plugs in the same room. Be creative in your distribution. Get a lot of extension cords and plug into different rooms, so you don't overload one individual circuit. You may have to have your electrician do a *tie-in*. This means that he plugs the lights directly into the fuse box and surpasses the electrical outlets at your location.

Chapter 12

Hear Ye, Hear Ye: Production Sound

*Y*ou've heard the expression "A picture's worth a thousand words." But with the right sound accompanying the picture, it can be worth 10,000 words! The right music or soundtrack can enhance even the dullest images. In this chapter, you see (and hear) how sound can make your film even more exciting.

Sound and picture should complement each other. It's kind of like a relationship: You may be all right on your own, but together you're a dynamite team. Radio dramas were exciting to listen to, and silent pictures entertained audiences, but it wasn't until radio and silent pictures were married that things really started to sizzle. And the honeymoon is still going strong. After you read this chapter, you too will be sounding good!

Getting a clear professional dialogue track on your film requires the expertise of someone skilled in the art of sound recording. A *production sound mixer* will have the knowledge of what microphones to use and how to control the audio levels to give you the cleanest audio tracks. If you don't have the budget to hire a professional sound mixer, you can train yourself, or hire someone interested in taking on the task of recording your audio — but you have to read this chapter first!

Testing, Testing, 1, 2, 3

Without sound you're just shooting a silent movie, and silent movies are a thing of the past. The sound elements for your film are made up of a series of sounds:

- Actors' dialogue
- Environmental atmosphere (ambience)
- On-camera sound effects

These elements have to be recorded properly to create a pristine soundtrack for your film. If you're making your film with a video camcorder, then you can record the sound onto the same tape in your camera that records your images, keeping picture and sound as one. If you're shooting with a film camera, then you'll have a separate sound system recording your audio, which will be married to your film in the postproduction phase.

Putting a Sound Team Together

Just as it's important to have someone who knows how to operate the camera and give you great-looking images (see Chapter 7), it's also important to have someone skilled at recording production sound so that the audience "hears" your film. You can record the sound yourself or hire someone eager to do sound for you, but if you can hire someone experienced in this field you'll have fewer headaches in the end (getting clear crisp sound for the final product). The other advantage to hiring a skilled sound mixer is that he or she may own a recorder and microphones, saving you the time and trouble of renting or buying them elsewhere.

Mixing it up with your mixer

No, a mixer is not your personal bartender on the set. A mixer mixes the sound elements on set, which consist of dialogue between actors and accompanying production sounds, like footsteps or doors closing, that help guide the addition of enhanced sound effects in postproduction.

A *sound mixer* uses a mixing board connected to the sound recorder when using film, or connected to your video camera when shooting video, to control and adjust volume levels and the quality of the sound — not too low, not too high, no interference, and so on. Sound mixers train their ears to pick up any distracting noise, such as background noise or hissing, that can ruin the recording of sound during a shot, and then they adjust it out of the sound mix.

JARGON ALERT

Wild and crazy lines

Dialogue has to be clear. If the audience can't hear an actor's dialogue, they'll lean over to the person next to them and say, "What'd he say?" and miss the next bit of dialogue. You don't want that to happen. If the sound mixer thinks that a line has been stepped on by another actor or that some background noise interfered, he or she has the actor repeat the lines, now called

wild lines, after the director has yelled "Cut!" and the camera has stopped rolling. Replacing those lines in postproduction is easier than reshooting the whole take if it's otherwise usable except for that line or two. Recording the actor's line on set ensures that the sound can be easily matched into the existing take.

The sound mixer's duties also include

- ✔ Recording usable actor dialogue and room tone (known as *ambience*)

- ✔ Announcing each take (called *slating* the take) and keeping a written log for the picture editor to follow in postproduction (see Chapter 15)

- ✔ Recording any necessary voice-over (off-camera narration heard over a scene) or *wild lines* (see the sidebar "Wild and crazy lines" in this chapter)

- ✔ Recording special sound effects on set that can be used in the final film, or replaced and/or enhanced with an effect from a sound-effects library

- ✔ Playing back music and lyrics for lip-syncing (on music videos)

Making room for the boom operator

The job of a *boom operator* is to hold the microphone attached to the tip of a pole called the *boom* (often referred to as a *fishpole,* because it resembles one) out over the actors (or just out of camera frame so it's not in the shot) and to find the best direction from which to capture the actors' dialogue. The boom operator works closely with the sound mixer and is usually guided by the mixer (through headphones) as to where to point the microphone for optimum dialogue recording.

The duties of the boom person include

- ✔ Directing the boom and mic in the most favorable position to pick up the best dialogue recording

- ✔ Being familiar with the scenes, knowing which actor speaks next, and pointing the microphone directly at that actor from above or below the camera frame

✔ Placing hidden plant mics or lapel mics on the actors when it's difficult to pick up good sound with the mic outside of the shot (especially in wide shots)

✔ Setting up and testing the wireless mics often used in wide shots where it's hard to pick up good dialogue audio from a microphone off camera

Don't underestimate the skill of the boom operator. On my film *Turn of the Blade,* we had someone fill in for my boom man one day. This guy was so bad, he kept creeping into every shot — he almost became part of the cast. Often, your mixer can recommend someone he or she has worked with before who doesn't need to be fitted by your wardrobe person.

Recording Analog or Digital Sound

Just as you have a choice of film and video formats (see Chapter 10), you have a choice of audio-recording formats: analog or digital. As you've probably discovered, your music CDs sound better than your cassette tapes. CDs are in the digital domain, and you don't lose any generation in quality when making copies as you do when dubbing analog cassette tapes.

With digital technology rapidly advancing, it's much easier to record your audio using digital equipment when shooting with film and spare the trouble of using older analog technology and lower audio quality. Digital machines are more compact, they use fewer batteries than some of the older bulkier analog recorders, and the tape is affordable. Finding a digital recorder in a small town is also easier than finding an analog recorder for film use. If you're shooting with a digital camcorder, your camcorder acts as a camera and a recorder all in one unit, and your sound will automatically be in the digital realm.

Analog: The sound of Nagra Falls

The Polish word *Nagra* means "to record." A Nagra, from the company of the same name, is an analog recorder that uses ¼-inch magnetic tape on reel to reel (Nagra makes digital recorders as well). Analog Nagras were once the choice of recording mixers on almost every film ever made in Hollywood, but now with the advent of digital technology, filmmakers have more choices (and less-expensive alternatives) when choosing a recording machine for their productions. An analog Nagra keeps in perfect sync with the film camera because it has a crystal-sync device within its housing. *Crystal sync* is an electronic device that is found in both the motion-picture film camera and the separate sound recorder and provides for precise speed control. If you're shooting with a video camcorder, you'll be able to use the audio on the same videotape that records picture, so you don't have to use a separate analog recorder.

A Nagra requires up to 12 batteries at a time, and those 12 batteries may have to be replaced every day. My advice is to move up to the new technology of digital audio recording and leave analog behind.

Digital: DAT recorders and dat's not all

DAT stands for *digital audio tape*. A DAT is similar in size to a mini-digital video-tape that you'd use in a digital camcorder. DAT recorders are compact and portable and work with batteries or an AC adapter. If you use the right micro-phone (see the following section, "Sounding like Microphones"), you'll get audio that's as pristine and professional as the audio in any studio feature film. You'll want to consider a DAT recorder when shooting film, but you can use your video camera's audio inputs if shooting on video. If you're in Los Angeles, you can take advantage of Equipment Emporium (`www.equipmentemporium.com`), which rents digital recorders like the Tascam DAP1 for around $40 a day. If you're in a smaller town, contact your local TV station and see if it can rent you a digital recorder or can recommend a sound rental house that will. If you hire a professional sound mixer, chances are he'll have all his own equipment, including a sound recorder and a set of appropriate microphones.

If you want to record digital but can't afford to buy an expensive system or rent one, you can purchase a mini-disc recorder at your local electronics store. It records onto mini discs (small CDs) and records up to 80 minutes per disc. Just make sure the mini-recorder has an input jack for a microphone. Mini-disc recorder/players start at $299, but prices are coming down.

Sounding like Microphones

Recording crisp, clear dialogue is an art because sound is a very sensitive element, moving in waves similar to the circular ripples that spread out when you drop a rock in water. Recording these sound waves — as dialogue or other audio elements — so that they can be heard with optimum quality requires the proper microphone. If you're shooting on video, you can plug the appropriate external microphone directly into the camcorder for better audio-recording results (and overriding the camcorder microphone — see the sidebar "Why digital camera microphones just don't cut it" later in this chapter). Dialogue, background sounds, crowd noise, or a live musical performance all require a different type of microphone. And a sound mixer is trained to know which type of microphone is appropriate for each situation. The sound mixer's arsenal of microphones includes

- Shotgun microphone (a directional microphone)
- Omni-directional microphone
- Lapel (lavaliere) microphone

The following sections describe how these microphones work.

Every type of microphone has a *listening pattern* that determines from which direction the microphone hears sound. For example, if you have a shotgun or directional microphone, its listening pattern is that of a narrow tube; it hears only what's directly in front of it. Anything outside this directional pattern can't be heard clearly by this type of microphone. Figure 12-1 shows what the listening patterns look like for omni-directional and directional microphones. You can often find an illustrated pattern of your microphone's listening pattern in the manual that comes with it.

A sound house or music store will normally rent you a very nice sound package at a really great rate.

Shotgun microphones

A *shotgun microphone* resembles Han Solo's light saber, only it doesn't light up — and it doesn't make a very good weapon. This type of microphone has a shock mount holder (suspended by rubber bands for shock absorption). It may also have a shoe for mounting the microphone on a boom, camera, or tripod.

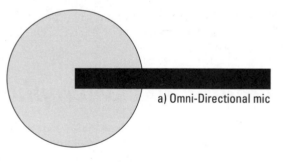

Figure 12-1:
Microphone patterns: (a) omni-directional, (b) directional (long), and (c) directional (short).

a) Omni-Directional mic

b) Directional (long) shotgun mic

c) Directional (short) shotgun mic

A shotgun is a *directional* microphone, meaning that it only picks up sounds directly in front of it, and it filters out sounds to the sides and back. It's like a bullet being shot from a gun — the line the bullet travels is the direction from which the microphone will pick up sound. Directional microphones are used to record actors' dialogue.

Shotgun mics come in two types:

- **Long shotgun** has a long, narrow directional pattern that picks up sounds at a distance directly in front of the microphone, which is effective when actors are in a wide shot and the microphone can't get too close without ending up in the shot.

- **Short shotgun** has a narrow directional pattern with a shorter reach for sounds closer to the microphone. It works well for medium and close-up shots when the microphone can be closer to the actors and still be out of the shot. This is the most common type of microphone used for recording actors' dialogue on set. If you can only afford to buy or rent one, this is it!

A shotgun microphone (see Figure 12-2) is usually covered by a *windscreen* (a tube-shaped piece of foam that slides over the length of the microphone). If you don't protect your microphone with a windscreen, you'll hear a shallow, soft banging from the air movement. A windscreen helps to absorb or filter out wind, as well as an actor breathing too closely to the mic. On windy, outdoor shoots, you use a windscreen resembling a furry ferret that absorbs wind before it hits the mic's sensitive diaphragm.

Figure 12-2:
A shotgun (directional) microphone from Azden.

Why digital camera microphones just don't cut it

The microphone that comes attached to your digital camcorder is not very good for professional sound recording. The main reason is that many camcorders have an omni-directional mic that picks up sound not just in front of the camera but from the sides and behind. That means the mic will pick up everything — from you behind the camera whispering to yourself, to Joe flushing the toilet in the next room. That's why most camcorders have an input to plug in an external microphone. The microphone that comes attached to your camcorder is usually appropriate only for recording events such as parades, birthday parties, vacations, and family get-togethers.

Omni-directional mics

Omni means "all," and that's exactly what an *omni-directional* mic hears. It is similar to how the human ear hears: It's unable to decide which sounds to listen to and hears everything at once — and at the same volume level. Omni-directional mics are used for events, crowds, plays, and environmental background recordings (see the sections "Sounding like Microphones" earlier in this chapter and "Recording On-Set Ambience" later in this chapter). Most built-in microphones on video camcorders are omni-directional.

Lapel microphones

A lapel microphone (also known as a *lavaliere,* or *lav* on set) can be worn on a lapel or cleverly hidden in a person's clothing, such as on a tie or in a pocket, and is small enough not be intrusive. Wireless lapel mics are often used on actors for distant shots requiring dialogue. Most sit-down interviews on television and documentaries utilize lapel mics.

The Azden Corporation (www.azdencorp.com) makes a high-quality broadcast standard WLX-Pro VHF wireless lapel microphone with a range of 250 feet.

Wireless microphones

Shotgun and other microphone types (including lapel mics) can be wireless and work on radio frequencies. Wireless mics are usually used only to pick up the actors' dialogue for distant shots, when a boom or mic cables would otherwise end up in the shot.

Using Your Headphones

You and your boom operator should always use professional cushioned *headphones,* which cup the ear and block outside noise to make sure that your sound is coming through clearly and that there's no interference or buzzing on the line. You can use *earbuds* (which fit in the ear), but you get a less accurate indication of the sound recording because some background noise will make its way in.

Always verify your sound recording through headphones. At the start of each day's shoot, record some test audio and play it back in the headphones to make sure your microphone and recorder are working properly (this includes your camcorder's audio if you're shooting on video). I've had too many shoots where I forgot to bring headphones or earphones, and just assumed that the camera was recording sound. One time, the microphone didn't have a battery and didn't record any audio. Another time, the external microphone wasn't plugged in properly to my video camcorder; instead the camera was picking up sound with the built-in camcorder mic, and you could hear everything in front of and behind the camera (all of it louder than the talent on camera).

Walkie-Talkies: Being Heard on Set

Even though walkie-talkies aren't used to record dialogue or sounds for a film, it would be difficult to run your set without them and so I mention them here. You would probably lose your voice after yelling back and forth on the set without them. Walkie-talkies or two-way radios are helpful for

- ✔ Communicating at a distance with actors
- ✔ Driving scenes (when the camera and the actors are in separate vehicles)
- ✔ Helicopter shots (for communicating with the ground crew)
- ✔ Signaling the police (or an assistant) to hold traffic or pedestrians during a shot

Instead of renting walkie-talkies for your shoot, go to your local electronics or department store and pick up some consumer walkie-talkies. They'll cost you less than a day's rental from a sound rental house — and you get to keep them! I've used two-way compact radios from Midland Radio (www. midlandradio.com) that have up to a 5-mile range and are priced at $24.95. An optional earbud and a lapel microphone allow for hands-free, voice-activated operation. Cell phones are another alternative, but don't forget to turn them off during a sound take!

Carting all that sound around

With sound recording, there's a lot of equipment to carry around. That's why professional sound mixers use a *sound cart,* which is a portable table on wheels that holds all the equipment, including cables, boom pole, adapters, mixer, and coffee and donuts, too. The sound cart serves as the mixer's moveable desk, with everything at his disposal. It also enables him to quickly wheel his equipment out of the way of the camera, should the director want to shoot in his direction!

Keeping Things Quiet

In addition to the windscreens used with shotgun microphones to keep the wind from becoming part of a film's soundtrack, sound teams use additional equipment to ensure that the actors' dialogue comes through loud and clear.

Shushing the camera: Barney hears you

A *blimp* or *barney* is a casing that fits snuggly over the camera magazine reels to muffle the sound of the camera — kind of like a silencer for the camera. If you use a video camera, you don't have to use a barney because camcorders are fairly silent.

Silencing footsteps with sound blankets and foot foam

If you have actors walking on hardwood floors or concrete, especially women in high heels, you need to put *sound blankets* on the floor. Sound blankets are like the heavy padded sheets used in moving vans for covering furniture. Sound blankets absorb the sound of the actors' footsteps on a bare floor, preventing the actors from stepping on their lines — literally. These blankets absorb errant sound waves and prevent your dialogue from sounding tinny or picking up too much reverberation. Of course, you only put sound blankets on the floor when the actors' feet are not in the shot. You can also drape sound blankets over vertical stands or hang from the walls to help absorb reverb off bare walls.

You can also purchase *foot foam* from any sound rental company. This product is a foam rubber of varying thickness that can be cut and adhered to the bottom of your actors' shoes, enabling them to walk on hard surfaces without making excessive noise and allowing the camera to show their feet as well.

If you're on a limited budget, you can silence your actors' shoes by attaching thin pieces of carpet underpadding to the bottoms of their shoes using double-stick tape or glue.

Getting Up to Speed

Tape takes time to get up to speed (whether it's analog or digital), just like it takes your car time to get up to 60 miles an hour. That's why the sound mixer has to yell out the word "speed" so you know that the audio will be usable. This is required when shooting film and using a separate sound recorder, but you should also give five seconds to get up to speed when shooting with a video camcorder, even though the sound and picture are one.

Slating with the clapper board

Slating is a familiar sight to most people, although many probably don't know what it's for. A person with a black-and-white board, called a *clapper board,* stands in front of the camera and says something like, "Scene 1, Take 3," claps the board down creating a loud "clap," and then ducks out of the way. Slating not only visually identifies the scene number, shot number, and production information, it also is used to sync up picture to sound when using a film camera (see the following section, "Using timecode to sync picture and sound").

When shooting film and separate sound, you match up picture to sound by matching the sound of the clapper clapping down with the image of the clapper board completely closed in the first frame. Syncing the clap with the picture in this one frame marries the sound and picture and puts it perfectly in sync.

If you've misplaced your clapper board or can't afford one, you can clap your hands together (just once — don't applaud!) to give a sync mark to match the sound to the picture. You won't be able to identify the scene number and shot number, though, unless you announce it or write it on your hand each time.

Acoustics and carpeting

Recording sound in a gymnasium or a house with hardwood floors makes it difficult to record proper sound without getting a tinny sound or reverb. The sound bounces off the reflective surfaces like radar. If you have a choice, film your scenes in carpeted rooms or be prepared to put down sound blankets. Also, hang some blankets over stands to absorb some of the sound that bounces off the walls and floor.

Silencing MOS

The abbreviation *MOS* comes from a German director (with contradicting opinions as to whom that German director was) who said, "Mit out sound," when a take was to be filmed without recording sound. If a scene contains no dialogue, you can often film MOS and not have to worry about disruptive sounds like planes flying overhead, dogs barking down the street, or the generator running the lights. You may even be able to let your sound mixer and boom operator go home early!

Using timecode to sync picture and sound

Timecode is a series of electronic-generated numbers — hours, minutes, seconds, and frames (for example, 10:28:22:06) — each representing a specific frame of your film when transferred onto videotape. Even if you have thousands of frames in your film, after it's transferred to videotape, each frame has its own personal identification number that can be punched into a computer to pinpoint that specific frame.

Timecode numbers can be used to sync shots (which is quicker than eye-balling the clapper board and matching it with the sound of the clap) if you're using a *timecode slate* (a clapper board that displays the timecode numbers read from a timecode audio recorder). You simply punch in the timecode numbers displayed on the special timecode slate, and the picture and sound will automatically sync up.

Recording On-Set Ambience

Ambience is the background sound of a particular environment. These distinctive, individual sounds accentuate a scene and help dialogue and sound effects blend together, while smoothing out the soundtrack to sound rich and full. Ambient sounds need to be recorded just like dialogue does.

While shooting on location, the sound mixer usually has the cast and crew be quiet for a moment or so and records *room tone* (recording outside ambience is called a *presence track*). Room tone can include the low hum of an air-conditioner, the almost inaudible sound of a refrigerator, or ocean waves. The ambient sound can then be *looped* (repeated over and over in postproduction) and layered under the dialogue, which is recorded separately, to create a realistic-sounding scene. Ambient sounds include

   ✔ Factory
   ✔ Carnival

✔ Library (yes, even a quiet library has ambient sounds)

✔ Freeway

✔ Meandering stream

✔ Restaurant

If you can't afford to shoot in an actual restaurant, you can fake it right in your own house or apartment. Set up a corner with a table and chairs and add ambient sounds that you've recorded at a busy restaurant. When you add the ambient sound in postproduction, it will seem like your actors are in a corner of a busy restaurant. Just don't pull back with the camera and reveal your dog sitting on the stairway waiting for table scraps.

Reporting Your Sound

Sound reports are production forms that the sound mixer fills out. They provide information about the audio recorded on set, including which tapes or reels contain which sound takes. Making sure that sound reports are filled out properly is critical for providing precise notes to the editor when matching up the sound to the picture. You can get sound report forms where you rent your sound equipment, but your sound mixer will probably have them.

Chapter 13

Directing Your Actors: Action!

*W*hen I was 8 years old, I was fascinated with magic and puppets. Then I picked up my dad's Super-8 movie camera and learned to manipulate my puppets on camera. The magic of filmmaking! Actors are kind of like puppets, and the director is the puppeteer pulling the strings through the magic of the movie camera.

The filmmaker in the world of low-budget filmmaking is often known as a triple-threat — producer, director, and writer. So when I talk about the "director," I'm referring to the filmmaker as well. Chances are you're at least one of these — or possibly all three.

This chapter uncovers the secrets of working with actors after you've cast them in your film. Your actors will look to you, the director, for advice and guidance. Discover how to create a comfortable environment in which the actors' trust you. Find out how to speak the actors' language, explore the story's subtext, and define each character's backstory with your cast. See how *blocking* (where your actors move on set) can enhance a scene, and discover how to pull the best performances from your actors.

A director needs to understand actors. Read about acting. Observe acting classes and study actors in films and on TV. Doing so conditions you to appreciate where an actor is coming from. Empathizing with your actors more helps you make better choices when directing your actors. Also, check out the book *Breaking Into Acting For Dummies* by Larry Garrison and Wallace Wang (published by Wiley) to get a better handle on the actor's side of things.

Getting Your Actors Familiar with the Material — and Each Other

The director's job is to understand the script and to make sure that the actors comprehend the overall story and how the characters they're playing fit into it. You as director need to discuss certain things with each actor to make the character clearer in the actor's mind:

- **The character's goals:** What drives or motivates the character and makes him or her tick?

- **The *subtext* (what the character isn't saying):** What is the character saying indirectly (not through right-on-the-nose dialogue)?

- **The *backstory* or *ghost* (the character's past):** How is the character affected by his or her upbringing?

- **Idiosyncrasies of the character:** Does the character have any unique quirks, special personality traits that stand out and make him or her different?

- **The introversion or extroversion of the character:** How would the character behave in a situation? (Would the character step back or step forward?)

- **The character's dress and grooming style:** Is the character neat or a slob? Does he or she care?

- **The character's views on life:** Does the character have strong opinions? Is the character a leader or a follower?

- **The theme of the story as it relates to the character:** Is accomplishing the goal necessary to the character's survival?

I talk more about helping actors prepare for their characters in the section "Preparing Your Actors before the Shoot" later in this chapter.

Remembering that familiarity breeds content

The director's first job is to make the actors feel comfortable because the actor/director relationship determines whether the performances and relationships on screen are believable.

An ensemble show like *Friends* has a successful cast that works perfectly together — they really are friends after working together for so many seasons. But when making a film, you don't have the luxury of the cast getting to spend a lot of time together, so arranging a few informal gatherings for your film cast is a good idea. A launch party for the film is always a good idea, because it gives everyone a chance to meet and greet before starting work on the film. Dinner with the main cast, coffee, or even a walk around the block helps break the ice and can make a big difference when the actors do scenes together.

Reading through the script: The table read

The *table read* is an informal get-together for the cast and director (and other prime production people) in which they sit down and read the script from beginning to end. This is the first time you'll hear the script come to life — kind of like a radio drama without the sound effects and music — and it's is an important stage during which the actors are heard together in one sitting. Have the actors read through the script several times and study their characters before coming to the table read.

The whole cast should be at the table read. This is the one rare occasion when the entire cast and the director are in the same room together. Because most films are shot out of context, it also may be the only time the actors hear the story from beginning to end, giving them, and you, a sense of the story's continuity. This helps the actors make choices and understand the story better when on the set and shooting a scene out of context. The actors can refer to the table read and know what came before and what follows after.

During the table read, you hear what works and what doesn't. If it's a comedy, does everyone find it funny? This is also the opportune time to answer questions from the cast as they read through the script together.

Changing dialogue to make it read naturally

Often, a screenplay contains dialogue that doesn't quite sound natural because the writer couldn't try it out with real actors. If an actor is uncomfortable saying a line, you should probably change it — you don't want an awkward performance that doesn't come across as believable. Use the table read to discover and correct these types of problems instead of waiting until you're on the set. The table read may also spark some additional ideas that the director may want to make a note of in addition to dialogue adjustments.

Life's a stage

We've all been actors at least once in our lifetime. At the age of 5, you probably put on your best performance for that trip to the ice-cream shop or feigned a temperature to get out of going to school. Remember that temper tantrum at 6, when you had to go to the dentist or get your hair cut? When you were young, you had no inhibitions and you weren't self-conscious — that's why children often make great actors.

Actors are really just hypnotizing themselves into believing that they are the character in the screenplay. (In high school, I tried hypnotizing all the girls in my history class, but it didn't work.)

What about in the courtroom? The lawyers who elegantly present their cases, and their clients — guilty or not guilty — often pour out believable performances to influence the judge and jury. Many people who are psychosomatic actually get sick because they've convinced themselves that they're sick. The mind is a powerful thing. William Shakespeare said, "Nothing is good or bad, but thinking makes it so." If you believe it, it must be true. An actor can use this power of the mind when adapting a character.

Being a Parent and Mentor to Your Actors — with No Allowance

Actors work from inside their character and can't see how their performance is being perceived. Even the most successful actors need guidance from their director. Many actors admit that they're like lost children: They need to be vulnerable, sensitive, and open to guidance to be a great actor.

Above all else, you need trust between you and the actors in order to get the proper performance. The more the actors trust you, the more they will allow you to dig in deep and pull great performances out of them. The actors also need to respect the director like they would a parent and a mentor. Without the actors' respect, gaining their trust and getting great performances from them is very difficult.

I recently adopted a puppy (during the course of writing this book, he's eaten five pairs of shoes). Without meaning to be condescending, I've found that raising a puppy is similar to working with an actor:

- The director has to be patient.
- The actors need discipline.
- The director must employ repetition to help the actors learn.
- The actors need to be rewarded (praised).

- ✔ The actors need to feel appreciated and loved.
- ✔ The actors need guidance.
- ✔ The director needs to be able to teach the actors new tricks.
- ✔ The director needs to show the actors the right way to do things.
- ✔ The director sometimes needs to reprimand the actors (civilly).
- ✔ The director sometimes needs to send the actors to their trailer (cage) when they misbehave.

Always remember that the actor should be treated with respect. A director gives guidance and support. The director is *not* a dictator!

Preparing Your Actors before the Shoot

You've done the table read and, if you're lucky, you have a little time to work with the actors one-on-one before everyone sets foot on the set. Preparing your actors includes rehearsing, but rehearsing is only a small part of the preparation. You need to share tips and tricks with the actors so that they give the best and most believable performances in your film.

As explained earlier in this chapter, the director makes sure that the actors understand the characters' goals, desires, and purposes in each scene. The actors and director need to be on the same page and agree on the meaning of each scene.

Casting is half the game. A director shouldn't have to teach actors to act. A director should guide and give direction only. It's up to the actors to come to the set as professionals and know how to utilize an actor's tools. See Chapter 8 for details about casting the right actors in your film.

To rehearse or not to rehearse, that is the question

Preparing your actors for the shoot involves some form of rehearsal. You can repeat each scene until it feels right. Or you can do exercises and give tips to loosen up the actors. Rehearsing can mean having the actors spend time with each other in order to become more comfortable around one other — especially those who have a friendship or association on screen. It can be *blocking* the actors' movements for the camera (see the section

"Blocking, walking, and talking" later in this chapter) and coming up with the right *business* for each actor in each scene (see the section "Taking care of business" later in this chapter). If you do rehearse with your actors, remember that the purpose of rehearsing is to make the planned look unplanned.

Too much rehearsing can take away a scene's freshness and spontaneity. Steven Spielberg, among many other directors, is not a big fan of rehearsing too much. In one of my films I had a musical number spoofing *The Pirates of Penzance,* and I wanted it to be an uncoordinated dance number. My sister Marlene asked when we were rehearsing, and I told her we weren't! The other problem with over-rehearsing is that if you see a better choice for blocking, dialogue, and so on during filming, it may be hard for the actors to change what they've conditioned themselves to do during rehearsals.

Not every scene needs a rehearsal, just like not every scene needs to be storyboarded (see Chapter 9 for more on storyboarding). Don't beat a scene to death. I like to let the actors give their rendition of the performance — that gives me something to mold and shape from a director's point of view.

Some actors require a lot of rehearsal, and others prefer very little. An actor may need rehearsals even if the director doesn't like to rehearse. Some actors' performances get better the more they rehearse, and some get worse (they become less believable, and their performance becomes flat).

An actor's training and experience can determine how much rehearsal time he requires, if any. By being observant, you can see whether the actor needs time to warm up or if she's up to speed on the first take.

When you rehearse with your actors, let them hold something back from their performance. Have them save a freshness for the camera.

Rehearsing the characters, not just the lines

The actors should think about the characters they're playing, not just the words they say. An actor needs to imagine himself or herself as the character and figure out what the character wears, what the character's opinions are, and how the character reacts in certain situations. An actor can rehearse a character while driving, having lunch, and so on without having to study the script or the character's dialogue.

Direct the actors to inject their personality into the characters — to imagine their blood pumping in the characters' veins. Encourage them to become their characters, to pull their characters off the page and bring them to life!

Actors should study people's quirks and idiosyncrasies and find little unique traits to add humanity and dimension to the characters they play. Frank Abagnale, Leonardo DiCaprio's character in *Catch Me If You Can,* always peels the labels off bottles, telegraphing his nervousness and youthful energy. It also shows Tom Hanks's FBI agent, Hanratty (who knows of Abagnale's label-peeling habit), that Frank is nearby. My friend Donald Petrie, who directed *Miss Congeniality,* was with Sandra Bullock at dinner one night when she laughed and let out a loud snort. Don told her that would be great for her character — and it ended up in the film.

Discovering the characters' backstories

Backstory is the history of a character. It's also referred to as the *ghost.* What haunts the character from childhood? What kind of family did he have? What type of upbringing?

The director should encourage each actor to imagine and develop the ghost of his or her character, but the actor doesn't need to share it with the director as long as the history works for the actor and helps bring dimension to his or her performance. The backstory can become the actor's personal secret, making the fictional character more real to the actor.

Knowing the backstory or ghost helps an actor make dramatic choices for the character during each scene when decisions need to be made. For example, if Jonathan was abused as a child, now as an adult he may flinch every time someone makes a sudden move around him.

Finding what's between the lines: Subtext

Subtext is what's being said between the lines. Rarely does a multidimensional character say things right on the nose (although they do it all the time in bad scripts). Subtext is an element that an actor's character will probably deliver through many passages of dialogue. It's important for the director to make sure that every actor understands the subtext of the scene.

When a character says that she doesn't mind, does she? When Sally says she's really happy that Noah's getting married, is she *really* happy for him? What does her body language tell us as we see her twisting a paperclip into a pretzel as she says, "Everything's fine"?

In *The Big Picture,* Kevin Bacon's character, Nick, is making lunch for his girlfriend, Susan (Emily Longstreth), whom he broke up with earlier in the film. The two are talking about their grilled-cheese sandwiches, but the dialogue and action in the scene are actually revealing the subtext of them starting up their relationship again. Subtext is relayed onscreen through the actors' body language and the dialogue metaphors that their characters choose during the scene.

Exercising and warming up your actors

Much like going to the gym, an actor needs to warm up both physically and mentally before getting into the real workout of filming. Stretching limbers up the body, and doing breathing exercises opens up the mind. Many actors forget to breathe properly before starting their scenes. It's amazing what a few deep breaths can do to calm an actor before performing a scene or getting into character.

Keeping it natural

A great exercise is to have your actors whisper their lines in rehearsal and then perform the scene again using normal volume. Overacting is much harder when you whisper, and it's always easier to bring up a performance than to bring it down. Bruce Willis was very believable in *The Sixth Sense,* and he virtually whispered his whole performance.

Another thing to note is the distance between your actors. If they're in close proximity to each other, they don't need to raise their voices for everyone in the room to hear. I was working with two actors who were speaking too loudly across a table, which made the performance unnatural. So I told them to pretend they were in a busy restaurant and didn't want anyone eavesdropping on their conversation. It worked like a charm. Lowering their voices toned down their overacting.

I discovered an exercise that helps actors play more naturally. If you're not getting a realistic performance from your actors, give each one a yo-yo. Have them recite their lines while trying to do tricks with the yo-yo. It's some kind of left brain, right brain (no brain) exercise that I've found takes the actors' minds off trying too hard.

Improving through improvisation: "I made that up"

An excellent exercise to get actors to think about what a scene is about, and not what's written in the script, is to have them ad-lib or improvise the scene. Doing the scene without the script — just making up what the scene is about — helps the actors feel the emotion and sense of the scene. When you feel that the actors have gained some insight by improvising, have them follow the script again.

Acting is reacting

Many actors are too focused on anticipating their lines and don't listen to the other actors. But acting is like Ping-Pong or tennis: You have to react to the ball coming at you or you miss it every time. Speechless characters can be just as intriguing in films as those who speak. Without dialogue, a character is a sounding board for another character, and someone who communicates through her physical expression, which can be as powerful as expressing herself verbally. Good actors emote without saying a word.

Act and react every waking hour. Acknowledge how everyday things affect your emotions. Which emotions are verbalized and which ones are shown through expression? Which ones are subtle and which ones are over the top?

Speaking with body language

Have your actors study body language. An actor not only speaks with words but with his or her body. Body language can be very powerful. People cross their arms when they're shy or being defensive. They slump when they're feeling down or have no energy. People move differently when they flirt. Turn the TV's sound off and watch for body language. It's a universal language without words. Notice how you can even tell how a dog is feeling by its body language.

Remind your actors that true character is revealed more by what a character's actions are when he or she is alone than when around others. The tough biker enters his apartment, sits down next to his cat on the couch, and pets the animal in a very caring manner — showing a sensitive side to the biker that no one sees when he's in public.

Directing Actors during the Shoot

Directing actors on set involves more than just helping them perform in character. It includes telling them where to move within the frame, giving them proper direction and motivation for the scene, and answering any questions that will help the actor better his or her performance. The actor should trust you and look to you for guidance.

Never yell at your actors. If an actor is doing a scene incorrectly or not to your satisfaction, take him or her aside quietly and discuss the situation in private. Do not correct or critique an actor's performance in front of the rest of the cast and crew. The actor will appreciate the fact that you discuss direction in private. Actors especially are self-conscious. You don't want to embarrass them in front of the rest of the cast and crew or upset them and have to deal with a moody actor who won't come out of his trailer.

Encouraging your actors to ask questions — but not too many

You want your actors to feel that they can ask questions, but you don't want them second-guessing things on the set. If an actor gets too dependent on the director and asks questions before every take, encourage the actor to start trusting his or her performance and answer some of those questions independently. To keep the need for questions to a minimum, be specific in your directions. Ambiguous directions can cost extra takes when an actor misunderstands you.

Remind the actors before shooting a scene where the scene is in the story and what came before it, especially if you're shooting out of order. This will help the actor recall how she felt in the scene before this one and match her emotions to reflect the former scene. If Mary was sullen in the last scene because Gary had to fly out of town, then Mary would still be holding her feelings in the next scene.

Reminding your actors that less is more — more or less

Sometimes it's better for actors to do less in terms of expression and emphasis in their dialogue. They should feel the emotion and let their body language and tone set the mood (but without exaggerating their body movements either — like waving their arms around or using their hands too much when talking). Stage actors have to *project* their performance to a live audience, which involves emphasizing dialogue and increasing volume because the audience is at a distance. However, when an actor projects in front of a camera, the performance can come across as stagy or not believable. A camera can pick up a blink, a tear in the eye, or a simple twitch. So giving less is more in film. Let the projector project, and not the actor.

I once read a newspaper review of a film that said, "Great acting!" To me, that's a contradiction. Great acting should be invisible. Last time I was in an office store, I complained to the store clerk that I couldn't find the invisible tape. Get the idea? If it's invisible, you shouldn't see it.

Being objective about subjective acting

Objective acting is when an actor is aware of his or her performance. The actor is conscious of the audience or camera and aware that he or she is being observed. The actor is not affected by the emotions of the character because he or she is being objective and can feel only sympathy, not empathy, toward the character. This is not the right way to carry a performance.

Subjective acting is when an actor is totally immersed in the feelings and emotions of the character in the scene, and the audience feels like they are voyeurs into the private life of the character the actor is portraying. The actor is acting internally, as if the audience and the camera don't exist. When the actor becomes the character and believes his own performance, so does the audience!

TIP

When it comes time for an actor to let loose for a big scene, make sure that you keep that actor fresh until the big moment. Save an actor's emotional performance for the close-up. If you know that you're going to go into a close-up when the actor wells up with tears, you don't want the actor to give her best performance in the wide shot. You still want to shoot the wide shot, so your editor can cut into the close-up on movement.

Also make sure that your actors flow each mood into the next. They'll need your guidance on this. When happiness turns to anger, the audience needs to see it building up — it can't just come out of nowhere. It's like a teapot coming to the point of boiling: It happens gradually until finally the steam shoots out under the pressure. When a singer carries a note higher and higher, it's a gradual ascension. A character would only "snap" from one mood to another if he were a crazy person.

Feeling the words, not just memorizing

What did you have for lunch three days ago? I can guarantee that you had to think about that. It took some *pre-thought*. Did you look down or away to catch your thoughts? As a director, remind your actors to use pre-thought when recalling things. Too many actors seem to roll off numbers and recall incidents without any pre-thought because they've memorized the script so well. They don't show that they're thinking — only acting.

Along those same lines, many actors enter a scene and put too much into a simple "hello." Direct your actors to have a more matter-of-fact delivery. Don't enter the scene saying "hello" like you've rehearsed it 100 times, and it's the most important thing in the world.

Also make your actors aware if they're enunciating each word too perfectly. Precise enunciation is reserved for narration, professional speeches, and presentations. Let the actors run their words together. Many actors tend to put too much space between words to make sure that they're being clear, but it doesn't sound natural or believable in films.

Blocking, walking, and talking

Blocking is how the actors move on set and how the camera covers that movement. The blocking for a scene is sometimes done in rehearsal, but often it's done on the set just before filming (see Chapter 14).

Establishing blocking is like breaking down a scene into separate blocks. An actor moves first from the window to the table, then from the table to a chair, and then from the chair to the door. Movement keeps a scene from becoming too static and makes the actors' performances seem more real. In real life, people rarely stand or sit in one place too long. The best time to decide on blocking is when you have the actors together for rehearsal, or on the set as the camera and lights are being set. Have the actors do their lines and see what motivates their movement. Often blocking comes automatically. It feels right for the actor to stand up at this point, or sit down, or move toward the window during a specific piece of dialogue.

Cheating is when an actor needs to turn slightly to one side for a better shot, or two actors need to move closer together to make a shot work. You cheat the lamp into the shot behind the actor's close-up so that it frames better in the picture.

Taking care of business

In addition to blocking, an actor's performance is made more real when he or she is preoccupied with moving and doing *business*. Business is what actors do with their hands, or the action that occupies them while they're performing a scene, such as drinking, fiddling with keys, doing the dishes, or tidying up. A director usually gives each actor an idea for his or her business, but sometimes the actor has a good suggestion as well.

Business takes away from an actor's self-consciousness. It gives the actor something to do with his or her hands. Some actors use their hands too much, waving them all over the place. By holding a book, a pen, or a drink, the actor doesn't have to worry about what to do with her hands. It's a diversion, like the yo-yo exercise mentioned earlier in this chapter.

Robotic performance

Without an on-screen personality, an actor comes across as a robot, programmed to recite words without feeling or expression. Encourage your actors to bring their uniqueness to the role, to plug their own DNA into the character they're playing. Look at successful and unique actors like Arnold Schwarzenegger, Steve Martin, Sandra Bullock, and Sylvester Stallone. All could have followed earlier advice to get rid of the accent, the white hair, the attitude, and so on, but they retained their own looks and personalities with great success.

Matching actors' actions

Make sure that your actors repeat the same blocking and business when filming from different angles. In postproduction, the editor needs to cut the two angles together, and as long as the actor does the same thing in both shots, the editor can have a choice of where to cut. If an actor is talking and raises a coffee cup to his lips, it has to match other camera shots taken from another angle. The actor has to raise the cup at the exact same line of dialogue, or the two shots won't cut together properly (and this will really frustrate the editor, who may not be able to cut the two shots together smoothly). The script supervisor helps the actors remember what their actions were in each shot so they match when the scene is shot from a different angle. (You can find more on the script supervisor's assistance to the actors and director in Chapter 14.)

Continuity mistakes can make a film look really unprofessional — even though the pros make them all the time. Continuity means that things need to remain consistent from one angle to another, or the audience will get confused. A sandwich has to have the same bites taken out of it when covered from a different angle. An unwrapped present shouldn't still be wrapped in a different angle. If an actor exits one room wearing a blue shirt, he should enter the next room wearing the same blue shirt.

Commending the actors

Giving your actors feedback after you shoot each scene is very important. An actor is always looking for a response — attention is one of the reasons people become actors. Actors often feel isolated and hurt if they don't receive acknowledgment.

Gorilla training

Sometimes an actor has to wear heavy prosthetic makeup (like a mask) or a complete body costume, like a monster or gorilla suit. Body language can have a big impact on a performance, especially when makeup limits facial expressions.

I did a cameo in the film *Naked Gun 2½* playing a gorilla when Leslie Nielsen comes crashing out of the zoo entrance in a tank followed by runaway elephants, giraffes, and two gorillas. (The gorillas had to be actors in suits because using the real animals wasn't safe.) For a week, I studied the mannerisms and body language of a gorilla — I was in "gorilla" training!

In a full body suit, an actor has to project his emotions to reflect how the character is feeling. Robin Williams had to perform as a robot in *Bicentennial Man,* and Jim Carrey gave an animated performance under the furry makeup of *The Grinch.* Sometimes an actor's mannerisms and body language are transferred to a computer-generated character, as was done with Gollum in *Lord of the Rings: The Two Towers.* Andy Serkis, acting as Gollum via computer motion-capture, received a lot of praise for his performance and was even nominated for awards.

If an actor doesn't receive any feedback from you, even a simple, "That was great," she'll feel that her performance didn't live up to your expectations. If you believe that your actors can do a better take, tell them, "That was good, but I know you can do better." Treat the actors delicately, and you'll get great performances from them.

A professional and thoughtful director compliments the actors' work and encourages them to give the best performances possible, but rarely will an actor return the compliment. The filmmaker usually gets his praise at the film's premiere.

Chapter 14

A Sense of Direction: Shooting Your Film

A director is an *auteur* — the true author of a film. He or she is not unlike a god, a creator, a leader who takes all the credit — or all the blame! If you as a filmmaker take on the task of the director, shaping and molding all the elements into a film, your passion for the story should be undeniable; you'll be involved with it for quite some time. A director lives film in the daytime and dreams film in the nighttime.

This chapter breaks down the mystery behind what a director does to produce a film. You see what makes a great director and how to translate a script to the screen. You discover the cinematic language of directors, from making decisions on the set to subtext, symbolism, and pacing.

You also find out when to move the camera (after all, it's a *motion* picture) and why, as well as what special equipment, including tripods, dollies, and cranes, helps you get the desired shot. Directing a film is a laborious task, so be prepared to run an exhausting, but exciting, marathon.

Focusing on Directing

The director of a film must work closely with the actors in a creative capacity, pulling the best performances from them (see Chapter 13, which talks about directing actors). The director also needs to have some knowledge of the camera and lenses, and how to use them to set a mood in a scene. Having the final say on the locations, casting, script, and often editing of the final picture makes the director the keeper of the film and stamps it with his or her personal signature.

I'm co-directing the film *They Cage the Animals at Night* with pop icon Michael Jackson. (I adapted the screenplay from Jennings Michael Burch's book of the same name.) This is Michael's feature-film directorial debut, but he's no stranger to film, with his music videos (which he likes to call short films) being the most successful mini-movies known worldwide. Michael wanted to share his thoughts in this book on the power of a director: "The painter paints, the sculptor sculpts, the songwriter sings — but the director, he makes monuments. It's the most expressive of all the arts. On film, you're affecting people's emotions, their hearts — they're living with you — you've got them! You've got them in the palm of your hand! That's the power of film-making."

Recognizing the characteristics of a great director

A director is a father, mother, psychologist, mentor, and ship's captain. To succeed in this role, you must be good at giving directions in an authoritative manner — without being a dictator. A great director:

✔ Is respectful and patient

✔ Has a sense of humor

✔ Is a perfectionist (but not a procrastinator)

✔ Is willing to take chances

✔ Is well read (a sponge for knowledge)

✔ Has an eye for detail

✔ Is understanding (both empathetic and sympathetic)

✔ Is sensitive and thoughtful

✔ Is mentally strong

✔ Is a decision-maker and a problem-solver

✔ Has a good eye for visualizing shots and framing

✔ Is trustworthy

As your film's director, you need to show confidence. You are the leader, and the cast (and crew) will look up to you.

Training yourself as a director

A director, no matter how experienced or successful, is also a student of film. You are continuously learning and studying — experiencing life and bringing those experiences to your work. To become a better director:

✔ **Read books.** Read voraciously, and on every topic; you never know what may come in handy.

✔ **Study films and cinematography.** See how others tell their stories cinematically, and figure out at least the basics of lenses and shot composition.

✔ **Watch people.** See how their moods affect their body language and how they react to strangers and to friends.

✔ **Experience life.** Take in the world around you. The more experiences you have, the more original ideas you can bring to your films.

✔ **Ask questions.** It's the only way to get the answers.

✔ **Observe acting classes.** See how acting coaches teach.

✔ **Take classes.** Force yourself to study subjects you normally would have no interest in. When you take active interest in a topic, you'll be surprised at the curiosity it generates in you.

✔ **Travel.** See the world and the lifestyles of other countries.

✔ **Study paintings.** Look for inspiration in terms of composition and lighting.

Seeing what other directors do can trigger new and original ideas, especially if you study films in your genre (see Chapter 2 on film genres). That's why you should watch films — not to copy, but to be inspired. Here are a couple tips to use when watching films and TV shows:

✔ **Read the script in closed caption.** One of my favorite things to do when I have time to watch TV or rent a movie is to view the closed-captioning. Doing so enables me to read the script on the bottom of the screen as the story unfolds. You can study performances (as well as camera moves) and see how the script is structured — literally.

✔ **Watch a silent film.** I like to turn the sound off once in a while when watching films (no one wants to watch films with me for some reason). Films are all about motion. If a film is done right, you can tell what the story is about by the visuals. If you watch *The Green Mile, E.T.,* or *The Sixth Sense* with the sound off, for example, you get a sense of what the characters are going through, the emotions, and so on. If you watch a soap opera on TV and turn the sound off, though, all you get are talking heads — and no idea what's going on.

Directing traits

Certain traits make up a successful director. Some people are born with these traits, others acquire them through observing and studying, and learning to be more aware of everything around them. The following list of traits will help you be a better director:

✔ **Being a problem-solver:** A big part of a director's job is problem-solving — and doing it on the spot. You need to make decisions quickly and wisely, because not making a decision is a decision. Take a deep breath, make a decision, and move on.

✔ **Setting the tone:** Setting the tone on set with the cast and crew is up to the director. A friendly family atmosphere creates camaraderie among the cast and crew that is reflected in the final production. Actors often subliminally mirror their director. If the director is frantic, uptight, and nervous, the actors' performances are affected. If the director is confident, organized, and decisive, the actors feel a sense of security. And if the director earns an actor's trust, the actor is more willing to try different things.

✔ **Having an eye for detail:** A good director has an eye for detail and can visualize the screenplay as a moving picture even before setting foot on the set. Help the actor find little nuances, subtle expressions to make his or her performance unique. When deciding on props and set design, look for details that add character and dimension to be used in your scenes.

✔ **Timing and pacing things right:** With the help of the script supervisor (see Chapter 7), the director makes sure that the shots and scenes are filmed at a proper pace. The script supervisor carries a stopwatch and accurately times each shot to get a better sense of how long the scene will run on screen.

The world tends to slow down on screen — probably because the audience's attention is concentrated solely on the screen and the camera doesn't blink. The director's job is to pace the film by controlling the pacing of the actors' performances and the number of shots in each scene. The more shots in a scene, the faster the pace feels and the less it seems to lag.

Translating Script to Screen

A screenplay is the blueprint of what ultimately becomes a motion picture. The director's task is to translate this blueprint to the screen — to "build" the film. Each scene can be interpreted in many different ways, and if the director is not the screenwriter, he or she must understand what the writer is trying to say. The director also needs to fix any holes in the story, know how to translate words into visuals, and add or delete scenes to make the story stronger.

As a director, you have to be passionate about the material — dissect it, understand it completely.

Understanding the screenplay

As a director, you need to understand exactly what the story is about, why the characters are doing and feeling what they do and feel, and what the motivation and goals of each character are. A director looks at each scene and asks, "What's the purpose of this scene? What's the underlining reason — to impress the girl, to prepare for the big race?" Just as the actor asks the question, "How does this scene relate to my character?" the director asks a broader question, "How does this scene relate to the story as a whole?" Sometimes the director finds that the scene doesn't add anything to the story and ends up cutting it. Other times, the scene may need to be enhanced, or another scene or two may need to be added before or after this particular scene to strengthen it and the story.

By asking questions, the director is forced to seek the answers. This adds more dimension to the story and characters. It helps the director make choices in his or her direction and step back to see the whole picture.

A scene's underlying purpose is often revealed by subtext. *Subtext* is the meaning behind the words — it's reading between the lines. You need to understand not only what the characters are saying, but also what the subtext reveals. What does the scene really mean? How do the characters really feel? Subtext can mean the opposite of what a character says verbally. A character may say, "I hate you!" when his actions reveal the opposite emotion. Instead of Karen saying she misses her daughter, it's much more effective to use a visual of her picking up her child's favorite doll and looking at it sadly.

Symbolism is a type of cinema metaphor. Visuals are often used in symbolism and can be very powerful. In the screenplay that I adapted for *They Cage the Animals at Night* from the novel by Jennings Michael Burch, I used the symbolism of little Jennings being locked in his room with the same key that was used to lock the stuffed animals in the cabinet at night — symbolizing that Jennings is just like a caged animal. I also used symbolism in the setting of the orphanage, which resembles a prison with barbed wire around it. Without ever stating the fact in words, the orphanage's setting symbolizes the imprisonment of the orphans.

Rewriting or adjusting the script

If the director isn't the screenwriter, he or she often embellishes the story and adds his or her own creative vision and style to the script. Enhancements to the script include adding or deleting scenes to support other scenes in the story, along with filling any holes in the story. In addition to strengthening the script in terms of better character development (Jimmy finally realizes he can do it on his own at the end) or story repairs (Sarah shouldn't run into Mark at the train station because it's too contrived to the story), you may also need to do some adjusting because of budget limitations.

As you're prepping the film, you may find that consolidating several locations into one makes the production more economical. You also may find that you can cut down some of the secondary characters that aren't crucial to the story, and save from having to paying additional actors.

Visualizing your screenplay

After you've done your directorial homework of understanding the emotional and psychological aspects of the screenplay, you now must turn the words on paper into visual shots. As you read your screenplay with your visual mind open, certain portions will jump out at you, calling for a specific shot or a certain angle to express what's going on in that particular scene. Sometimes it's a simple *close-up* or *two-shot* (see later in this chapter) or it's a dramatic image that calls out, like the powerful end shot in the original *Planet of the Apes* (1968) when the camera pulls back to reveal the Statue of Liberty half-submerged in the sand by the ocean's shore.

Translating the script into visuals is something that the director does alone, unlike the table read, which involves the entire cast (see Chapter 13 on actors). To get the creative juices flowing and to better understand the characters and story, isolate yourself from civilization and escape into the world of the screenplay.

Take a pencil and a ruler and partition the individual scenes in the script. Draw a solid line across the page at the beginning of each scene. Separating your film into separate blocks makes tackling the scenes one at a time easier.

Mapping Out Your Plans for the Camera

Part of a director's homework includes making notes, sketches, or diagrams of how he or she envisions the shots in each scene. You can use various techniques to plan shots, including storyboards, written shot lists, schematics, notations on the script, and models.

Designing storyboards

Some directors start directing even before stepping onto the set by creating a comic-book version of the film utilizing *storyboards.* Storyboards are visual frames that outline the composition of each shot. Some directors prefer to design shots with storyboards, but they require a lot of time and an artist's hand (although you can draw stick figures). Other directors prefer to save storyboarding for special-effect shots and action scenes only (see Chapter 9 for more on storyboarding).

Creating a shot list

A shot list, sometimes referred to as a *dance card,* consists of written directions that describe the details of each shot. Usually, it is scribbled on index cards for convenience. Sometimes the director prepares the shot list well in advance, and sometimes it's done right before the next day's shoot. A shot list contains the scene and shot number, which the director checks off as shots are completed. Here's an example of a shot list for Scene 45 from my film *Undercover Angel* (more on types of shots in the section "Taking Your Best Shot" later in this chapter):

Harrison looks up from typewriter — **camera dollies** in for a **close-up**.

Jenny gets up and goes to the door — **camera follows** her and stops.

Harrison gets up — **camera leads** him to *Jenny* at the door.

Two shot — **over the shoulder** of *Harrison* talking to *Jenny*.

As the director, you may want to do both a shot list and storyboard your scenes to illustrate the actual framing and position of the action.

Sketching schematics

Schematics show a basic floor plan with an overhead view of where the camera and actors will be placed for each shot within a scene. I use dotted lines with directional arrows showing actors' movement. If you have several camera angles, number each camera shot in the schematics to show exactly where the camera will be placed.

You can draw schematics on separate pieces of paper and numbered to each shot and scene or you can sketch them on the page opposite the scene in the screenplay. In Figure 14-1, the director's schematic shows the actor's position and direction of movement with the camera placement and movement as well. If you prefer to use a software program, Smartdraw ($69) provides various floor-plan layouts and hundreds of images, including a camera icon that you can use to design your shots from an aerial point of view. For a free 30-day trial, go to www.smartdraw.com/downloads/download/asp.

When planning your schematics, you can use different-sized coins (pennies, dimes, and nickels) to represent different actors and move them around on your floor plan. After you decide on the actors' movement within the scene, circle the coins in place and then choose the best camera placement to cover the action (but then put those coins into your budget — you're going to need every penny!).

Making notes on the script

You can circle, box, underline, and highlight certain words in the script to show different instructions, such as when to use a close-up, dolly-in, or tracking shot. (See "Taking Your Best Shot," later in this chapter, for information about the different types of shots directors use.)

Planning with models (not the high-fashion kind)

To get a three-dimensional idea for your shots, you can place dolls or miniature plastic soldiers on a tabletop to find the best camera angles. Doing so helps you visualize where to position the actors to get the best coverage. Just be prepared to explain why you're playing with dolls when someone walks into the room unexpectedly.

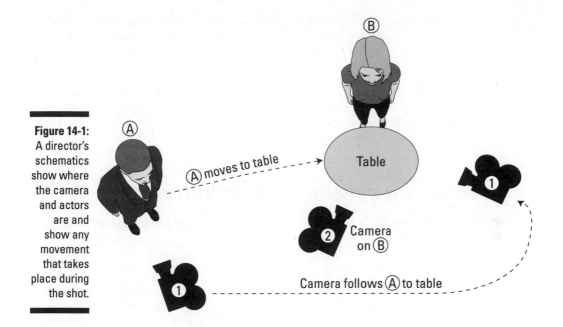

Figure 14-1:
A director's schematics show where the camera and actors are and show any movement that takes place during the shot.

Continuing Continuity with Your Script Supervising

Directing a film is like piecing a jigsaw puzzle together. It's up to the director and the script supervisor to make sense of it all (see Chapter 7 for information about hiring your crew). The *script supervisor* works alongside the director, keeping track of *continuity* (the logical order of things or actions, wardrobe or characters that need to be consistent from shot to shot or scene to scene*)* and following the script to make sure that the director doesn't miss a scene or a planned shot. Forgetting a scene is very easy, because a script is usually shot out of sequence. Without a script supervisor to mark the script and follow what has been shot, it's not uncommon for a scene or two to be forgotten. Even the lowest budgeted film should have a script supervisor. The director has enough things to worry about, and forgetting whether the actor exited right or left in the last shot is very easy to do — but it's the script supervisor's job to remember those types of details and more. The script supervisor can be the director's best friend.

Got a match?

The director sometimes has an actor repeat his actions so they match when the same action is filmed from a different camera angle or with a different shot size. This is called *matching*. It's important for the actor to match his actions exactly so that the two shots can be cut together seamlessly, ensuring continuity. An effective way to cut shots together is during movement on camera; if an actor lifts a coffee cup to his lips in a wide shot, the filmmaker (or your editor) may choose to cut to a close-up of the cup coming up to the actor's lips. But the action must be repeated exactly in the wide shot and again in the close-up for it to match in the editing room. The script supervisor takes note of the actor's *business* (see Chapter 13) and reminds the actor to repeat the same action at the new angle.

Inserting coverage and cutaways

As the director, you should be versed in the power of coverage, cutaways, and inserts — and know the difference.

Coverage

Coverage is catching the same action from different angles so that the continuity of the shots is logical. It can be done with several cameras or, as is often done on low-budget productions, by placing the camera in different positions and repeating the action.

When covering the action, the director needs to set a shooting ratio (how much film to usable footage). An average shooting ratio on a low-budget film is 3:1 — three takes to get one good one. Setting a shooting ratio is important, because this will let you pace how much film you will need to purchase (and what to budget for). A production that is budgeted for 3 takes per shot will need to have approximately 270 minutes of film to end up with roughly a 90-minute finished film (3 takes × 90 minutes = 270 minutes of raw film needed).

If you're shooting on video, you have more leeway because tape is cheap — and you can even play back the shot right away to see if it worked to your satisfaction and then decide if you want to try another take.

Cutaway

A *cutaway* is a shot of something the actor looks at, or something that is not part of the main shot — such as a clock on the wall or another actor reacting to what's going on in the scene. You can use a cutaway to save a shot that doesn't work in one take and to hide what would otherwise end up being a *jump-cut* (the action appears to be missing frames and jumps). You can use part of Take 1 before the cutaway and the end of Take 2 after the cutaway. Cutaways are often used in interview situations: the guest speaks, and then there's a cutaway to the interviewer nodding (this allows tighter editing of the guest's answers).

Use a cutaway after a gag to show a reaction. It helps to emphasize a funny moment for the audience, allowing them to share their reaction with an on-screen character. Showing a reaction also lets the audience know how to react to something if it can be interpreted in several ways. An effective use of a cutaway is the Wicked Witch in the *Wizard of Oz* watching Dorothy and her friends through a crystal ball. You can also use a cutaway to condense time — he walks toward the exit, cut to a cutaway of him being watched by the cat from the stairs, and then cut back to the actor now on the street and getting into his car.

Insert

An *insert* is similar to a cutaway, except that it's usually part of the same location where the dialogue or action is taking place, but often shot separately from the main shoot or after the actors have left the set. An insert is usually a close-up of a watch, a letter (like the one Harry Potter received notifying him he was accepted at the Hogwarts School of Witchcraft and Wizardry), or someone holding an object, like the remote control for the time-machine Dolorean that Doc operated in *Back to the Future*.

Screen direction: Your other left

Screen direction is an important element to be aware of. If a car is driving right to left in one shot, the car should continue to travel in the same direction to its destination. If the camera crosses the *line of action* to the opposite side of the car and shoots it going left to right, it will appear to be going in the opposite direction, as if it were heading back to where it started from. Paying attention to the line of action, also known as the *action axis* or *180-degree rule*, helps keep the direction of your actors and movement consistent so as not to confuse the audience.

When one actor speaks to her left, you expect the actor to whom she's speaking to look to his right. You create an imaginary line and keep all your elements on one side of the line or the other — but you have to remain consistent, otherwise you'll be *crossing the line* and the on-screen direction will be flipped. If you film both actors as though they're looking to their left, it will appear as though they're looking at something to their left, and not at each other. The camera should not cross the line of action. Many amateur filmmakers often make the mistake of *crossing the line*. See Figure 14-2 for an example.

You can cross the line of action while the camera is in motion (where the change of direction is seen on-screen) because then the audience sees that the camera has stepped over the line, and you don't have an abrupt cut that can be disorienting.

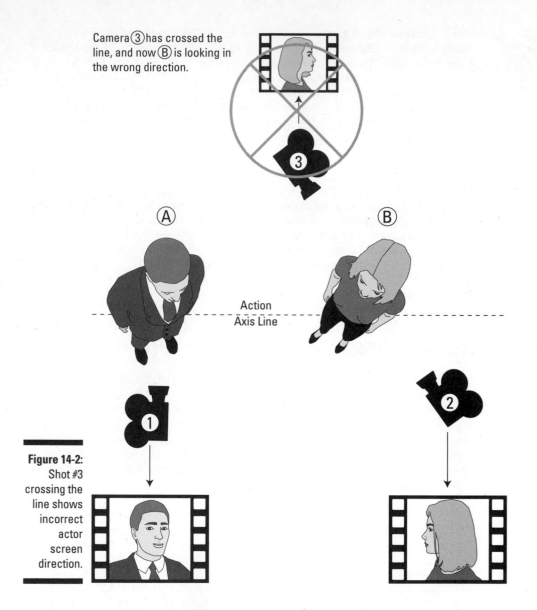

Camera ③ has crossed the line, and now Ⓑ is looking in the wrong direction.

Ⓐ

Ⓑ

Action
Axis Line

Figure 14-2:
Shot #3
crossing the
line shows
incorrect
actor
screen
direction.

Taking Your Best Shot

The camera never blinks. That's what cuts (changing from one shot to another shot) are for. But to cut from one shot to another, you have to vary your shots by size and angle so that you don't end up with a *jump-cut*, which would appear as if the shot were missing some frames (see Chapter 15 for more on film editing). Shot compositions, sizes, and angles enhance how you tell your story. You may want a close-up when two actors are talking if the conversation is an intimate one. A wide establishing shot may be appropriate if you want to show that the actors are surrounded by a barren wasteland.

As a director, knowing at least the basics of the camera and lenses is advantageous. You should hire someone who is skilled in shooting video and/or film if you want your production to look professional. The cinematographer's job is to be educated about lenses, exposures, and how the camera functions (see Chapter 10), but you'll be better able to convey your story visually if you have a sense of what the camera can do.

Each cinematographer and director has a slightly different definition of framing and shot sizes, but the definitions are similar enough to warrant the following list of traditional shots, explained in the following sections:

✔ Wide shot (which can also work as an establishing shot)

✔ Medium shot

✔ Two shot

✔ Close-up

Where the heck are we?: Establishing a wide shot

A *wide shot* (WS) reveals where the scene is taking place. Also referred to as a *long shot* or *master shot,* a wide shot helps orient the audience. A wide shot also gives the actors room to move within a shot, without the camera having to follow them. Medium shots and close-ups (explained later in this chapter) are often cut into a wide shot for variation.

An *establishing shot* is a type of wide shot that can establish a building before the camera cuts to an interior office. Figure 14-3 shows a wide shot from my film *Undercover Angel* in TV format (close to the dimensions of a square) and a wide shot from my film *The Random Factor* in the wider theatrical format that is an oblong rectangular frame size.

You don't have to be a psychic to get a medium shot

A *medium shot* (MS) is a standard shot that usually shows a character from belly button to slightly above the actor's head. A medium shot is more intimate than a wide shot, but provides more breathing space for the actor than a close-up. It's also used when you have an actor holding something in the frame or elaborating with his hands. Figure 14-4 shows a medium shot from my film *Undercover Angel*.

Figure 14-3:
A wide shot in TV format size (left) and an establishing shot in theatrical format frame size (right).

Photo of Dean Winters and Emily Mae Young in Undercover Angel, courtesy of Sunland Studios/Stellar Entertainment
Photo of Andrew Divoff and William Richert in The Random Factor, courtesy of Showbuzz and Gloria Everett

Figure 14-4:
A medium shot.

Photo of Dean Winters in Undercover Angel, courtesy of Sunland Studios/Stellar Entertainment (UA photos by Bill Grimshaw)

Two shot: Three's a crowd

A *two shot* can either be a form of a medium shot that has two actors standing or sitting next to each other or an over-the-shoulder shot where one actor's back or profile is closer to the camera than the other actor facing the camera. A two shot can save time and money when you have a dialogue scene between two actors by having them both in the frame as they carry on their conversation. The audience diverts their attention to each actor as they speak, instead of having the camera cut to individual shots of each actor speaking. This is also effective when two characters are walking and talking side by side in a two shot. Figure 14-5 shows a two shot from *Undercover Angel*.

I'm ready for my close-up

A *close-up shot* (CU), or *single,* is usually from above a person's chest or the nape of her neck to just slightly above the top of her head. If you get in closer, so that the actor's head fills most of the frame, you have a *tight close-up.* Going in even tighter, to a person's eyes or mouth, gives you an *extreme close-up.* Close-ups create a sense of intimacy and the feeling that you're involved in the scene. They also reveal emotion in the eyes or the hint of a smile. Figure 14-6 shows both a close-up and a tight close-up.

Figure 14-5: A two shot.

Photo of Dean Winters and Yasmine Bleeth in *Undercover Angel,* courtesy of Sunland Studios/Stellar Entertainment

The director often chooses a close-up to emphasize the intensity of a scene. Emotional or sensitive dialogue is often shot in a tight close-up to emphasize the importance of what's being said.

Figure 14-6:
A loose close-up (left) and a tighter close-up (right). Notice the breathing room to the left of the actors.

James Earl Jones in Undercover Angel, courtesy of Sunland Studios/Stellar Entertainment (photo by Bill Grimshaw)
Crystal Owens in Turn of the Blade, courtesy of Northstar Entertainment

When framing an actor in a close-up, give him some *breathing room.* Breathing room puts more space in front of the actor's face in the direction he's looking or talking than behind him. If you don't allow this space, the shot will have a claustrophobic feel to it. Also, never center a head in the middle of the frame unless it's a news reporter talking into the camera. Centering someone in the middle of the frame creates an awkward composition and creates an off-balance feeling to the shot.

Teeter-tottering angles: Are you high or low?

A *high angle* is usually shot using a crane, standing on a hill, or looking out a window of a high-rise to get an angle looking down. When you shoot from a high angle, your subjects look smaller and therefore insignificant.

In contrast, you shoot a *low angle* from below your subject's height — as low as the ground (or lower if you dig yourself a hole). Low angles tend to make subjects look bigger and more powerful. A character appears intimidating if you use a low-angle shot. Figure 14-7 shows an example of each type.

Here's an inexpensive way to get a low-angle shot from the ground: Get one of those beanbag pillows and lay your camera on it. Shape the pillow to cradle your camera safely and align it so that the shot isn't crooked (unless you want it to be).

Figure 14-7: High-angle shots make subjects look smaller and less significant (left). Low-angle shots make subjects look more imposing (right).

I'm high on you: The God shot

In a *God shot,* the camera looks straight down on a scene, symbolizing God's point of view looking down on his creation — also showing the audience the big picture. This can be an interior shot or a very effective exterior shot from the sky. It is often used in films to remind us that a central character is human and sometimes insignificant. The God shot was used effectively in *The Truman Show* to symbolize the God complex of Christof who created and directed the ultimate reality show documenting the real life of Burbank Truman and televising his personal life unfolding in front of the entire world.

To accomplish a God shot, you'll need a camera crane, or a cheaper way to go is to shoot looking down from a tall structure.

Finding the director's viewfinder

Kish Optics makes the Filmmaker's Finder, a precision mini-viewer that enables you to see the world through the eyes of a lens — and it's available in designer colors. The Filmmaker's Finder has built-in interchangeable aspect ratios that you can resize with a simple twist (for framing TV or theatrical-screen shots). The finder allows you to "see" through different size lenses that a film camera uses without having to carry a camera around with you. These mini-finders are light enough to hang around your neck or keep in your pocket or handbag. Kish also has a finder that corresponds to camcorder lens sizes — the first of its kind. Check out www.kishoptics.com for other types of finders, including the Ultimate Director's Finder, the Personal Director's Finder, and the Mini Director's Finder.

Picture This: Deciding When to Move the Camera and Why

Fred Astaire said that if he didn't dance in a scene, the camera should. Keeping motion in a shot is like choreography for the camera. If you stand still too long and your camera remains static, your audience gets restless. It's as if you're having a stare-down with the image because the camera never blinks. A moving camera, however, brings energy to the scene. So, when you have a good reason to move the camera, let it dance! It's appropriate to move the camera when

- ✔ Following a character
- ✔ Revealing something
- ✔ Emphasizing a character's reaction
- ✔ Underlining a dramatic effect
- ✔ Creating a sense of chaos or excitement

An actor's actions should motivate the camera. Start to move the camera at the same time the actor moves to create seamless camera motion.

Playing with dollies

A camera that needs to be moved is placed on a *dolly* so that the motion is fluid and doesn't bump around. You can rent a professional dolly with a hydraulic stand that acts as a motion tripod, or you can make your own by fitting a flat board with rugged wheels. Put a tripod on the board, and you have yourself a dolly. I use a Bogen Manfrotto tripod (www.bogenphoto.com), which I secure to the dolly. It's a lightweight but sturdy tripod that has a great fluid head for effortless panning and tilting of the camera.

If you're working on an uneven surface, you need to lay down *dolly tracks*. You can rent them with the dolly, or you can put down boards or mats on the ground to create a smooth surface for the dolly wheels to roll over. ProMax Systems (www.promax.com) makes a lightweight tracking dolly with super-smooth dolling motion. The package comes with 15 feet of track that breaks down into 5-foot sections for travel or storage. It's priced at $399.

If you can't afford a dolly, borrow a wheelchair. Sit in the wheelchair with the camera (get one of those beanbag pillows to rest the camera on to absorb the shock) and have someone push you for a smooth dolly shot.

I once needed a shot that moved in over a conference table during a scene of the boss talking to his board members. I wanted the camera to move toward the boss at the head of the table. We put the camera on an inexpensive skateboard and slowly moved it over the surface of the table toward the actor. It was one of the smoothest shots in the film!

Craning to get a high shot

A camera *crane* allows you to raise or lower ("boom") the camera while filming to get a more dramatic shot. ProMax Systems makes a series of cranes that includes the *CobraCrane,* a 5-foot crane (it can reach up to 9 feet in the air, depending on the height of your tripod). The CobraCrane uses a cable-and-pulley system with roller bearings, allowing you to tilt the camera for extremely smooth angles in all directions. Check out the CobraCrane, which starts at $199, at www.promax.com.

When using a crane, you need to run a video cable from the camera to a TV monitor when shooting video, or to a *video assist* unit when using a film camera so that you can see to manipulate the shot properly. (Jerry Lewis invented video assist — see Chapter 10 for more information.) I use a portable LCD mini flat screen from TV One to watch and play back the crane footage (you can find it at www.tvone.com). You also need a set of free weights (from a sporting goods store) to counterbalance the crane to keep your camera in the air, kind of like a teeter-totter.

Steadying the camera

A camera steady device attaches to your body (or the cinematographer's) with a harness and turns the camera into a fluid floating machine. Think of it as a shock absorber for the camera. The brand commonly used in Hollywood is called a *Steadicam,* made by the Tiffen Company (www.tiffen.com). Instead of laying down dolly tracks, the camera operator just walks with the camera "floating" in the Steadicam harness. A Steadicam is great for walking and talking shots with your actors. Tiffen also makes a Steady Stick (compact version $179.95, professional version $249.95) for cameras weighing less than 30 pounds.

ProMax puts out the impressive Steadytracker that works for video camcorders. It balances the camera, giving it weightlessness and the appearance that it's effortlessly gliding through your shots. You can purchase a Steadytracker starting at $199 at www.promax.com.

Part IV
Finishing Your Film in Post

The 5th Wave   By Rich Tennant

THE NEW HOLLYWOOD

CUT! PASTE!

In this part . . .

Welcome to the world of postproduction. Editing a film has become easier and less expensive over the last few years as filmmaking has entered the digital computer age — this is a marriage that will last forever. You discover in this part that you can edit your film like the big studios do — right on your desktop computer.

Postproduction audio, like sound effects and musical compositions, is an important element for making your film sizzle with great sound. Special visual effects have been greatly influenced by the computer age, but with some ingenuity, you can still create some incredible effects with the camera without exploding your budget. In this part, I also discuss the title of your film and the proper credit recognition for all the cast, crew, and contacts who help bring your film to fruition.

Chapter 15

Cut to: Editing Your Film Frame by Frame

. . . .

In This Chapter

▶ Working in a linear or non-linear environment

▶ Editing your film on a computer or a turnkey system

▶ Cutting creatively

▶ Burning your finished film into the digital domain

. . . .

After you've shot your film, you're ready to *cut* (edit) it together. You can edit your film on your computer and do it affordably. In this chapter, I introduce you to the various software programs that enable you to cut your film without leaving your desk.

In this chapter, you also see how the worlds of linear and non-linear editing work and discover the secrets to cutting your picture for the optimum effect — by controlling the story, changing the sequence of events, and playing with time. Sound editing is also important when cutting together dialogue, sound effects, and music; so you see (and hear) all about that, too. I also introduce you to the duties of your film laboratory and show you how to *develop* a great relationship.

Cutting Your Film: Putting One Frame in Front of the Other

Editing is more than just piecing together shots into scenes. Understanding the story and the best way to tell it is an art. Great editing controls the feel of your film and can often make or break the illusion. It means knowing on what frame to start your scene and on what frame to end it, knowing when to cut to the *reaction shot* (a visual response from another actor in the scene) and when to stay on the main character.

You need to decide whether you're going to edit the film yourself or get a fresh pair of eyes to do it for you. Many directors avoid editing their films because they're too close to the material and want to bring another perspective to the story. That's why, on a big studio film, a picture editor starts assembling your shots and scenes together as you're shooting, and a sound editor edits the dialogue and other sound elements. You can place an ad seeking an editor in the classified section of many film and trade magazines like *Backstage West* (`www.backstagewest.com`) or search online at `www.crewnet.com` for an editor near you! Look for someone who has at least a few films under his belt and ask to see a sample of his work — does he cut scenes tight so they don't lag? But if you're on a small production, you're probably your own editor. You're in good company, though. Robert Rodriguez *(Spy Kids I* and *Spy Kids II)* prefers to cut his own films. For more on hiring an editor for your team, check out Chapter 7.

One of the advantages of hiring an editor is that he or she can start assembling what you've shot immediately after the first day on the set. This means that your editor can tell you while you're filming whether you need extra footage: a *cutaway* (a reaction shot or something that helps piece two other shots together seamlessly) to make a scene work better, a close-up of some person or object, or an *establishing shot* (a wide shot of the location that orientates the audience to where the scene is taking place).

Cutting creatively

Some of the elements you need to consider when editing are

- **Pacing:** The length of shots and scenes gives the entire film a pace — a feeling of moving fast or slow. You don't want the film to lag.

- **Scene length:** Keep scenes under three minutes, if possible, so that scenes don't drag on and seem monotonous.

- **Order of shots and scenes:** See the "Ordering your shots to go" sidebar later in this chapter.

- **Clean entrances and exits:** Show actors entering and leaving the shot.

- **Cutting on action:** Most shots cut (or edit) better on action. If your actor is picking up a coffee cup, have him or her repeat the action while you film it from different angles or shot sizes (such as a close-up or a wide shot). You then can overlap the shots as you cut on the motion. This is also called *matching,* and it helps hide the cut, making the transition appear seamless.

- **Matching shots:** You want to join static shots with static shots, and moving shots next to other moving shots. If you have a fast-paced car-chase scene and the camera is moving wildly to follow the action, a sudden static shot of a car sitting quietly at a stop light will be jarring. (Of course, that may be the effect you want.)

✔ **Varying the angle and size of shots:** A *jump-cut* happens when shots that are too similar in appearance are cut together, making the picture look as if it has jumped, or that the actor has popped from one spot to another. In order to avoid a jump-cut, you need to vary the angle and size of the next shot. One way to avoid a jump-cut is to shoot a cutaway of an actor's reaction or of a significant object on set that you can use to tie two different shots together. An appropriate cutaway can often save the day.

✔ **Showing simultaneous action:** You can cut back and forth between scenes happening at the same time. This is called *cross-cutting.* Or you can make a *parallel cut,* which is showing the simultaneous action with a split screen.

✔ **Choosing the best take (or combining the best of several takes).**

Shooting enough coverage

You need to shoot enough *coverage* so that you have plenty of different takes and interesting angles to choose from. Every time you add another angle to a scene, you make it more interesting and less monotonous. Using just one shot in a two-minute scene is like having a stare-down — and that's just dull and annoying (unless it's a bet to see who wins). The camera never blinks — that's what cutting is for. Cutting is like blinking from one shot to the next. When you watch a play, you don't stare at the stage as a whole the entire time; you concentrate on the individual actors as they speak, or on a prop or action sequence that catches your attention.

If you don't have time to shoot several angles, then create movement in the shot, such as having the camera follow or lead your actors as they're walking and talking.

Some directors shoot a ratio of three takes to get one shot, and some shoot ten or more. The editor's job is to find the best take or to combine the best of two takes with a cutaway. As you start to piece the film together, it magically begins to take on a shape of its own, and the story starts to make sense.

Assembling a first cut

The first step is piecing together what is called an *assembly cut* or *first cut.* This is the most basic cut possible, showing the story in continuity (because often the scenes are shot out of order, out of continuity).

Editing the picture of your film is very similar to writing a screenplay. The first assembly of footage is like the first rough draft, putting things into perspective and giving you a feel for your film. After you have your basic cut, you start shaping, trimming, and cutting until your piece feels complete. Like dancing, there's a rhythm to cutting — it flows, and everything feels like it's falling into place.

Don't be discouraged if the first cut doesn't excite you. The pacing may seem too slow, the performances may appear dull. I've often been disappointed with a first cut. After your first cut, you start to get a sense of how to tighten up the picture. You start to cut out long boring exits to the door, pauses that are too long between lines, or a scene that isn't working and that won't be missed if you cut it out entirely. You need to do a lot of shaping and adjusting before your masterpiece shines through. It's like molding something out of clay — you have to keep chipping away until you like what you see.

Creating a director's cut

The director's contract usually stipulates whether he gets to make sure his vision is followed in the editing room by approving the final cut of the film. This final, director-approved cut is called a *director's cut*. The director usually views an *assembly cut* (scenes assembled loosely in continuity according to the screenplay) by the picture editor. The director then gives the editor suggestions on where to place specific shots, close-ups, and establishing shots; how to change the order of things; how to tighten a scene; and so on. Usually, a director gets a director's cut based on his clout in the industry. Ultimately, the studio has the final say in the cutting of a picture if the director doesn't contractually have final cut. Steven Spielberg always gets his final say because he's earned that honor and proven himself to know what works and what doesn't. George Lucas always has the final cut because he doesn't report to anyone but himself!

With the release of most films on DVD now, many directors who didn't have the clout to get a director's cut theatrically in their studio contract, now have the opportunity to get a *director's cut* featured as one of the bonuses on the DVD.

Photo finish: Creating a final cut

Many times a studio screens a version of the film to a *test audience* (a group of people paid to watch and rate the film). The audience members take notes, and the studio (or the director, if she has final cut) evaluates all the comments on the picture and may re-edit accordingly.

After all the editing is finished and approved, you create the final, *locked* picture approved by the studio — or by the director if he has the authority to make the final cut (which you probably do have if you're an independent director). Now the postproduction work on sound begins, and the composer can start timing the scenes that will be *scored* (set to music).

The cutting-room floor

Many actors in Hollywood have unfortunately only made the *cutting-room floor*. This expression started in the days when editors physically cut film and literally threw the discarded scenes on the editing-room floor. Today, very few film scenes are discarded. Instead, these unused scenes are saved on a computer hard drive and often incorporated into the bonus section of the film's DVD release (including outtake flubs by the actors).

Listening to the sound editor

In addition to editing the picture on your film, you have to assemble and edit the sound elements. These elements are prepared by the sound editor, who is most often the picture editor and even the final postproduction sound mixer on an independent film. The sound elements are put onto separate audio channels (called *tracks*) and then mixed down into a final soundtrack that combines all channels mixed together. Some of those edited sound elements include

- ✔ Dialogue (may have separate dialogue tracks for each actor)
- ✔ Sound effects (can have unlimited sound-effects tracks)
- ✔ Music (usually one or two tracks for music)
- ✔ Ambience (background sounds like birds chirping, an air-conditioner humming, ocean waves crashing, and so on)

Dialogue editing is as important as your picture edit. The sound editor has a variety of elements to consider, such as overlapping conversations or starting a character's dialogue over the end of another character's shot. Check out Chapter 16 for more on dialogue and sound editing.

Considering Your Editing Options: Linear versus Non-Linear

Imagine that you've sorted through a set of your recent vacation photos and slipped them into a photo album, one picture per page. You just created a sequential order to your sightseeing photos. But say your mood changes or you decide that the picture of the huge fish you caught looks much better facing the photo of Uncle Bob's minnow, even though he caught it several days before your catch and before the trip to Disney World. No problem. You can just slide the photos out of their pockets and rearrange them. This is non-linear organization. Of course, if the photos are glued into the pockets, you can't rearrange them. They're now treated together as a whole, and not as individual shots — they're stuck in a linear world and can't be rearranged.

Editing in linear

Linear editing means that you assemble your shots one after another in consecutive order. Linear editing takes longer than the alternative (non-linear editing — see the following section).

The only time you *have* to edit linearly is if you shoot on videotape. A video deck, used as a *player,* allows you to transfer footage to a video *recorder* deck that puts one shot at the end of another shot. Videotape can't be cut physically so if you want to remove or add just one shot somewhere in the middle of your edits, you have to start over again.

Editing in non-linear

Digital non-linear editing, first pioneered by George Lucas's Editroid system, has opened a new world for the editor. A single editor can now quickly experiment with different variations of picture that would otherwise have taken a dozen editors many hours to perform.

Moviola and the flatbed

Just a few years ago, editors would cut their films by actually handling the film itself and physically cutting it, where necessary. They would trim the celluloid and glue or tape the scenes together on a moviola or flatbed, which would run the film at the proper speed to see what the final results looked like, and how the picture timed out.

A *moviola* is an upright editing system that resembles a projector. The actual film is projected into a viewer as it spools onto a top reel. The picture editor physically cuts the film into individual shots and hangs the film strips in a bin for reassembling. A *flatbed* editing system works similar to the moviola, but instead of being vertical, it's a horizontal table with the film reels lying on the surface.

Although physically cutting the film is considered non-linear editing because the individual shots and scenes are rearranged like individual blocks, the process isn't nearly as quick and effective as rearranging the clips digitally on a non-linear editing system. Editing on a moviola or a flatbed has pretty much been replaced by digital non-linear editing on a computer.

In *non-linear editing,* each shot, each scene, is its own separate compartment and can be moved around in any order within your film. Even the opening scene can be moved to the end in the editing room. Non-linear editing is easier and quicker; it also allows you to be more creative than linear editing does. This book is organized in a non-linear fashion. You don't have to read the chapters in order; you can skip back and forth, and no matter what section you read, it works on its own.

When you shoot footage with your camera, you're shooting in a linear fashion. For example, if you're filming the birth of a baby, everything you film shows the birthing process in order. But if you go into the editing room and decide to edit in non-linear, you can change the order of real time and have the baby go back to the mother's womb (go to your womb!). With digital technology, you can shoot in linear fashion and cut in non-linear style.

Editing Your Film on Your Computer

The same computer on which you write letters, organize your bank account, surf the Internet, and maybe even write your script can now easily be turned into a powerful editing machine. Most computers, both PCs and Apple computers, are able to edit a film in a non-linear environment and are limited only by the size of their hard drives.

In non-linear editing, you take all your separate shots, arrange them in any order, and then play them consecutively to form a scene. Every frame has its own individual set of *time-code numbers* (numbers generated electronically on the video image or in a computer) or *edge-code numbers* (numbers printed on the actual film stock) that pinpoint its exact starting and ending frames. Computer software can then generate an *edit list* that accurately contains the hour, minutes, seconds, and frames of your shots and identifies each cut made by the editor. With the right editing software, you have the capability to edit your film without leaving your computer.

For tips on setting up your own editing studio, check out *Digital Video For Dummies* by Martin Doucette (published by Wiley).

You can also purchase third-party software programs to perform additional functions like special effects, mattes, and process video footage to look more like film. (See "Simulating cinema with software" later in this chapter. Also see Chapter 17 for more on software used for special effects in the postproduction phase.)

Ordering your shots to go

Sometimes the order of your shots is dictated by the obvious — like the order of events when getting dressed: You put on your underwear first and your pants second — at least I hope you do. But if you rearrange the order of shots or events, you can change the psychology of your scene. For example, here are three shots in a particular order in your film:

1. A baby crying

2. The family cat hanging from the ceiling fan

3. A baby laughing

If you start with the baby crying, then the effect is the cat has stopped the baby from crying, and the child is now amused. Now see what happens when you change the order:

1. A baby laughing

2. The family cat hanging from the ceiling fan

3. A baby crying

Having the baby laughing at the beginning and crying at the end creates the effect that the child is now frightened for (or of) the animal. Quentin Tarantino put the ending of his film, *Pulp Fiction,* at the beginning of the film, and let the story progress until it picked up the beginning at the ending.

Hard driving

Your computer hard drive stores all your picture information. Because you'll probably need more hard drive space than the amount that's in your internal hard drive, you may want to purchase an external hard drive. An external hard drive is compact — about the size of a small paperback novel. Iomega (www.iomega.com or 888-4-IOMEGA), which makes the popular Zip drives and discs, now makes slick-looking, dependable external hard drives that plug into your computer. EZQuest (www.ezquest.com) also makes a line of hard drives called Cobra, which are extremely reliable and easy to set up. External hard drives connect to your computer via USB cables, and some use *firewire* for speedy data transfer (see the "Understanding firewire" sidebar in this chapter for details).

Most external hard drives come with setup software and usually work for both PC and Mac platforms. When set on *broadcast-quality mode* in your computer (the highest quality picture for television broadcast), you can capture anywhere from five to ten minutes of film per gigabyte of hard drive space. Therefore, an 80GB drive lets you hold up to 11 hours of footage. (I have a 120GB drive from EZQuest.)

Editing system software

Without software, a computer has no personality. Add film-editing software, and it becomes a complete postproduction editing suite within the confines of your desk space. You can choose from a myriad of editing software that allow you to affordably edit your film or video footage in a non-linear environment. Many computers even come with editing software.

Most software-editing programs use these basic components of non-linear editing:

✔ A bin to hold your individual shots

✔ A timeline that allows you to assemble your shots in any order (it resembles storyboard panels — see Chapter 9)

✔ A main window that plays back your edited footage

iMovie

Many Macintosh computers come with iMovie, a simple-to-use, non-linear editing software that allows you to cut your film on your computer (see Figure 15-1). Check out *iMovie 2 For Dummies* by Todd Stauffer (published by Wiley), which guides you through the steps of using this effective and easy-to-use software to edit your projects.

Avid

Avid, a name synonymous with non-linear editing, now makes Avid 3.5 software, which works with Mac or PC platforms. Many studio feature films have been edited on Avid non-linear systems. The software is more sophisticated than other lower-priced editing software, and with a price under $1,500, you can't beat the professional editing it lets you perform. It also includes titling and graphics, along with a variety of real-time effects. You can get more details on the Avid editing software at www.avid.com.

Understanding firewire

Firewire is a digital connection (a special cable) that transfers the information from your digital camcorder to your computer, to an external hard drive, or to other equipment with no degradation in picture quality. Most computers now have firewire inputs so that you can plug your camcorder directly into them and transfer your footage. The data speed transfer of firewire is up to 400 Mbps (megabytes per second). The higher the Mbps, the faster the data transfer — which is a good thing if you get impatient easily.

Firewire external drives are able to move information faster than USB drives (which transfer data at least 30 times slower than firewire), and are almost a necessity when working with large project files.

Scene bin with imported footage from video

View edited shots in order of storyboard below

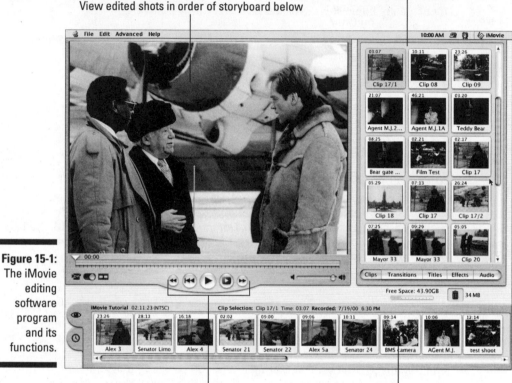

Figure 15-1:
The iMovie
editing
software
program
and its
functions.

Buttons that function like a VCR to play your edited footage

Shots in storyboard - arranged in any order

iMovie screenshot reprinted by permission of Apple Computer, Inc.

Final Cut Pro

Final Cut Pro, available for Macintosh for under $1,000, is a professional non-linear software program. It's much more sophisticated than iMovie or some of the other non-linear software, and it can produce some amazing results, including titles, effects, and transitions (check out www.apple.com/finalcutpro). Apple has also come out with Final Cut Express, a simpler and easier-to-use version of Final Cut Pro, for $299. This is a perfect non-linear editing software for the independent filmmaker.

Adobe Premiere

Adobe makes popular software programs for the editing world with Adobe Premiere 6.5 (priced at $549) and with After Effects (at $699), which is kind of like Photoshop, but with motion. Check out Adobe's products at www.adobe. com. Primatte Keyer is a software program that works with Adobe After Effects to do some amazing postproduction work, including seamless mattes and picture correction (www.redgiantsoftware.com).

Simulating cinema with software

Many independent filmmakers desperately want to make a film that looks like it was shot on film — but they can't afford the expense that comes with shooting film. There are now software programs that will process your video footage in the postproduction phase, and create the illusion that you shot the footage on film. These programs emulate the characteristics associated with the look of film such as grain, softness, subtle flutter, and saturated colors. The software also pulls down the equivalent 30-frame video footage to the 24 standard frames used with film.

CineLook from Digie Effects (www.digieffects.com) and Magic Bullet by the Orphanage (www.toolfarm.com) give your harsh-looking video footage the soft romantic look of film. Third-party film-simulation software works with most editing programs, such as Final Cut Pro and Avid 3.5.

The biggest difference between shooting with a 24p video camera that instantaneously gives you the look of shooting film in the camera and the choice of emulating the look of film to your video footage in the editing room is that the software requires rendering time that can take a while if you're processing a feature-length film (90 minutes or more).

Another way to get your video to look more like it was shot on celluloid is to check out a company called FilmLook (www.filmlook.com). It takes your original video footage and reprocess it to look like you shot it on film (and not video). It's similar to the new software that's available, but FilmLook has mastered this process and carefully monitors your video footage from the first to the last frame.

Turning the Key on Turnkey-Editing Systems

If you don't want to use your current letter-writing computer to edit film, you can purchase a stand-alone editing system often referred to as a *turnkey system*. This type of editing machine comes with its own operating system and software, which is different from Mac and PC, that's solely for the purpose of editing. You literally take it out of the box, plug it in, master the basic operation of the machine, and you're ready to edit. It's as simple as driving a car — just turn the key, and you're off!

The Editor's Tool Kit

Digital Juice puts out *The Editor's Tool Kit* (starting at $499), an invaluable tool for creating titles and credits. Each of the nine DVDs in the set provides seamless animated backgrounds and lower thirds (where you key in titles and credits), along with royalty-free graphics and animations. You also get 50 fonts to choose from for your credits and titling needs. This is a great tool for any editor!

Digital Juice also puts out *Jump Backs* (starting at $249 per volume on DVD-ROM), which provides lively animated motion backgrounds that can be looped seamlessly (repeated without a definitive end to the footage) to enhance any video or film project in the editing room (see Chapter 18). Jump Backs comes on DVD-ROM and Juicer software, which lets you process the animations on any computer. Jump Backs is also available on regular DVD for immediate playback without the use of a computer. To discover more about what The Editor's Tool Kit and Jump Backs can do for your project, go to www.digitaljuice.com.

A great turnkey system is the Casablanca Prestige by MacroSystem. This magical machine is one of my favorite editing tools; I've edited many broadcast projects on it. Resembling a VHS deck that you can hook up to a TV or monitor, it comes with a keyboard and mouse, much like a standard computer does. You input your film or video footage electronically, and the Casablanca captures the footage, allowing you to cut your film or video footage into individual shots and reassemble in a non-linear environment. You can then output your final footage (in pristine broadcast quality) in virtually any format, including VHS, Beta, DigiBeta, and mini-DV; you can even burn your own DVDs, which lets you make your own customized menus like the studio films you buy or rent. The complete turnkey system costs approximately $3,500 — all you add is a TV or monitor. Check it out at www.casablanca.tv.

One advantage to a separate turnkey system is that you're not using the same device to write your letters and surf the Internet. You can be reassured knowing that this machine is used only for your editing projects and that no third-party applications or hungry Internet viruses can corrupt or damage your hard drive and files.

Posting Your Production in Your Computer

After you finish editing all the dialogue and picture elements for your film in your computer, you're ready to marry your picture and sound together. If the final production is going to television and home video (and not a theatrical release), then you can continue to do most of your final preparations in the computer (color correcting, titles, and so on). If you plan on getting a theatrical release for your picture, then you'll be working further with your film laboratory to prepare the appropriate film elements for a theatrical release (see the following section).

Developing a Relationship with Your Film Lab

If you shoot on film and then edit in your computer, you need the services of a film lab to develop your film negative and then transfer that footage to videotape so you can then input that footage into your computer containing your editing software.

If you shoot your movie on film, or on digital video, with plans to transfer to filmstock (for a possible theatrical release), you'll still need to establish a relationship with a motion-picture film laboratory. A film laboratory develops your film negative and makes a separate film print if you're cutting the actual film or going for a theatrical release. The process is not unlike the process of taking still photos and having the negatives developed to make photo prints. You can find a film laboratory in the Yellow Pages under "Film Laboratories" or "Motion Picture Film Services." If your town doesn't have a film lab, you may want to call a laboratory in Los Angeles or New York. In L.A., try Deluxe Labs (www.bydeluxe.com) or Technicolor (www.technicolor.com). In New York, try Colorlab (www.colorlab.com) or DuArt Film and Video (www.duart.com) and arrange to have your film shipped for developing.

When I shot my film *Undercover Angel* in Ottawa, Ontario, I had my film shipped by bus to Deluxe Laboratories in Toronto. The lab developed my film stock and shipped back the *dailies* (see the next section "Dailies or telecine") by overnight express. A good relationship with your lab ensures that the services it performs — including developing your film negative, transferring your film to videotape (for dailies as well as the final product for TV and home video release), transferring your film shot on videotape to filmstock (for a theatrical release), and printing your film — are performed properly and on a timely basis. Also, don't be afraid to negotiate for the best price you can. Laboratories often give discounts to first-time or independent filmmakers. All you have to do is ask!

Dailies or telecine

If you're going directly to TV or home video, you can skip the process of printing your film and actually turn your developed negative into a positive image in the telecine stage. *Telecine* is the procedure of transferring your film footage directly onto videotape. Many film labs have telecine bays (or work closely with companies that do) where you can transfer your film footage to videotape. In telecine, you can play with the colors, correct the exposure, and do lots of other picture enhancements, as well.

Dailies consist of the footage that you shot the day before, which has already been developed by the lab. If you're shooting with a camcorder, your results are immediate, and you have no dailies to speak of — you just rewind the tape and watch what you've shot.

Positive input: Hiring a negative cutter

Cutting the film negative (if you originally shot on film) is one of the last steps before you're ready to make prints of your film for theatrical distribution. The negative cutter follows your *edit decision list* (EDL), which is an electronic printout of numbers that relate to each edit if your film was cut on a non-linear system, or the actual edge-code numbers printed on your *film work-print* (a print of your film that can be handled) if you're physically cutting the actual film.

The EDL on computer disc can also instruct a computer in a professional post-production editing bay to assemble your project into a final edited production on videotape. It finds the shots that are to be edited together and matches up the correct numbers at the end of one cut, and the numbers assigned to the new cut (this is usually done in a professional editing bay if you off-lined your film on your computer in a lower picture resolution — possibly because you didn't have the hard drive space to do higher picture resolution).

The best place to find a negative cutter is through your film laboratory's recommendation. You want a good negative cutter who will delicately cut your film negative, keeping it safe from dust and scratches.

Color-correcting your film is as plain as black and white

Before you make your final film print, your film footage has to be color-corrected scene by scene, so that the shots match perfectly. For example, when you're shooting outside, the sun is constantly moving and changing the color temperature of your footage (see Chapter 11 for color temperature stuff). One shot may not match a previous shot because the tint is slightly different.

You may want to enhance the color of your scenes, such as make your skies bluer or add more saturation of colors to your footage that requires shot-by-shot adjustment. If you're making a Western or period piece, you may want to pull out some of the color or infuse a sepia tone into the entire production.

When color-correcting the actual film negative, a machine called a *hazeltine* or *color analyzer* calibrates the settings of color correction and exposures, which the printing department follows. Your negative footage appears on a monitor showing how the positive picture and color will look when projected on the screen. The person working for the lab who corrects the color is called the *timer*. If you color-correct your film for video or TV release, the color corrector is called a *telecine operator* or *colorist*.

If you're editing your film or video on a non-linear system in your computer, you can also control and correct the image color with the editing software or with a third-party software. Video doesn't require extensive color-correcting because you can do the adjustments in the camera and see the results immediately. The correction that you make in the postproduction stage is usually to enhance the image colors or to change them completely for effect.

Answering your first film print

After your negative cutter puts together your final negative cut (if you're planning a theatrical release) and your color corrections have been made, the film lab develops the first positive print of your film, which is called an *answer print*. You usually get to screen the film in one of the lab's screening rooms to check the picture for proper exposure and color correction. You make a note of any adjustments and send the notes to the lab to correct.

After you accept the adjustments to the answer print, you then make your final *composite,* which contains the picture and sound together. You're now ready to make theatrical prints for your distributor or to send to the theaters, depending on your distribution plan (see Chapter 19). This process is used only if your film is going to be screened in movie theaters.

Cloning, Not Copying; Cloning, Not Copying

In the past, making a *dub* (copy) of your VHS tape was as simple as taping from one machine to another, or taking the tape to a video-dubbing company (which makes dubs in quantity at one time). But the dub never looked as good as the original. It was always grainy and softer in focus — kind of like a photocopy of a photocopy that gets more and more fuzzy.

But now, when you make a copy from a digital tape to another digital tape or to a DVD, you're making an exact duplicate, a mirror image of the original material (of course, without being reversed). You're actually making a *clone* — an exact copy of the original with no degradation in picture quality. So the clone you send to people looks as good as the original footage. Most film laboratories also offer this service either in-house or through an affiliated company.

Most PCs and Macs make it easy for you to burn your own DVDs right on your computer. Macintosh makes a program called iDVD that lets you create menus and chapters and put an entire film or project, up to two hours in length, on a DVD-R. MyDVD for the PC by Sonic retails for $79 and does all the DVD authoring you need.

Many DVD burners include the DVD-authoring software by Sonic, (www.sonic.com), so check that out before buying the two separately. DVD blank discs are also coming down in price. You can now purchase one for around $3, close to the price of a VHS tape. Edgewise Media in Hollywood sells Princo blank DVDs at a great price. Visit the company's Web site at www.edgewise.com.

You can make your own DVD labels with CD label kits and personalize your DVDs with a selected still photo printed on the CD label from your film.

If you don't have a DVD burner in your computer, or you're still afraid of the technology of DVD burning, don't worry. DVD player/recorders are starting to pop up on the market. These DVD player/recorders look like regular DVD players, but they can burn DVDs as easy as making a VHS dub. They have analog and firewire inputs (for true digital transferring with no picture loss). Philips (www.philips.com) makes a DVD player/recorder — the DVDR 985 — that burns your projects onto DVD+R discs, which play in most DVD players. Making DVD copies of your film is as easy as pushing the record button!

Chapter 16

Posting the Sound for All to Hear: Mixing Sound and Adding Music

● ●

In This Chapter

▶ Mixing dialogue, sound effects, and music together

▶ Sounding off on sound effects

▶ Adding music that's music to your audience's ears

▶ Marrying picture to sound

● ●

More than 80 percent of the sound in a film is added *after* shooting, during postproduction. All the different types of sound — dialogue, sound effects, music, and so on — are recorded separately and then mixed together to create one soundtrack. If you really want to take notice of sound that's been added, watch an animated film like *Shrek* or *The Lion King,* for which 100 percent of the sound was created (because an animated picture requires all sounds to be created from scratch to match the images).

Even if your film features live actors, you need to add sounds effects, music, and other sound elements in order to strengthen the production value of your film. Sound effects enhance visual elements, putting some real *punch* into a punch, for example. Music, whether it's licensed popular songs or composed specifically for the picture, enhances the mood of a film. This chapter explains what these other sound elements are, how to record or acquire them, and how to mix it all together yourself, or find a professional sound mixer to make your film's sound sound great.

Mixing Sound in Postproduction

After your film's picture is *locked* (picture editing and timing of the film will not change, and dialogue is synced up with the picture), you're ready to start adding another dimension to your baby: sound design.

The *re-recording mixer,* also known as the *postproduction sound mixer,* takes all the sound elements of your production and mixes them down into one master soundtrack that complements the picture. On a tiny budget, you may be the sound mixer, but the job will require some technical know-how and artistic skills and may be too ambitious an undertaking. If you can find someone with experience, that's the best route to go. On bigger budget productions, you may have a team that includes three mixers working together. One controls the music, one mixes effects, and another handles the dialogue. The key to mixing the final elements is knowing how and when to feature different sounds and controlling the volume of each element. When dialogue comes in while music is playing, the mixer needs to find an appropriate mix so that the music doesn't drown out the dialogue or disappear behind the scene. A sound that is too loud or too soft can distract from the action. Sound-mixing a film is similar to sound-mixing a song in which lyrics and instrumentation are combined and balanced so all the elements are heard clearly.

The more layering of sound you have, the more professional your soundtrack will seem. The effect is subliminal. A good sound mix is invisible to your audience — but they're sure to notice a bad mix.

Looking in the mixer's toolbox

The mixer brings artistic and technical skills to the mix, but the following tools make the job easier:

- ✔ Mixing board (if not part of your sound software)
- ✔ Computer (most home computers can accommodate sound software)
- ✔ Sound mixing software
- ✔ Digital audio tape (DAT) recorder for output to your final film or video project

If using a computer, you input the separate audio tracks — containing dialogue, sound effects, and musical score — into the computer and mix them by using special sound-mixing software (again it's recommended you hire a professional mixer if you're not versed on the technical aspects of sound mixing). The tracks are then balanced and output to a final recording device. From there, the sound can be transferred to a finished video master or to the optical track of your film print. (See the section "Outputting Your Final Mix," later in this chapter, for more information.)

Pro Tools is the sound-mixing software of choice, used by 95 percent of professional sound designers. It's the sound equivalent of a picture-editing system like Avid or Final Cut Pro (see Chapter 15). You can download Pro Tools for free at www.digidesign.com.

If you're not computer savvy or you're afraid to use an intricate software program to design your film's soundtrack (and you can't find or afford to hire a sound mixer), you can do your own sound mixing the old-fashioned way on an analog video editing bay and an actual mixing board with sliding knobs — you just have to control the audio levels manually, and it may take a little longer. Though this is a more primitive route to go, it requires less technical knowledge (not having to be versed in sound-mixing software), but you still have to listen carefully and mix the audio level of your tracks properly so that dialogue is not drowned out by the music score.

If you want (or need) to hire a seasoned postproduction sound mixer, you can call local sound studios and ask for contact numbers. You can also look for a sound mixer at `www.crewnet.com` and `www.media-match.com`, which lets you search for any crew position by city or state.

Finding the right balance

The sound mixer plays each scene of your film repeatedly as he or she mixes and syncs the sound elements. These elements consist of

- ✔ Dialogue
- ✔ Sound effects
- ✔ Foley (footsteps, falls, fight sounds, hand props, and so on that are matched perfectly to the actor's on-screen actions by Foley artists — see "Getting to know Jack Foley" later in this chapter)
- ✔ Musical score
- ✔ Voice-over narration
- ✔ Ambience (background environmental sounds)
- ✔ Source music within the scene (on radio, TV, or a performing band), which has to be recorded specifically for the film or with permission to use the source from the originator or owner of the source music

The sound mixer must make sure the dialogue, music, and effects aren't competing with each other, controlling the audio levels so that the sounds balance one another. On a small production, the sound mixer is usually in charge of mixing all the elements, which include dialogue, music, sound effects, Foley, and ambience. The key to a good sound mix is staying focused on the picture so that the audience can stay focused on your story.

The mixer controls a separate track for each individual element, including several tracks of dialogue. The dialogue editor prepares a separate audio track for each actor's dialogue so that the sound mixer can control each actor's dialogue in terms of audio level and equalization individually to get clear-sounding dialogue. On a small production, your dialogue editor is often the same person who edits your picture. Each sound category is marked on the mixing board so that the mixer knows which volume slider controls which track. A film soundtrack can have unlimited individual audio tracks on top of each other containing different sound elements, as the mixer can keep layering and mixing (adjusting appropriate audio levels), on as many different tracks until you've got one complete master soundtrack.

The sound mixer can emulate certain effects through the mixing board or a software program; for example, a *telephone filter* can make a voice sound as though it's coming through a telephone. *Reverb* can add an echo to a voice to make it sound like the actor is speaking in an auditorium, and even make voices sound like they're a fair distance away. In addition to these specialty effects, audio can be adjusted to minimize any *noise,* or hissing, that may be on the recorded audio track.

The mixer also prepares *music and effects* (M&E) *tracks* without the actors' dialogue so that, if the film is purchased for distribution in a non-English-speaking country, it can be dubbed in the language of choice and still retain the music and sound effects. You can find further details on M&E in the section "Separating music and effects tracks for foreign release," later in this chapter.

A qualified sound mixer has an "ear" for mixing the right volume levels and finding a happy medium between the dialogue, music, and sound effects so they aren't competing with each other. To help ride the proper audio levels of each sound element, the sound mixer will refer to a cue sheet prepared by the sound editor that will indicate when each effect will be coming up (so the mixer can anticipate lowering or raising the volume of the upcoming sound element).

Looping the Loop

Looping, also called *ADR* (automatic dialogue replacement), is the art of replacing dialogue that wasn't recorded clearly on the set or couldn't be recorded properly because the location was too noisy to get good audio. The actor watches on a monitor or movie screen the shot or scene for which dialogue needs to be replaced. Through a set of headphones, the actor listens to the unusable audio replayed over and over again (looped) and then repeats the lines for re-recording, trying to match what's on the screen. The best audio take is kept and edited to match the picture as closely as possible. The mixer works magic with equalization and reverb to make it sound as close to the previously recorded on-set dialogue as possible.

If an actor steps on a line, stutters, or screws up a word during actual filming, it can be re-recorded in an ADR session and mixed back into the dialogue tracks.

Creating Sound Effects with a Bang

Try turning the TV sound off, and you realize how much less dramatic the action seems without sound effects (or music or dialogue). Sound effects can be very subtle, like a key jiggling in a lock, or very dramatic, like a thunderous explosion of a missile strike. Almost all the sound effects that accompany a film are added or re-created in postproduction. Dialogue is the only sound from the actual filming that's retained all the way to the final picture — but not without enhancement.

Using a sound effect to suggest an action or event that you can't afford to shoot is often just as effective as showing the whole event. For example, say you want to include a car crash in your film. Your actor's car slips off a ridge as we hear him yelling, and then we hear a loud splash (a sound effect). Or a car drives out of the frame, and a few seconds later you hear a terrible crash (another sound effect) — and then a lone tire rolls into the frame. You've created a believable effect — without totaling the car! You can create your own sound effects or license them from a sound-effects library.

Checking out sound-effects libraries

You can find almost every sound effect imaginable in sound-effect libraries. Sound Ideas is one of the world's largest publishers of sound-effects libraries. I'm currently using one of its sound packages called the General 6000 Series. This series contains every imaginable sound effect; you have 40 CDs' worth of sounds to choose from. Check out the Web site at www.sound-ideas.com to see the different sound-effects libraries offered. The sound effects are all digitally mastered and include these categories:

- **Animals:** Dogs, cats, birds, exotic animals
- **Devices:** Telephones, cell phones, fax machines, coffee makers
- **Fights:** Punches, jumps, falls
- **Locations:** Airports, restaurants, schools, playgrounds
- **Office environments:** Office machines, printers, elevators
- **People:** Crowds, applause, footsteps, laughing, crying

- ✔ **Toys:** Wind-up toys, race cars, spring-action toys
- ✔ **Vehicles:** Planes, trains, automobiles, boats

I like to have the actual CDs and use the category listings and track numbers, but you can also download Sound Ideas' effects at www.sounddogs.com or www.sonomic.com.

Some sound-effects libraries let you download individual sound effects for as little as $6 an effect. You can also buy individual sound effect CDs at most record and CD stores for under $20. A professional sound-effects library on CD can cost you $800 and up, depending on how extensive it is.

Another sound-effects company, Hollywood Edge, carries some great sound-effects libraries online at www.hollywoodedge.com. This site enables you to search for the exact sound effect you're looking for, listen to it, and download it to your hard drive immediately (after using your credit card and paying for individual sound effects or entire CDs, of course). You can then output it to a digital editing program or tape source or onto a recordable CD.

If you're mixing your film at a professional mixing studio, most times you'll be able to use its sound-effects library for a minimal charge — usually by the individual sound effects or a negotiated flat fee.

Creating and recording your own sound effects

If you want to save some money and have some fun, you can record your own sound effects. I did that for my independent film *Turn of the Blade*. I went to the airport and recorded sounds of planes and helicopters taking off and landing, along with other airport sounds, on a portable DAT (digital audio tape) recorder. These tapes are similar in size to mini-digital video (DV) tapes. Because DAT is in the digital domain, you get pristine, high-quality audio when recording and don't lose any quality when making dubs of your sound mix (because, in the digital world, dubs are clones; you get an exact duplicate of the master).

Can't afford a DAT recorder but own a digital video camera? Record your sound effects onto the audio portion of your mini-DV tape. Just make sure that you use a good external microphone appropriate for recording the particular sound effect you want. (Use directional for concentrated sounds like keys dropping on the ground, and omni-directional for recording ambient sounds like the ocean. See Chapter 12 for more on microphones.) You may want to keep the cap on the camera so you know that you were recording for audio purposes only (but remember to take the cap off while shooting your actual film!).

You can also record on a portable CD recorder for professional digital quality.

Don't be afraid to be creative when creating sound effects. Emulate skaters on an ice rink by scraping knives together and punches by slamming dough on a counter. Make alien sound effects by slowing down, speeding up, or mixing several sounds together. Need the sound of a roaring fire but the real thing doesn't roar? Try crumpling paper into a ball close to a microphone. Waiting for the thunder in a rainstorm? Wait no longer; get a piece of tin or even a cookie sheet and flap it around. Voilà — thunder inside your house!

Getting to know Jack Foley

Named after its innovator, Jack Foley, *Foley walking* is a precise sound-effects technique where an artist (also called a Foley artist) watches the screen and reenacts the actors' interaction with items to re-create the sound effects that accompany the images on the screen. Foley effects include footsteps, clothes rustling, objects being handled, and body impacts.

Foley is different from using a sound-effects library because it's easier to emulate someone walking up a flight of metal stairs and matching it in one take with a Foley walker. With a sound-effects library, you would have to find individual footsteps and match each one every time the actor moved up one step. This would take more time and more work to sync up.

A sophisticated audio postproduction facility usually has a *Foley pit* available. A Foley pit consists of separate floor panels with different surfaces such as hardwood flooring, carpeting, concrete, and even water. The Foley walker has different surfaces at his or her disposal and walks "in place" on these surfaces while watching the actors on screen. A skilled Foley artist usually watches the scene a few times before acting out the action and then creates the Foley sounds at the same time as the action is playing out on the screen while it's being recorded to audio tape.

A Foley artist often brings a large suitcase containing items to assist him or her in re-creating sound effects to match the picture, such as various shoes, an assortment of hand props (paper, cutlery, stapler, and so on). Letting the Foley artist know what special elements may be helpful to bring when adding Foley to your picture (for example, coconut shells cut in half can emulate horses hoofs trotting across the pavement) is also helpful. I've seen a few burly Foley walkers put on high heels to emulate a woman on screen trekking down the street in heels.

The best way to locate a Foley artist is by contacting a local sound studio or TV station and asking if it has a list of professional Foley artists. You can also log on to www.crewnet.com and see if there's a Foley artist in your neighborhood. I can imagine a Foley walker's business card with the slogan, "I'm not a cross-dresser, but I may need to put on high heels."

If you can't afford a professional Foley artist (which could cost upwards of $25 an hour), you can have fun doing your own Foley. You'll just have to do a lot of practicing. You can put together your own Foley pit by using a square foot or two of different surfaces like tile, wood, concrete, and carpet, plus a bucket with water (for splashing sounds) that you can find from around the house or at a home supply store. Create your own fight sounds by punching into a bag of flour or sand. You can use household items to enhance sounds made by your actors interacting with items on screen, like keys jingling, pens clicking, and cutlery clinking.

Adding room tone: Ambience or background sound

Ambience is the background sound that gives your soundtrack fullness and enhances the location environment. Ambient sounds can be the buzzing of an air-conditioner working overtime, dogs barking in a neighborhood, or water dripping in the kitchen sink. Often, the production sound mixer records a loopable ambient track at the shoot (see Chapter 12). The postproduction sound mixer can also enhance a scene by adding ambience from a sound-effects library that may have a fuller sound than the original location-like sound of lots of birds chirping in a park, or a nearby waterfall.

Scoring Big with Music

Turn on a classical radio station and close your eyes while the orchestral pieces play — you can't help but imagine visual images created by the music. Instrumental music can help evoke a mood in each scene of the film and create an underlying emotion that the audience can feel. Add some songs with lyrics, and you've got a film soundtrack.

Hiring a composer to set the mood

A *composer* can write an original music score to fit your film perfectly. He or she composes a theme that identifies your film and enhances the emotion and subtext of your story. The composer should write music appropriate to each scene. You don't want pounding rap music during a romantic interaction of two people having a candlelit dinner, for example. Some musical scores, such as the scores from *Jaws, E.T.,* and the emotional orchestral score of *Schindler's List,* have become easily identifiable because they capture the style and theme of each film so well.

Nowadays, composers can record an entire film soundtrack without leaving their garage or studio — and without hiring a single live musician. But although synthesizers and samplers have gotten better, they still can't replace the sensation of human breath filling an acoustical instrument. Hiring musicians can be expensive, however; so a synthesized orchestra is often a cheaper way to go. Or you can combine synthesized music with real musicians. That's what composer Greg Edmonson did on my film *Turn of the Blade* to create a score that sounded more like a real orchestra.

With the sophistication of today's computers and digital technology, almost every film's music design is done digitally (on a computer) by using a software program like Pro Tools. Sound can be processed, manipulated, and adjusted quickly, so the composer can hear the results immediately and continue to make adjustments if necessary.

The best way to look for a composer is by calling the local radio stations or sound-recording facilities in your area. Your local TV station may recommend a composer who works in your town. *The Hollywood Reporter* (www. hollywoodreporter.com) has special film and TV music issues that come out several times a year. The issues list composers alphabetically along with their credits. You can also contact the various music organizations (BMI, ASCAP, and SOCAN) and get a free list of their members — composers, musicians, and songwriters. Crew Net (www.crewnet.com) is a free service that lets you search for a composer (and other crew positions) by city or state. Media-Match (www.media-match.com) also provides a similar service via the Internet. You could also e-mail composer Alan Fleishman at arfmusic@datzart.com — he's scored over 30 projects of mine. Tell him Bryan sent you.

Composing your own music

You can use music software programs that put you at the keyboard — and you don't even have to read music or have ever played a note in your life.

Sonic Pro makes two products, SonicFire Pro (for professional use) and Movie Maestro (for consumer and educational projects — additional music licensing is required for broadcast purposes), that enable you to become your own composer by using your computer. The programs give you control over genre, style, and duration. You don't have to be a musician to get professional results. Movie Maestro (see Figure 16-1) is easy to use and costs just $49. No knowledge or understanding of music is required — just choose from the selection presented to you for the style of music (scary, happy, energetic, romantic, thriller), along with tempo and length, then point and click. Check out SonicFire Pro and Movie Maestro at www.smartsound.com.

Figure 16-1:
Movie
Maestro
makes it
easy to
compose
your own
music. Here
I am with
Michael
Jackson —
he's had
a little
success
with music.

Checking out music libraries

If you're on a limited budget, you may not be able to afford a composer to write and score original music for your film or video project. That's where music libraries come to the rescue. Just as you can get sound effects from a CD library, you can get music of every conceivable type, which you pay a fee to use in your film. Some music libraries charge a *needle-drop fee,* which is a fee charged literally every time a music cue starts and stops. Your project will sound very professional if you utilize music from a music library.

Most music libraries provide *royalty-free* music, meaning that after you buy the CD, you get a lifetime of unlimited use of the music on that CD — so get out your library card!

Companies such as Music Bakery (www.musicbakery.com) provide CDs with a wide variety of music cues to choose from for your film project. CDs start at $59. I've been using Music Bakery's CDs for years, and I've always been impressed with the selection. Some of the categories that Music Bakery offers include

✔ Jazz and blues

✔ Orchestral

✔ Corporate image music (short music intros appropriate for logos)

✔ Rock and urban

> ✔ High energy and sports
>
> ✔ Drama and suspense
>
> ✔ Classical

Some music libraries allow you to sample their music via the Internet so that you can select tracks for your project without having to buy the CD before you hear it. For example, Creative Support Services (CSS) is another music library that provides a broad range of music for film and video projects. At the Web site (www.cssmusic.com), you can listen to up to 10,000 tracks — if you have the time.

Using original songs

You can enhance your film and add some energy to certain scenes by slipping in some songs. Finding new talent in clubs and showcases (maybe you'll find the next Beatles) can be a lot of fun — not to mention cheaper than having to license a well-known song from a major recording label. You're sure to find bands that will be excited to have one of their songs in your film. If you offer to let them keep the rights to the song, they may let you use it for free.

Always have some written agreement between yourself and the band. It's best to have an attorney versed in entertainment or music contracts write it up for you. You can find music and song agreements in *Contracts for the Film & Television Industry* by Mark Litwak, which I talk about in Chapter 7, along with other staff and crew contract information. Your agreement should clearly state that the band is providing you the original lyrics and music in a recording that you can use in your film (for no charge, or a nominal fee), and the band owns the song that can be used in the context of your film. Any royalties paid by the band's music association (BMI, ASCAP, or SOCAN) is paid from the TV network that licenses the film and follows the music cue sheets to see who gets paid for the music (see the "BMI, ASCAP, and SOCAN" sidebar in this chapter).

BMI, ASCAP, and SOCAN

BMI, ASCAP, and SOCAN (a Canadian association) are music performance rights organizations that collect royalties for songs, soundtracks, and any other music sources created by their members (composers, songwriters, and musicians) that appear in any published work. They monitor the information through the cue sheets (see "Cueing up cue sheets" in this chapter) that the film's composer or production company provides to each buyer or distributor. These performance rights organizations send their members quarterly statements listing the distribution of the projects in which the members' music has been heard. The composer or songwriter receives a royalty (a fee paid each time his or her work is heard) in a particular production.

Getting the rights to popular music

Record companies have dedicated licensing departments for the very purpose of licensing songs for use in films, TV, and commercials. A well-placed song can be as lucrative for a band and its record company in a soundtrack that sells at a music store as it is having the song in the finished film. But record companies don't just let you use their music for free; you have to pay a licensing fee. Every record label has a licensing department that deals specifically with licensing their songs to film, TV, and commercial properties. Using a recognizable song in your film can cost upwards of $20,000 for the *synchronization rights* (connecting musical recordings up with film or TV works). You can save some money if you use the lyrics from the song but have your newly discovered band do its own rendition. Many bands have their own garage sound studio where they can record a song or two for relatively little money, or they have contacts with professional sound studios that may give them a discount.

Even the song "Happy Birthday" is protected by copyright. You would need permission to use the lyrics or music in your film even if one of your actors sings it or any part of the song. It's easier to write your own birthday song — and then copyright it so that no one else can use it without paying you!

Cueing up cue sheets

When you sell your film to a distributor, you need to provide a *cue sheet*. This sheet, usually prepared by the composer, is simply a listing of all the music cues in your film. A cue sheet lists the cue number, the time length of the cue, and a brief description of what the music piece relates to in the film (for example, David turns around — and he sees her!). Cue sheets are used to help the music organizations like BMI, ASCAP, and SOCAN monitor their members' contributions to various projects and receive proper royalties for the use of their music.

Using songs in the public domain

Seventy-five years after a song is written, its copyright expires, and the song enters the *public domain*. Anyone can use material in the public domain without having to license it from the owner or get permission to use it for professional (and profitable) purposes. Most of Gilbert and Sullivan's famous songs, such as "The Modern Major General," are in the public domain. Titles such as "Pop Goes the Weasel" and "Row, Row, Row Your Boat" are other well-known ditties in the public domain. For various titles that are currently in the public domain, check out www.pdinfo.com.

A song may be in the public domain, but the actual recording may be copyrighted, so make sure to do your research. The best thing to do is to have a composer rescore it and hire original singers and musicians to perform it.

Outputting Your Final Mix

Your sound mixer prepares separate tracks known as *stems* for your film. Each set of stems consists of different mixed elements that make up your final mix. One set of stems contains the dialogue, one set is dedicated to music, and another set is for sound effects and Foley. When played together, these stems represent your final mix and are used in the making of your final release.

After you have your dialogue, sound effects, ambience, Foley, and music pulled together into your final mix, or *printmaster,* you're ready to sync sound to picture by transferring the sound to your film negative at the lab. If your sound has been mixed for a digital video production, the final soundtrack can be transferred directly into a digital-editing system or onto a DAT audiotape.

The final output is usually done by someone at the film lab when transferring to film. If you're going to video or into a non-linear editing system, you can input it yourself, or if you're using an editor, she can input it and sync it up to the final picture.

When finishing on film, the final sound mix is printed to the *optical track* of your film print. The sound and the film become one — for better or worse! However, if you want to use a popular sound format that will make your soundtrack really come to life, you'll need to take your printmaster through a format-specific encoding process. Dolby Labs licenses its popular Dolby Digital 5.1 surround encoding technology, giving a unique dimensional sound quality to your soundtrack.

Surround sound

Sound can be exciting to the ears, especially with the advancement of surround sound formats, which include Dolby Digital 5.1 and Sony SDDS 7.1, a three-dimensional sound experience. With three front speakers (left, center, and right), two surround channels (left surround, right surround, and a separate feed for a subwoofer for low-frequency material), you can make your audience feel like they're part of the action. After you've mixed your multichannel surround, you usually also create separate printmasters for four-channel surround (Dolby SR) and stereo masters as well. This is another option if you want to spend the extra dollars and feel that your soundtrack will benefit from utilizing the surround sound technology.

Separating music and effects tracks for foreign release

If you know that you're going to have a distributor sell your film in the foreign markets (overseas), you will also need to make two separate printmasters: one that contains only the music and sound effects (M&E tracks) and another with just the English dialogue. Having this version of the printmaster enables a foreign distributor to dub the language of its country into the picture and still have the original music and sound effects tracks behind the dubbed voices. The English dialogue track is used only as a guide.

Next time you're on an airplane that flies to a foreign country, check the audio channels on the in-flight film. You can often switch back and forth between languages, but you'll notice that the music and sound effects are the same on both channels.

Chapter 17

Creating Effective Special Effects

· ·

· ·

A special effect is something out of the ordinary that entertains, amazes, and adds wonder to the story, whether that's dinosaurs in your kitchen or a car blowing up downtown. In other words, special effects can't just happen immediately in front of the camera without proper preparation and skill.

Special effects are kind of like the masterful illusions of a magician on stage that leave the audience in awe. A magician creates effects that defy the world of reality. You can do the same thing with the magic of film — with special effects on set through the camera, or in postproduction, you're able to fool your audience by making something look like it really happened!

Special effects can be created in several ways:

✔ **In the camera:** By using lenses and filters or by controlling exposure (see Chapter 10).

✔ **On the set:** This can include explosions, fire, and gunshots. Levitation and superhuman leaps can also be created on-set with wires attached to your actors (like Spider-Man leaping from building to building); the wires are removed (erased) in postproduction. You can also use *matte paintings* (elements painted on glass in front of the camera) or front and back projection of locations onto a large reflective screen behind your actors.

✔ **With make-up:** This can include horror make-up, latex appliances to the face, and special teeth and contact lenses. Full-body costumes, such as a gorilla suit or the creature costume in *Alien* also fall under this category.

✔ **In postproduction:** Using *opticals* (adding images together in the film lab) or compositing images together using blue or green screen. Also CGI (computer-generated images) are very popular (and much more affordable nowadays) for generating special effects and creating images during the postproduction phase.

Generating computer effects

Almost every film you see nowadays has at least some computer-generated effects — even if you don't notice them. *A Beautiful Mind* has seamless digital effects, such as the seasons that magically change right before the audience's eyes while John Nash (Russell Crowe) sits by his window working on his thesis. Another invisible computer effect is the scene of Nash's baby in the bathtub with water filling up over his head — the water was created in the computer. Then you have films like *Men in Black* that have hundreds of computer-generated effects created in postproduction, after the main photography of the film has been shot. These amazing illusions can be created entirely on a desktop computer.

Adobe makes a software program called After Effects that can be used with non-linear editing systems (see more on non-linear editing in Chapter 16) to create many amazing effects. If you're familiar with Adobe's Photoshop, which lets you manipulate photos and images, then imagine After Effects as Photoshop in motion. You can take a still image of a truck, animate the wheels, add suspension in the cab, and create a moving image on film or tape. For more information, go to www.adobe.com. Studio Artist from Synthetik lets you *morph* (transform one image into another, like the antagonist in *Terminator II* or Dr. Banner in *The Hulk*) and do *rotoscoping* (turning your live-action actors into the line drawings often seen in commercials and music videos). To get more information on Studio Artist, go to www.synthetik.com.

Using and Creating Backgrounds

Often on an independent budget you can't afford to travel to a distant location to be used as a backdrop for your film, or the location only exists in your mind (like a desert planet with three moons and a pink horizon). There are techniques to placing your actors into backgrounds that have either been filmed separately (without any actors in the shot) or creating backgrounds completely in the world of the computer. This is known as compositing, where several elements shot at separate times can be combined to look like they were shot together and are part of the same shot (not several other shots).

Turning blue and green

John Fulton was one of the first effects creators to use what today is known as the *traveling matte* using *blue screen* (*green screen* is popular now, too). Fulton designed the effects for *The Invisible Man* in 1933 (an updated version, *Memoirs of an Invisible Man,* in 1992, starring Chevy Chase, used the same blue-screen techniques over have a half-century later). George Lucas uses blue screen in his *Star Wars* epics to blend his live-action actors into wondrous sci-fi fantasy locales from his imagination.

In the blue-screen process, the actor does the scene in front of a blue (or green) background, which is later replaced with a picture, painting, or computer-generated background (also known as a *background* plate — see the following section on plates). Imagine taking a pair of magic scissors and cutting away everything that's blue or green. You end up with what looks like a cardboard cutout of your actor that is then placed in front of a background. Your actor looks like she's really there and not in front of a screen at all. Green is used a lot now for the screen color, because that particular hue is not a common color that your actors would be wearing. Black is not used in this process because then an actor's pupils, black clothing, or dark hair would disappear.

Figure 17-1 shows the prehistoric pig, Jurassic Pork, generated on the computer. The second image is me in *Miss Cast Away* against a blue screen (even though it's a black-and-white photo, I swear it was blue). When the two images are merged together, you have what is called a *composite* with the action hero and the dinosaur in the same shot together.

You don't have to use a professional blue or green screen — you can just use a plain-colored bed sheet, as long as you don't have that same color in your subject's clothing or hair coloring. Then in postproduction, you remove the screen or sheet color and bring in your background plate to merge the elements together. If you want to purchase an effective and inexpensive blue or green screen (like the one I used in the composite shot in Figure 17-1), Photoflex makes one called Flexdrop that pops open to a 5-x-7-foot blue and green screen (it's double-sided). It's a great deal at $140 and is light and portable so you can take it to the set or stage. Check out the Photoflex Web site at www.photoflex.com.

Dishing out special-effects plates

You can't eat off these special-effects plates. I'm referring instead to a background *plate* — a still photo or a motion picture shot of a particular location. This still photo or moving footage is then inserted in postproduction behind an actor or characters who performed the scene in front of a blue or green screen. Plates are usually shot before the main photography of your film so you know how to line up your actors so that they blend into the plate photos.

Digital cameras are great for taking high-quality pristine photos of locations for background plates. I use the Kyocera Finecam S4 digital still camera (www.kyocera.com). It's a 4-pixel camera, meaning that you can enlarge the photos without losing detail. Most digital still cameras range from 2 pixels to 4 pixels.

Computer generated
Jurassic Pork

Hero Adventurer against
blue screen

Figure 17-1:
The author
in a com-
posite shot
created
from two
images.

Final composite of images blended together

© Zandoria Studios/William Sutton
© Concept by Bryan Michael Stoller 2003

Matte paintings: Painting scenery into your shots

Instead of constructing or destroying real cities, buildings, and other backgrounds, you can paint them! In the *Wizard of Oz,* the famous Emerald City
is actually a *matte painting.* The grass and field of flowers in the foreground
are part of a real set, but the background with the Emerald Castle and sky is
painted on glass. A matte painting can actually be in front of the camera, the
painted image can be positioned so that the glass is not seen on camera, and
the painting on glass looks to be part of the actual shot. A matte painting can
also be photographed in postproduction and merged with previous scenes
already shot.

JARGON ALERT

Composing a composite

You can combine several different special effects, such as matte painting, blue screen, and background plates, by *layering* them upon each other. It's like laying clear plastic sheets on top of each other, but each one has a different element that complements the previous plastic sheet and its element. After all the elements are blended together, you have a *composite*. Primatte Keyer is a unique software program (that also includes Composite Wizard and Image Lounge) that lets you make seamless composites (check out www.redgiantsoftware.com for more information).

The Gotham City skyline featured in *Batman* also utilized matte paintings. And the film *Earthquake* used matte paintings to simulate earthquake damage to the high-rise buildings by placing paintings over the existing exteriors to simulate gaps, caved-in walls, broken windows, and partially collapsed buildings.

Have you scene scenic backdrops?

Almost every television show or film uses billboard-sized scenic backdrops that either are blown up from an actual location photograph or are painted onto a light, durable material like vinyl and positioned behind the actors on the set. Scenic backdrops are different from matte paintings that are positioned in front of the actors, close to the camera lens — but not blocking the actors in the background, or matte paintings added in postproduction. Scenic backdrops are often seen through the windows on stage sets. Or the high-rise building with the huge picture windows and the beautiful city skyline could be a scenic backdrop. An example of a city backdrop at night is the one seen every weeknight behind David Letterman's desk on *The Late Show*. Scenic backdrops are sometimes translucent so they can be backlit to give the image vibrancy. Backdrops save time and money in the long run because they're cheaper than actually going to Paris when you can use a scenic backdrop (in a warehouse in your hometown) of the Eiffel Tower outside the restaurant set window.

Scenic backdrops can also be projected from behind or from the front onto a reflected screen behind the actor that accepts a deep sharp image from the projector. This can be cheaper to do because you don't have to find a life-size backdrop. The projected image can be from a 1-Inch slide or transparency. With the advancements in computer effects, however, most productions (that have the budget and computer equipment and software) prefer to create the backdrop in the computer instead of using front or back projection.

Using a touch of glass

You can position a painting, miniature, or photograph on a piece of glass in front of the camera to create the appearance of that element being an actual part of the shot. Glass, if lighted properly, is invisible to the camera, so the audience won't see the glass. Remember that you see in three-dimensions, but the camera has only one eye and sees in two dimensions (a flat surface) only. A photograph or painting has the illusion of looking three-dimensional through the camera's single lens, therefore it appears to be part of the actual shot.

Cutting up your magazines

You don't have to be an artist to insert amazing features into ordinary shots. Go through your magazines and cut out images that would work in your shots. For example, if you have an actor venturing across the world who comes upon a beautiful castle, find a photograph of a castle in a magazine and cut it out (don't venture across the world, unless you really want to for this shot). If you need to enlarge it, go to the color-copy place or scan it into your computer. Then stick the image on a piece of clear glass or mount it on cardboard, stand it up between the camera and your actor, and frame it appropriately in the shot. In Figure 17-2, you see a magazine picture placed on glass and incorporated into an actual location with the actor. The princess is standing 20 feet *behind* the camera and slightly to the left of the castle cutout. If the princess were to move closer to the castle, she would end up behind the cutout.

Weathering the storm

Weather is considered a special effect in film because you have to imitate Mother Nature (she doesn't storm on command). Many screenwriters don't think twice about starting a scene with, "It was a dark and stormy night." But unless you want to sit and wait for it to really rain, you have to create the storm yourself, and it's not cheap. Same with wind and snow. So unless it's crucial to the scene, leave it out.

Creating snow or rain outside a window for an indoor scene is a much easier effect to accomplish. Rain is as simple as having someone outside spraying a regular garden hose above the window — the water will fall and look like raindrops against the pane (just don't forget to close the window!). Rain is also easier to see if it's backlit. For snow, you can find various substances like laundry detergent and have someone above the window (on a stepladder)

sprinkling the dry soap flakes evenly from above. From inside, it looks like silent snowflakes are falling. Just make sure you don't mix your soap snowflakes with your garden hose rain — you'll have an outdoor bubble bath flooding the neighborhood!

Figure 17-2: Magazine picture on glass.

Making Use of Miniatures

Many amazing effects have been achieved on film using *miniatures* (which are relatively small, and usually built to scale). The film *Earthquake* had miniature towns, cities, and landscapes built so they could be destroyed easily on film. Steven Spielberg used a myriad of miniature sets in his film *1941*. (If you saw that film, do you remember the scene of the Ferris wheel breaking off its axis and rolling down the Santa Monica Pier into the ocean? That was a miniature built to scale. It would have been too expensive, too dangerous, and nearly impossible to do that with the real thing — plus, I think I was on that ride a few years ago.) Spielberg also used miniatures combined with actor close-ups when Elliot and his friends steered their flying bicycles across the sky above their neighborhood in *E.T. The Extraterrestrial*. He also used stop-motion animated models (see Chapter 2) in his *Indiana Jones* sequel during the coal-mining cart chase.

Shooting miniatures

You need to keep several things in mind when shooting models and miniatures:

- ✔ **Use pinpoint lighting (because you're lighting small objects) when filming indoor miniatures.** For exterior miniatures, such as towns, landscapes, and roads, build the miniature set outside and take advantage of the real sunlight, as well as the real sky and clouds.

- ✔ **Keep the camera on level with the miniatures, as if you and your camera are to scale with your miniature.** Only shoot higher if you're simulating a shot from a helicopter or tall building.

- ✔ **If you're using miniature vehicles, water, or anything with movement, slow down the action so that the miniature doesn't move unrealistically.** If the miniature is half the size of the real object, you slow the film down by half. This means that you shoot at 48 frames per second, which is twice the speed of the normal 24 frames per second (thus, compacting double the frames in the same amount of time, which creates the illusion of slow motion). By speeding up the frame rate, you're slowing down the real-time action when it's played back at the regular 24 frames per second. If your miniature is one-quarter the size of the real thing, slow it down by four times the actual speed — get the idea?

  Speeding up the camera to get slow-motion sounds like a contradiction, but don't be confused. If a film camera is sped up and shoots 120 pictures (frames) a second, it will play the action back as slow motion because the projector is playing back at a constant speed of 24 frames per second. It will, therefore, take the projector about six seconds to show the action that took place in that one second — thus, creating slow-motion effect.

  Keep in mind that the larger in scale your miniature is, the more realistic it will look, and the lesser chance your audience will think it's a miniature.

Forcing the perspective, forcefully

If you stand at the end of a long road and look off into the distant horizon (which I don't recommend, especially if it's a busy highway), the road will appear to narrow as it reaches the horizon. With miniatures, you want to create this effect without the distance. This concept is called *forced perspective*. If you want to build a miniature road, for example, you cut out a long triangle instead of a long even strip of road. Position the triangle on the ground and put the camera at the widest end of the triangle. The point of the triangle will look like the road is going off into the distance (see Figure 17-3).

Wired for special effects

Wires are a great way to have your actors achieve superhuman feats. Wires were utilized in all the *Superman* films to make it look like he was flying. Harry Potter flew successfully on his Nimbus 2000 with the help of wires. *Crouching Tiger, Hidden Dragon* assisted its actors in leaping higher, running along rooftops, and shooting through the trees with the help of wires that were erased during postproduction. Keanu Reeves in

The Matrix performed some anti-gravity acrobats with the skilled work of wires. Tobey Maguire would have been grounded, if it weren't for the application of wire work in his film *Spider-Man*. You can erase the wires from the footage either by having a computer artist simply erase them or by using blue or green wires that can be removed when the image of the actor and the background plate are composited together (like the blue-screen process).

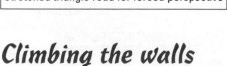

Figure 17-3: A miniature road.

Stretched triangle road for forced perspective

Climbing the walls

In my teenage days, I made a short film called *Superham*. In it I had a scene of a Spiderman-type character climbing what appeared to be the side of a brick building. The effect cost me all of $3. I bought a plastic sheet pressed with miniature bricks at the local hobby store. To defy the laws of gravity, I turned the miniature brick wall sideways, lining the edge up with the top of a short concrete wall 20 feet behind the miniature wall and had my actor crawl across the top of the short wall in the background. I turned the camera sideways, so it looked like my actor was crawling up the brick wall — and of course the miniature bricks turned sideways closer to the camera helped to complete the illusion (see Figure 17-4). The original *Batman* TV series utilized this simple technique in every episode where the caped crusader used his bat rope to climb to the top of a building (and his cape was held up by a wire).

Storyboard your special effects so that the entire production team can see exactly what the effect is. See more on storyboarding in Chapter 9.

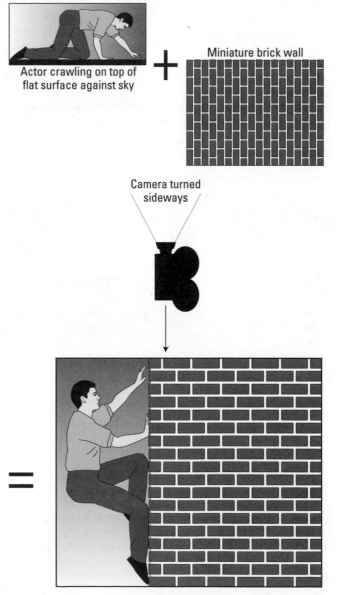

Figure 17-4:
An actor "climbing" a wall.

Creating Effects Right in the Camera

Many of today's digital cameras have built-in effects such as fade-in and fade-out, *wipes* (which "wipes" the image to black with a sliding black shape), mosaics, and negative black-and-white images.

Many of these effects work great as transitions (smoother cuts) between scenes, such as the wipe (which you can also create by sliding a piece of cardboard across the lens). When shooting with film, the film lab often creates these effects for you, which are referred to as *optical effects.* Another simple transition is having an actor walk toward the lens until he covers it completely. I once did a film where I had the actor throw his laundry over the lens, causing the scene to go black.

Another effect you can do with the camera is to use a *beam splitter,* which is a half-mirrored piece of glass between the camera and your subject. The glass is positioned at a 45-degree angle to reflect an image that's off-camera into the glass that the camera is shooting through. The half-mirror is invisible to the camera except for the image it's reflecting into the glass. This makes your actor appear in the original shot as a transparent ghost.

Backward about reverse photography

Reverse photography can be as obvious as somebody having a meal backward (you film him or her normally and then just reverse the film) — it can get a hilarious (or gross) response from your audience. Or you can be more subtle and create an effect that doesn't immediately appear as if the footage were reversed.

I was shooting a commercial in which a superhero emerged from a phone booth and, like Superman, leaped up into the sky. It was a simple effect. My actor stood on top of the phone booth (remember phone booths?), and the camera only framed to just below the top of the booth. The actor then jumped off the top, entering frame, and then straightened up and walked backward into the phone booth. I simply reversed the footage and it appeared as if he walked out of the phone booth and leapt straight up into the air.

In the opening credits of *Austin Powers: The Spy Who Shagged Me,* Austin Powers emerges from an outdoor swimming pool after a synchronized Busby Berkeley–type water folly and rises up into the air — with his hair and clothes completely dry. This was achieved by lowering him into the water, and then simply reversing the footage.

Split diopter lens

One of my favorite special-effect lenses is the split diopter, which Orson Welles used for many of his scenes in *Citizen Kane* to keep both the foreground and background images in perfect focus. When filming at night or indoors, keeping everything in focus is hard. It's like being near-sighted, and not seeing things at a distance — or being farsighted and not seeing things close up. A split diopter lens is exactly what it sounds like: It splits up the picture so that a distant object on one side of the frame and a close-up object on the other side can both be in focus in the same shot. It's kind of like a bifocal lens turned sideways.

I used a split diopter on a comedy short I did called *Monkey USA* where I spoofed *King Kong*. I had an actor sitting in a giant King Kong hand (rented from a studio), which was 30 feet away from the camera on one side of the frame. On the other side of the frame, I had an actor in an ape suit stand about 2 feet away from the camera. Both sides of the frame remained in focus and created the illusion that the giant King Kong hand wrapped around the actor was connected to the gorilla head (see the following figure).

Double exposure, double exposure

A *double exposure* puts two different pictures or scenes together at the same time, and runs them parallel to each other. You create a double exposure on film during postproduction in the film lab, or with software on a non-linear editing system. The difference between a double exposure and a true blue or green screen (see the "Turning blue and green" section earlier in this chapter) is that the double exposure causes the person to look transparent and not a solid part of the scene that it is double-exposed against.

Speeding slowly

Undercranking and *overcranking* refer to manipulating the speed of a camera. You can usually change speed on a motion-picture film camera by adjusting the camera itself. To change the speed of a digital video camera, you have to change the speed during the editing postproduction phase.

You can create interesting effects by controlling the speed of the film running through the camera or changing the speed during the editing postproduction phase:

- ✔ *Overcranking,* **or speeding up film, creates the illusion of slow motion.** The faster the film runs through the camera, the slower the motion will be. Running the film through the camera quickly gives you more individual frames to play back at regular speed — creating the illusion of slow motion. Overcranking the camera is also a necessity when you're filming miniatures in slow motion, as I mention in the section on miniatures earlier in this chapter.

- ✔ *Undercranking,* **or slowing down film, speeds up the action in your scene.** Car chases are often undercranked slightly to make cars appear as if they are traveling dangerously fast. *Undercranking* also refers to clicking frame by frame, similar to stop-motion animation (see Chapter 2). Because the frames end up missing some of the actual action, the actor or vehicle on camera appears animated or sped up.

- ✔ **Using time-lapse photography captures motion often imperceptible at real-time speeds.** An *intervalometer* is a timer (either attached to or a part of the camera) that can be set to click a frame at specific intervals, such as every second or every 24 hours. You've seen this effect with flowers blooming, clouds twirling through the sky, and buildings being constructed in a matter of seconds.

Using lenses and filters to create effects

Special lenses and filters that you screw onto your camera or use in a matte box (see Chapter 10) can alter or create a special element that you couldn't achieve using a normal lens.

The difference between a lens and a filter is that a lens changes the shape of the picture in some way (such as distortion with a super-wide-angle lens — see Chapter 10). A filter usually plays with the color, exposure, or glare coming into the camera.

Special-effect filters change colors in unique ways (these aren't the color-correcting filters that I talk about in Chapter 10). For example, if the bottom part of the lens or filter is blue and the top part is yellow, the ground will appear blue and the sky yellow. Tiffen, one of the top developers and manufacturers of lenses and filters, makes a variety of these effects. Check out www.tiffen.com. Here's a list of common special-effect filters and lenses and what they do:

- ✔ **Star:** Makes reflective objects in the picture twinkle
- ✔ **Fog:** Creates a soft fog effect in the scene
- ✔ **Prism:** Creates multiple images of objects or actors in the frame
- ✔ **Split diopter lens:** Divided lens that can focus on near and far objects at the same time in the same shot
- ✔ **Gradual:** Changes the color of the sky or the upper part of the frame only

Explaining Explosions and Fire

A lot of special effects look dangerous on film, but are harmless effects created in the mind of the filmmaker. Explosions, fire, and guns, on the other hand, can be very dangerous.

Never attempt any fire effects or explosions on your own. Always enlist the skills of a qualified pyrotechnician. You're also required to have a firefighter on set to make sure that everyone remains safe.

A *pyrotechnician* is trained to work with elements that could be extremely dangerous on your set. Creating explosions and fires and using ammunition are some of the skills a pyrotechnician has been trained for.

You can add fire later with a computer or superimposed by overlapping several images. Or you can actually set a fire in a controlled environment. *Backdraft,* Ron Howard's firefighting film, used many controlled situations to simulate the danger of fire. This was done with a firefighter supervising on set along with a skilled pyrotechnician.

At Halloween time, you'll see fog machines in almost every novelty store. They're small vaporizer-type devices that heat up and expel a harmless smoke-like steam into the air — similar to dry ice but much simpler and safer to use. They cost between $35 and $100, depending on the size of the machine. You can buy fog juice that heats up in the device, causing the juice to turn into fog that can be controlled to shoot out a nozzle in small or large bursts. Great for shooting a foggy night scene or smoking up a bar. Do you remember the flashlight beams cutting through the misty forest in *E.T.?* Fog machines were used to catch the rays of light and enhance the mood of the scene.

Making Up Your Mind about Make-Up

Special effects aren't just limited to illusions that look real only through the camera lens or after the postproduction stage. Make-up is make-believe that can walk and talk without the magic of the camera but through the magic of talented make-up artists. Many people think of beauty makeovers when they think of make-up artists. You don't normally think of monsters, alien creatures, and flesh — but the world of the make-up artist is a broad one.

Procedure of prosthetics

Prosthetics is a term associated with artificial limbs. In the world of special effects make-up, however, *prostheses* are used to create additional limbs, burn victims, and monster effects (all the sick, gross stuff). Prosthetic pieces, also called *appliances,* are usually made of foam latex, which can move much like human skin and muscles. Make-up effects artist David Miller designed the conehead makeup for Dan Aykroyd and the entire Conehead population in the film *Coneheads.* It took Miller and his team several hours to apply the conehead make-up to Aykroyd, painstakingly blending the edges seamlessly into Aykroyd's real forehead. Miller also designed Freddy Krueger's make-up for the *Nightmare on Elm Street* films. Miller was working late one night trying to decide on the look of Freddy Krueger and glanced down at his melted cheese pizza — inspiration hit!

You can also do mechanical make-up effects, like a head-cast made from an actor with features added to a fake head. I made a cameo appearance as a werewolf in one of my short films several years ago. My sister Marlene, a professional make-up artist, and make-up artist Jack Bricker took a cast of my head by pouring plaster over my face, leaving straws in my nostrils so I could breath (that was the only time in my life that I've ever been plastered). When the plaster dried, they used the mold to design the werewolf head in latex and added hair and an extended muzzle to the *dummy head* (now you know why I'm the one writing this *For Dummies* book). To save money, they only made a half-head because the final shot was a profile, and the camera would never see the other side (see Figure 17-5).

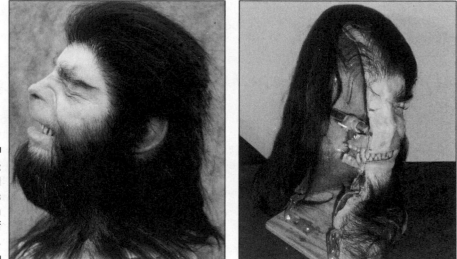

Figure 17-5:
Front and profile shots of a foam werewolf head.

Here's looking at scleral lenses

Remember Michael Jackson in *Thriller?* Jim Carrey in *The Mask? The Incredible Hulk?* The apes in *Planet of the Apes?* Or Linda Blair in *The Exorcist?* They all had weird eyes. These eyes are achieved by special contact lenses, called *scleral lenses,* which have funky pupil designs and are fitted to cover the actor's eyes like conventional contact lenses.

You should purchase scleral lenses from an optometrist or from eyewear specialists like Dr. Morton Greenspoon and Dr. Richard Silver (www.provisioncare.com), who have designed and provided special scleral lenses for many Hollywood blockbusters (including *The Grinch* and *Men in Black*). Although specialty stores, especially during Halloween, carry designer effects lenses, you don't know if they're made by a reputable company, and the lenses aren't fitted to your particular eye shape. You don't want to take a chance by putting just anything in your eyes.

Linda Blair wore scleral contact lenses for *The Exorcist* and then again when I revisited her possessed state in the comedy spoof *The Linda Blair Witch Project* (see Figure 17-6), where Linda finds out she's possessed by famous comedians (did you know that possession is nine-tenths of the law?). You can stream my short on Steven Spielberg and Ron Howard's Counting Down Web site at `www.countingdown.com/theater/short_films/detail/316272`.

Take a bite out of this

Another skill of the special-effect make-up artist is designing and creating teeth that fit over the actor's own bite. A mold is taken of the actor's real teeth — very similar to how a dentist takes a mold to fit you for a crown. The artist then sculpts a new set of molars — from ghoulish monster or vampire teeth to rotten buck teeth like Austin Powers. Refer to the right-hand image in Figure 17-6 for an example of vampire teeth that fit over the actor's own incisors.

Figure 17-6:
An example of scleral lenses and vampire teeth.

Chapter 18

Giving Credit and Titles

● ●

In This Chapter

▶ Giving credit where credit is due

▶ Designing titles and credits to fit your film

▶ Creating inexpensive, effective titles

▶ Preparing film for foreign release

● ●

*C*redits (a person's name with his or her position) are important to your cast and crew because everyone likes to be recognized for their hard work, and people who work on films are no exception. Receiving credit on a film gives your cast and crew members credibility, and can help get them their next job working on another film after yours. In this chapter, you discover impressive ways to give credit to everyone who worked on your film.

Choosing a main title for your film is important, too. It can be compared to deciding what to name a baby — after all, your film *is* your baby. Giving your film the right title can help market your film to the right audience. The name of a film can influence what people perceive it to be about. It can be an intriguing title like *Fatal Attraction,* or an identifiable title to let the audience know exactly who the film is about like *Batman, 101 Dalmatians,* or *The Blues Brothers.* In this chapter, you see how to create inexpensive titles that can be shot right in the camera or hire a title house to design your titles. You also find out how to prepare a textless version of your film before it's sent to foreign distributors — in this chapter, I explain what textless is and how to do it.

A main title and credits can be presented in many creative styles, limited only by your imagination. Start thinking about a unique style that fits your film. An appropriately designed main title and credits can convey the feeling of fun with a free-style font, seriousness with a plain unencumbered font, or wild and crazy with letters that look like they want to break free.

Keeping a Running List of Names and Positions

From the minute you start thinking of making a film, start jotting down the name of every person and company involved in your production. Remembering to place a name in a credit roll in the first place is always much easier (and cheaper) than finding out later that you forgot someone and having to deal with the consequences.

Spelling it write

Make sure every name in your opening credits and ending credits is spelled correctly. Years ago I made a short film spoofing *Friday the 13th* where Jason joins a hockey team. My composer Alan Fleishman wrote a fantastic orchestral score, and I was really proud of how the music came out. Alan is also a very good friend, and when the film premiered to a large audience, Alan pointed out to me that his name was spelled wrong. I felt terrible. Well, now I have a chance to make it up to him. Here's the correct spelling: Alan Fleishman. (I'm proofreading this chapter before it goes to press, just in case.)

Spelling names incorrectly is easy to do. Many names sound the same but have different spellings — always check and double-check. Here are just a few examples:

- ✔ Geoffrey and Jeffrey
- ✔ Susan and Suzanne
- ✔ Steffanie and Stephanie
- ✔ Brian and Bryan
- ✔ Terry and Teri
- ✔ John and Jon

Get the idea? Be extra sensitive when it comes to a person's name.

Entitled to a credit

For every favor, product deal, or donation you get, you need to thank these people and companies in your film's ending credits. It's cheap to use up a line — it could cost you relationships and friendships if you forget. People and companies like to see their name up on the big screen, and recognizing them in this way shows your appreciation of their contribution to your film (they may contribute to your next one, too!). So credit — don't forget it!

Designing Your Titles and Credits

When you decorate your house or apartment, you pick a style. You should do the same when you design your opening title and credits. If it's a murder mystery, you don't use cartoon lettering in your opening credits. For example, in my film *Undercover Angel,* my lead character, Harrison, is a struggling book writer. I chose the Courier font, which looks like it came from a typewriter, for the opening credits of the film. It worked especially well because the film starts off with Harrison at his typewriter shortly after the opening credits end.

Often, an audience doesn't pay too much attention to the fonts of your title and credits, but they do have a subliminal effect on the viewer. In Michael Jackson's *Thriller,* the title looked like it was scratched in blood — definitely creating a mood. The opening credits to *Spider-Man* were caught in an animated web. Next time you go to the movies or watch a video, notice the stylish fonts used in the title and opening credits; you'll be surprised how different and creative they are.

Digital Juice makes a line of colorful and effective animated backgrounds called Jump Backs, which add a professional flair to your video or film title and credits. You've probably seen these backgrounds on many TV shows with credits and titles superimposed over them. Instead of setting your title and credits on plain black, you can have them pop and breathe with life, accentuated with lively Jump Backs as your background. Twenty volumes are available, which add up to more than 800 backgrounds. Each animated background is 15 to 30 seconds in length and can be seamlessly looped to go on forever. Digital Juice also makes a series of nine DVDs called the Editor's Tool Kit, which includes animated backgrounds, *lower thirds* (for adding names and titles anywhere on the screen), and 50 font types to superimpose over your images. Checkout www.digitaljuice.com for more details and to request a free demo.

I've used a company called VT2 Media Design and Communications (www.vt-tv.com) of Texas, which has designed and created opening titles and credits for some of my films, including the animated logo for one of my projects with Michael Jackson. It usually designs storyboard panels illustrating how the titles and credits will look in the final frames of the finished film.

Setting the style with fonts

You can choose from thousands of different font styles to make up your title and credits. You've probably got a few hundred on your computer right now. Each font has a feeling and sets a mood. Take a look at some different font styles in Figure 18-1.

Figure 18-1:
The font
style you
choose for
your film
credits
creates a
mood for the
audience.

You can find some great font software at Web sites like www.fonts.com and www.broderbund.com (click on "ClickArt"). Broderbund offers its ClickArt Fonts 2 package (with over 10,000 different font styles) for only $19.99.

Animating your main title and credits

Animation adds life and character to your opening and ending title and credits. *The Pink Panther* films were popular for their amusing animation credits and helped spawn the *Pink Panther* animated cartoon series. Steven Spielberg utilized a stylized cartoon opening for his film *Catch Me If You Can*. Although a full-length animated film is expensive to produce, a few minutes of animation for opening title and credits is usually affordable enough (especially if you utilize stop-motion or cut-out animation — see Chapter 2). Spending your money on animation at the beginning of your film rather than the ending is better because most people leave as the end credits begin to roll anyway.

The Animation Factory provides a fun angle on presenting your titles and credits. On its Web site www.animationfactory.com, you have a choice of over 150,000 cycled animations, including high-resolution video clips that can be incorporated into a Web site announcing your production or used in the opening or ending credits of your film. It has every themed animated image imaginable. For a small annual fee starting at $59.95, you can access the entire library of animations. It's a really fun site — check it out.

Electronic or optical credits

If you're shooting on video, you can design your credits right on your computer and transfer them to your video footage. These are called *electronic credits*. Most new computers today have a video card or can have one installed that allows you to input and output video.

Optical credits are done at a title company that specializes in designing and photographing titles and credits. They are then printed to film and *superimposed optically* (placed over the appropriate scenes by the film lab) over the opening or ending footage of your film. They can also be printed as white letters on a black background, which is often the way ending roll credits are presented.

Hollywood has many title houses, including one actually called Title House, that can do your opening titles and ending credits. It's done many of the titles and graphics you've seen on the big screen. Check out its credits and information at www.titlehouse.com. You don't have to live in Los Angeles to hire a title company like Title House. You can e-mail and fax all the information, and it can shoot your titles and ship them directly to you. Many title companies are eager to help independent filmmakers.

Most title companies can convert Microsoft Word or WordPerfect files containing your titles and credits, and selected font styles, and print or *telecine* them (electronically place them into your film using a video editing bay) into your finished film or video production.

When working with a professional title house, you'll always be sent a sample of the copy to proofread. Be sure to read closely — overlooking the obvious is all too easy.

Crediting without a computer

If you don't have a computer to create your own title and credits and you can't afford to hire a title company, you still have hope.

Go to your stationery or art-supply store and pick up some lettering stencils or vinyl stick-on letters by Letraset or Formatt. You can even get three-dimensional letters from an art-supply or toy store.

If your film is a beach film, write your title and opening credits in the sand and let the tide come in and wash them away. If it's a college or high school film, write your title and credits on a blackboard with chalk.

I did a stop-motion animated film many years ago that retold the story of the Frog Prince. My ending credits looked like they were at the bottom of a pond that rippled between credits. Here's what I did: I placed my credits on a card and took a clear dish and filled it with water. I shot through the water in the dish with my camera and jiggled the water in between credits. The credits looked like they were under water! You've also probably seen many films use the turning pages of a book for the opening credits — it's easy to do, and it never gets old.

Rolling Your Title and Credits

After your film is completed and you've assembled all the elements for your main title and credits, you need to concentrate on the timing, order, and legibility of those credits.

Titles and credits bookend a film, clearly identifying the beginning and "The End" of a film. The opening title and credits begin before the film gets into the meat of the story. The ending credits roll when the film has come to a satisfactory conclusion (at least that's what you hope for!).

If you make your ending credits interesting, you may be able to keep the audience in their seats. Most people get up and leave the theater (or head to the kitchen or bathroom if they're watching on TV), but you can do some of the following to keep them glued to their seats:

✔ Have some type of animation or movement to the ending credits.

✔ Intercut scenes from the film in between the credits.

✔ Stop the credits to feature funny *bloopers* (flubs or mistakes) from the film (like *Monsters, Inc., Toy Story,* and *Rush Hour* have done).

Timing the opening and ending credits

The best way to organize and time your title and credits is to storyboard the opening of your film (see Chapter 9 for more on storyboarding). This allows you to pace your opening credits to the visuals of your film's opening scenes. If you have your title and credits over black (that is, without scenes from the film running in the background), you don't have to worry about storyboarding them.

Keep in mind, when timing your ending credits, that you don't want them to roll by too fast or too slow. They should be slow enough to read, but not so slow that you put your audience to sleep.

Non-contractual credits

If you make up an advertising poster for your film before the film has been shot and before the actor contracts are signed, you want to be aware of the disclaimer *non-contractual credits.* You can put actors' names on the posters (a good idea if some recognizable names are considering roles), but the words, "credits are non-contractual" must be on the poster. This means that you have not contracted the actors to be in your film (but they have given you verbal permission to put their names on the poster), and their names are only appearing on your poster in good faith. This protects you if a distributor demands that you use the actors listed on your poster, or if you have to replace an actor featured on the poster. Put the words "credits are non-contractual" at the bottom-right corner of your poster in very small lettering — just like the fine print the attorney doesn't want you to notice in a contract.

Ordering your title and credits

The order of opening credits has no real norm, except that usually a big-name star's credit is one of the first to appear (after the distributor logo). The last credit to appear is usually the director's credit. But in between, a myriad of variations exists. Here's one example of a typical opening-credit order:

- Distributor logo
- Production company presents
- The director or production company's possessory credit ("A film by . . .")
- Title of the film
- Starring cast
- Casting by
- Executive producer
- Producer
- Co-producer(s)
- Music by
- Costumes designed by (usually reserved for period pieces or wardrobe-heavy films)
- Visual effects designed by (if a heavy visual effects film)
- Production designer
- Edited by
- Screenplay by
- Directed by

If you're making an independent film, chances are you may be a triple-threat, meaning your credit will read, "Written, Produced, and Directed by. . . ."

If you are a triple threat, you may be possessed by the possessory credit. I directed Linda Blair in a spoof I wrote called *The Linda Blair Witch Project* (the film spoofed *The Exorcist* and *The Blair Witch Project*). Not only was Linda Blair possessed in this parody, she also found out it was hereditary. Actually, a possessory credit has nothing to do with being possessed. It's a possessive ownership (auteur) credit that usually belongs to the director of the film, such as "A Steven Spielberg Film." Sometimes it's not a director or individual, but a production company, for example, "A Northstar Production."

Ensuring the safety of your credits

One very common mistake that even the professionals make from time to time is forgetting to check for *title safety*. Everyone's TV set shows a different image size in terms of the edges of a picture. Most of the time you never know that the edges of the picture are cut off, except when there are titles or credits. A universal safety zone was established to protect titles and credits from being cut off within the frame. Figure 18-2 illustrates the space you need to place around your credits before they fall off the screen, so that they remain legible. These safety lines are usually visible through the eyepiece in motion-picture film cameras. Television sets have slightly different viewing areas at the edges, so always allow an invisible border around your titles and credits to ensure they're safe.

Television Film Safe Areas

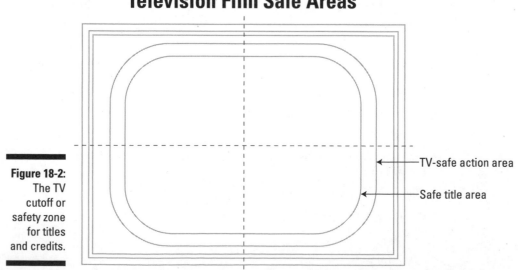

Figure 18-2:
The TV cutoff or safety zone for titles and credits.

TV-safe action area

Safe title area

Subject to subtitles

Subtitles are usually reserved for foreign films coming into the English-language market. The English translation appears in the lower part of the screen as the actors speak in their foreign tongue. This is similar to turning on the closed-caption feature on your TV, which amounts to English subtitles in English-speaking films so that the hearing impaired can follow the dialogue.

Chances are you're not going to use subtitles in your film, unless you're doing it for comedy purposes or an alien or a person speaks a foreign language among English-speaking characters (like the natives in *Raiders of the Lost Ark*). Most American films are not subtitled overseas; instead the voices are usually replaced by voiceover actors speaking in their own language (see Chapter 19).

Make sure your credits are big enough to read if your film is broadcast on TV. This was a problem of many of the films I made as a kid. My mom always reminded me to make the lettering legible. To this day I stop to remember her advice — so now my credits are always legible on any size screen.

Covering Your Eyes: Stripping Titles for Foreign Textless

Textless opening and ending footage is simply the footage from your film before you add the title and credits over the picture. When your film goes to the foreign markets, your cast and crew names remain the same, but the names of each position and your main title are translated into another language.

After your film is completed, the lab or video operator makes a *textless* copy of your opening and ending credits footage. It's exactly your opening and ending film footage, but without any titles or credits over the picture (they are removed). When the foreign distributor receives your film, it places the translated title and credits over the picture. Voilà!

Part V
Finding a Distributor for Your Film

The 5th Wave   By Rich Tennant

"You know that 'buzz' I said our film created here at the festival? Short in the theatre's sound system."

In this part . . .

This is one of the most important parts of this book because, without distribution, the world will never see the masterpiece you worked so hard on. Distribution is getting your film into theatres, onto video cassettes and DVDs, and into video stores, as well as airing on TV screens all across the globe. With the right distributor, this is all possible.

Film festivals are another avenue for getting your film out in the public eye. You can gain some great recognition as a filmmaker and maybe even win some well-deserved accolades for your creative cinematic endeavors. Film festivals are also a great way for distributors and potential buyers to discover you and your film, and this part gives you the lowdown.

Chapter 19

Distributing Your Film

. . . .

In This Chapter

▶ Defining distribution

▶ Finding a distributor

▶ Distributing domestically and overseas

▶ Negotiating a fair distribution contract

. . . .

Distribution is the final stage of the filmmaking process, and it's definitely the most important one. If it isn't distributed, your film will sit on a shelf, and no one will ever see it.

In this chapter, I explain the secrets of film distribution. You find out how media rights for theater, television, and video, as well as ancillary rights for merchandising products inspired by your film, are broken down. You see how a distributor markets a film and what you can do to help. I also offer invaluable tips on what to look for in a distribution contract and help you discover the secrets of negotiating the best distribution deal for your film. You also see the advantages of hiring an attorney who's well versed in distribution agreements.

This chapter provides information about finding a foreign distributor who has relationships with worldwide buyers. I tell you about all the possible markets for your film, what each territory pays, and what to expect for your film. I provide firsthand information about the film markets that can introduce your film to foreign buyers, including Cannes in France, Mifed in Italy, and the American Film Market in Santa Monica, California. And make sure you check out the invaluable lists of the top domestic and foreign distributors.

Understanding How Distribution Works

Distributing a film is similar to selling a product. The product needs to get to the customer, and a distributor puts the two together. The world is your potential customer, with global distribution separated into two divisions: domestic and foreign.

Many times securing a distributor before it can see a finished product is difficult. When you do have a finished film, you send them a screening cassette (covered later in this chapter) for distribution consideration. Finding a foreign distributor first and then concentrating on finding a domestic distributor to cover the United States and Canada is often easier, because there is more demand for product worldwide. (See "Finding a Reliable Distributor," later in this chapter.) Enter your film in the various film festivals (see Chapter 20) and let the distributors track *you* down. You can also hold your own screening and premiere your film to invited distributors.

Including the United States and Canada, more than 65 countries could buy your film. Each country or territory is a potential paying customer. When a territory purchases your film, it sells it to the various TV, video, and theatrical markets within its country — and it has to negotiate a price with your distributor to do so.

When a film is distributed overseas, it usually has to be converted to a different running format that will be compatible with the electrical power currents that are different from those in the United States.

The two standard worldwide formats are NTSC and PAL:

- ✔ **NTSC,** which stands for National Television Standards Committee, is the standard broadcasting format in North America, most of South America, and Japan. It is based on 525 lines of resolution and is equivalent to 30 frames of video per second.

- ✔ **PAL,** which stands for Phase Alternation Line, is the analog television display standard that is the predominant video system used in Europe, Asia, and other parts of the world. PAL transmits 25 frames each second and uses 625 individual scan lines of resolution.

For an NTSC video to be viewable overseas, it has to be transferred to PAL format. Your foreign distributor arranges for the conversion of your film for sale in the overseas territory.

A third option, *streaming* via the Internet, is a universal format that can play footage on virtually any Internet-equipped computer. Streaming is more appropriate for showcasing short films on specialized sites. Steven Spielberg and Ron Howard's CountingDown.com showcases one of my parody shorts called *The Linda Blair Witch Project.* Check it out at `http://countingdown.com/theater/short_films/detail/316272/`.

Presenting Your Film to Distributors

Studio distributors are always on the lookout for little gems to distribute, so creating awareness for your film before and after you shoot it is essential. A film trailer is a great tool to get buyers excited about your film, and designing a poster for your film is the first thing you should think about — even before you start shooting your film.

Post (er)ing your film

An intriguing poster can excite buyers and raise interest in your film. You may be thinking, "Why make a poster? I haven't even made my film yet." But many films are pre-sold by posters that exist way before the film is ever shot. Give your investors (see Chapter 5) or a potential distributor a taste of what's to come.

Adobe PhotoShop (www.adobe.com) is a great software program that you can use to design a poster. Synthetik (www.synthetik.com) makes another great program called Studio Artist that gives you painting and drawing power.

When you make a poster before the film, the credits on the poster are considered *noncontractual*. This means that the people whose names appear in the starring roles and production credits are not officially signed to do the film (but have verbally given you permission) and could change by the time the film is made. Stating this protects you and the people whose names are on the poster from any legal disputes between each other, especially the distributor and/or the buyers.

Even though your poster may help attract a distributor, after you find a distributor the company may want to design its own poster. Your distributor knows what kind of graphics, colors, and images appeal to global buyers. A domestic distributor will usually design a different style poster than what would appeal to foreign buyers through your foreign distributor. Figure 19-1 shows two posters for my film *Undercover Angel* — one for the domestic market and the other for foreign.

Picturing the set photographer

Having someone take professional photos on your set while you're shooting your film is important. These photos will be invaluable when it comes to marketing your film; they're also a mandatory requirement of any distributor. The distributor needs photos showing stills from your film for the promotional flyers. It also uses photos to design your main poster. Don't rely on taking stills off the original footage — the quality isn't very good, and your poster will look cheap and unprofessional.

Figure 19-1:
The *Undercover Angel* domestic and foreign posters are quite different.

Courtesy Sunland Entertainment/PM Entertainment

If you can't afford a professional photographer, get a digital still camera like the Kyocera Finecam (www.kyocera.com) and have someone on your crew with a good eye snap some photos. (Your cinematographer could do this before and after shots.)

Pulling your audience in with a trailer

After you find a distributor and have completed your film, the distributor will want to create a professional film *trailer,* which packs the exciting moments from your film into a commercial. Sometimes a filmmaker will shoot a trailer to try to interest an investor in putting up money to make the actual film. A trailer usually runs one to three minutes in length and features highlights from the film that will spark the interest of buyers.

Premiering your film

Showing your film on the big screen in front of a captive audience is a good way to influence potential distributors (as long as the audience's reaction is positive!). If you live in or near Los Angeles or New York, set up a premiere for domestic and foreign distributors, theatrical distributors, TV stations, and home-video distributors. If you live outside L.A. or New York, you may want to venture there for the big premiere. The main costs associated with setting up a premiere include rental for a theater, and printing and mailing invitations.

If you can't bring buyers to your film, you have to take your film to the buyers. You can get professional-quality dubs of a feature-length film on VHS for less than $5 a tape, including label and video box. Now that DVD copies are coming down in price, you may even be able to send a DVD that has better picture resolution and CD-quality sound (and requires less postage than a VHS tape).

Compelling artwork on your DVD or VHS cover can go a long way toward catching the eye of potential distributors. You can design your own video artwork on your computer or scan a color photo from your film. Buy the plastic video boxes that have a clear plastic sleeve (like school binders) and slip your artwork into the sleeve. Ten or 20 dubs of your film should be enough to send to distributors. For lists of distributors, turn to "The best domestic distributors" and "The best foreign distributors," later in this chapter.

Before you send screening copies of your film, have the dubbing place superimpose a visual disclaimer across the bottom of the picture that says something like "Screening Copy Only." This disclaimer prevents thieves from stealing your film and selling it to television or home video — there's no way to get rid of the visual warning unless you cut off the part of the picture that has the disclaimer.

Distributing Your Film Domestically

Domestic distribution is the licensing of your film to media outlets in the United States and Canada. Domestic usually encompasses Canada as well as the United States because television broadcasts spill over the border, and satellite can be picked up in both the United States and Canada. TV and satellite are part of the media rights for which a distributor negotiates.

Seeing stars

If you can get a name actor in your film, even in a small part, your film will get more attention and help you get financing or a distributor (depending on the actor you get). Casting directors can usually use their relationships with agents, managers, and talent to help you land some stars.

Casting Yasmine Bleeth and James Earl Jones helped get my film *Undercover Angel* off the ground. Having Dan Aykroyd as the voice of Dexter the computer in my film *The Random Factor* helped the film find distribution.

I did self-distribution my way

When I made my first feature film, I was frustrated because I couldn't find a distributor to pick it up. One day I went into my local video store and, for fun, put a copy of my film (in a video box with artwork) on the shelf so I could tell people that my film was in the video store. A week later, I went into the video store, and my video was gone! I asked the clerk, who looked on the computer and told me that it had been rented! It was an exciting feeling to know that someone actually rented my film. About a year later I finally found a distributor, and the company put my film in major video stores — saving me the trouble!

Domestic distribution can account for 50 percent of your film's profits, the other 50 percent being from foreign profits. If your film is picked up by a major motion-picture distributor in the United States for theatrical release, you could receive an advance of $500,000 or more, plus a share of the profits (which is negotiable and varies depending on the distributor, anywhere from 20 to 50 percent). The distributor will usually deduct what it paid in an advance from any profits owed to you. Miramax paid $5 million for the independent film *Swingers,* produced on a budget of only $250,000.

Home-video rights with a major studio distributor can pay an advance of around $300,000, depending on the material and whether any recognizable names appear in the film. In addition to an advance, you could also see profit participation as well. You can get anywhere from $10,000 to $500,000 for a one-time television licensing fee.

 Domestic studio distributors may give you a *negative pickup agreement* for your film. A negative pickup guarantees that the distributor will buy your film when you deliver the final product. Raising the money is easier when a studio distributor gives you a negative pickup offer in writing. You can then approach investors and show them the negative pickup agreement from the studio insuring that the film will have distribution when you deliver it.

Media rights

When you sign with a distributor, the distributor negotiates *media rights* (which clarify what outlets your film can be seen) in the following order for your film in each country (also referred to as a *territory*):

- ✔ **Theatrical:** For theatrical screenings to audiences.
- ✔ **Home video:** The distributor distributes your film to video stores on VHS and DVD.

- ✔ **Pay-per-view:** For broadcast viewing on a pay-per-view basis.

- ✔ **Pay television:** For broadcast on pay television that has paid subscribers. Pay TV, such as HBO or Showtime, usually has no commercials.

- ✔ **Satellite:** For TV satellite markets within a territory (broadcast at the same time that pay TV starts).

- ✔ **Cable television:** For broadcast to basic cable television subscribers.

- ✔ **Free television:** For broadcast on television networks like NBC, ABC, CBS, and FOX.

- ✔ **Closed circuit:** For limited exposure in hotels, airplanes, and cruise ships.

- ✔ **Internet:** For viewing or downloading off the Internet.

A *window* is the period of time during which a film is available for each media right. For example, a theatrical release usually goes to home video after a window of six months; home video usually has a window of 30 days before pay TV can broadcast it. Some broadcasters negotiate for an extended window of up to a year or two, depending on what they pay for the licensing of the picture. Each buyer needs to abide by the window so as to not infringe on another buyer's window in a different medium.

When a film is licensed for a particular medium and has a defined window, the distributor may request a *holdback,* meaning that your film cannot be shown on any other media until a negotiable period of time has lapsed.

Ancillary rights

Ancillary rights bring in additional income derived from other sources, such as a soundtrack, novelization, comic books, toys, or any type of merchandise inspired by your film. *Star Wars* figurines, *Harry Potter* books and games, and *Teenage Mutant Ninja Turtle* dolls are all part of this merchandising bonanza. You can find *premiums* (inexpensive toys and gadgets) in cereal boxes and kids' meals at fast-food restaurants as cross-promotion for films. Additional ancillary rights can include a sequel to your film, a spin-off television series, or even a stage play (like Disney's stage adaptation of *The Lion King*).

Successful ancillary merchandising on an independent film is much more difficult without the backing of a major studio. However, my independent film, *Undercover Angel* had a character named Mr. Dodo in the film, which created a following and led to the marketing of Dodo dolls and books (see Figure 19-2).

Mr. Dodo © 1998 Bryan Michael Stoller (www.mrdodo.com); Miss Cast Away mug at www.zandoria.com

Finding domestic buyers at the VSDA convention

The Video Software Dealers Association (VSDA) holds conventions in July in Las Vegas and Los Angeles that bring domestic buyers and sellers of films and programming for home-video entertainment on VHS and DVD to resellers. The owners of both the big video chains and ma-and-pa retail stores gather under one roof. This is usually after a domestic distributor has signed a distribution deal with you to represent your film to all the video retailers. If you haven't found a distributor for your film, this is a good place to network and meet potential video distributors to distribute your film on home video.

Distributing Your Film around the World

Foreign distribution is the licensing of your film to theatrical, TV, and home-video buyers overseas in the global market. Your foreign distributor represents your film to more than 65 countries (also known as *territories*). Each country has individual buyers who purchase film rights for their territory. Foreign sales can account for 50 percent of all worldwide sales (with domestic representing the other 50 percent). Europe accounts for up to 70 percent of all foreign sales. Finding a foreign distributor is much the same as finding a domestic distributor — you send a screening cassette of your film to the various foreign distributors (see "The top foreign distributors" later in this chapter), or browse through The Hollywood Creative Directory's distributor guide (www.hcdonline.com) for a listing of every foreign distributor (and domestic ones as well).

Some territories group together multiple countries. Check with your foreign distributor for details.

Selling your film at the super markets

When you secure a foreign distributor, that distributor is likely to take your film to a market to connect with potential licensors. Four international film markets allow foreign distributors to showcase their library of films for licensing to the global market. These markets are a necessity for foreign distributors to attend, although films are sold between markets as well.

- ✔ **The American Film Market (AFM)** takes place in February in Santa Monica. Producers, distributors, buyers, sellers, actors, and filmmakers flock to a beachfront hotel for eight days of dealing and networking. More than 300 exhibitors set up offices in suites at the hotel. Local theaters screen films so that buyers can view the distributors' products.

- ✔ **The Cannes Film Market** takes place in mid-May for approximately 12 days on the French Riviera, running simultaneously with the Cannes Film Festival (see Chapter 20). The festival is a competition of films, and the market is a film-selling convention. Buyers, distributors, and filmmakers enjoy the festive European culture along with distributor parties on rooftops and luxury cruise boats.

- ✔ **The MIFED Market** takes place in the beautiful Italian city of Milan for five days in late October. This market is more business and less festive than the Cannes Market. But the pasta is fantastic — it sure beats my macaroni and cheese!

- ✔ **MIPCOM,** another popular overseas market, is held in mid-October for five days in Cannes and concentrates on TV series and movies for international television markets. Your foreign distributor can get additional TV sales for your film by taking your film to this market. MIP-TV is put on by the same organization and takes place in March.

Your foreign distributor may agree to pay your way to one or more of the markets in exchange for distributing your film, or it may deduct your traveling expenses from your film's profits. But hey, wouldn't it be fun to go to Italy and France with your film?

If you've made a 35mm print of your film, your distributor will set up screening times for buyers to see your film in a nearby theater. If you don't have a 35mm print, your distributor may pay to have a print made.

If you shot and cut your project on video, you may need to blow it up to 16mm or 35mm if your film is getting a theatrical release, or your foreign distributor wants to screen it for buyers at the various film markets. The delicate and expensive process called *film scanning* can cost from $30,000 to $60,000 for a theatrical-length piece to be blown up to 35mm. To save on this cost, see if your foreign distributor can project your film from a video projector instead, unless the distributor is willing to incur the cost to blow it up.

Negotiating: How much for your film?

Your foreign distributor makes separate and exclusive deals with each country for all media rights or combinations thereof to your film. As with domestic media rights, each media right is for a certain window of time so as not to infringe on another market's window. Buyers pay a heftier price if your film has a theatrical release before home video and television.

Usually, filmmakers give foreign distributors all foreign rights, including all ancillary markets, so the distributor can enter into agreements for TV, theatrical, and home video overseas. Domestic works differently, because the filmmaker has more control in distribution at home and can do individual deals for TV, theatrical, and home video, which would be difficult to track on foreign sales.

Each country pays a different licensing fee for your film, negotiated by your foreign distributor. The fee depends on the size of the country and other factors, such as:

- ✔ **The state of the global economy.**

- ✔ **The genre of your film.** Action and horror, which translate well visually overseas, tend to bring in higher prices than comedies and family fare.

- ✔ **Whether any name stars or recognizable talent appear in your film.**

- ✔ **The production values of your film.** Does it look like it was made on a higher budget?

- ✔ **What's popular at the time at the world box office.** Is science-fiction popular at the time because of a major sci-fi film doing well at the box-office? Next week it could be fantasy or crime, depending on the success of major studio releases (everyone likes to follow in the trail of a successful genre).

Table 19-1 shows the low and high rates paid by a selection of foreign territories for television and video rights. It gives examples of prices that have been paid for independent films with the production values of a $1 to $3 million film. As you can see, the numbers really add up. Theatrical rights could pay significantly higher numbers. Note that foreign distribution companies usually deal in U.S. dollars when selling overseas.

Projecting your image

Because more and more productions are being shot on video, many theaters are now equipped to project video. This is a plus when a distributor wants to project your film to potential buyers and you don't have a theatrical print, but only a finished copy of your film on video. Your video production can be transferred to DVD or digital tape and projected in a theater without the expense of blowing it up to 35mm film stock. Most people won't know the difference, especially if you make your video look like film, either with software that emulates film, like Bullet (www.redgiantsoftware.com), or with one of the new 24progressive digital cinema camcorders, like Panasonic's AG-DVX100. George Lucas is working on ways to beam film to theaters electronically and do away with the heavy film reels and cans that are currently shipped. It would be similar to how you receive cable television channels or satellite TV. The future holds some exciting possibilities!

Table 19-1	Prices Paid by Foreign Buyers for a Low-Budget Film for TV and Video Rights
Territory	*For a Film That Looks Like a $1 to 3 Million Budget*
France	$70,000 to $200,000
Germany	$50,000 to $300,000
Italy	$50,000 to $200,000
South Korea	$40,000 to $100,000
Japan	$75,000 to $300,000
Mexico	$30,000 to $100,000
Poland	$10,000 to $50,000
Turkey	$10,000 to $20,000

Speaking their language

After your film is sold to a foreign territory, it's dubbed in the language of the country that purchased it. The filmmaker has prepared a music-and-effects track (see Chapter 16) that allows the language of the foreign country to be dubbed while retaining the original music and sound-effects tracks. The foreign buyer or territory that licenses your film incurs the cost of translation and dubbing and performs the work in its country. Each and every country may not have to do a separate dub. If your film is sold to France and dubbed in French, your distributor can use that same French version to sell to French-speaking portions of Canada. If you sell to Spain, your distributor will inform the buyers for Mexico that a Spanish version is available for licensing.

The English-language dialogue isn't the only thing that has to go when dubbing a film; the English words that visually appear in the film have to be removed as well. When your film goes to another country, you must provide the distributor with a *textless* version with the title and all credits missing. The receiving country translates your film's title, as well as all production credits (of course, the crew and actors' names remain unchanged), into its language. See Chapter 18 for information about credits and titles.

Finding a Reliable Distributor

Finding a distributor can be easy if you've made a very commercial film, or difficult if your film can't seem to find an audience. The first thing to do is get a list of distributors (see The Hollywood Creative Directory in the following list) and make an introductory call to see if it may be interested in screening your film. If there is some initial interest, send a screening cassette of your film with a letter stating that you spoke with them on the phone and thanking them for their consideration.

Another way to get a distributor interested in your film is to submit to film festivals. If your film is accepted to screen at a major film festival, like the Sundance Film Festival or Toronto Film Fest, then you have a very good chance of having a distributor discover your film. If your film doesn't get accepted or discovered at a film festival, there are other ways to find a distributor for your film:

- ✔ **Film Finders:** This service tracks film rights and availability throughout the world at no charge to you. List with this service, and distributors may be calling you to inquire about your film! Go to www.filmfinders. com to list your film.

- ✔ **Producer's representative:** A *producer's rep,* also called a *sales rep* or *sales agent,* is an individual or a company, similar to a manager or agent, who helps you find a distributor. Producer's reps have relationships with various distributors and attend all the major film markets. They can also advise you on distribution contracts and help negotiate the best deal. Bruder Releasing (www.4bri.net) is a producer's rep and a distributor who has represented some of my films for domestic television.

Pre-selling a film

Pre-selling is when a distributor sells rights to your film to foreign buyers even before it's made (see Chapter 5). The distributor takes *advances* (down payments of at least 20 percent), which are presented to the bank or to investors to confirm that your film has buyers waiting to license it after it's completed. Doing pre-sales is much more difficult than it used to be, unless the film has some major stars attached to it.

✔ **Other filmmakers:** Other filmmakers who have films in distribution may be able to provide you with an introduction to their distributors.

✔ **Trade papers:** *The Hollywood Reporter* and *Variety* put out annual foreign-film market issues and domestic distributor listings.

✔ **Distribution directories:** The Hollywood Creative Directory (www.hcdonline.com or 800-815-0503) puts out reference directories, including one on film distributors. It lists the contact information for more than 800 companies, including film and TV distributors, foreign film buyers, networks, financing companies, and producer and distributor representatives. The directory is updated several times a year.

See also the lists of the top ten domestic and foreign distributors later in this section.

If a distributor is interested in your film, always ask for referrals. Talk to other filmmakers whose films they distribute. This lets you know if the distributor is reliable and honest.

The best domestic distributors

The following are the top ten domestic studios that distribute films for theatrical, television, and home-video release in the United States and Canada:

✔ **Dreamworks:** 1000 Flower St., Glendale, CA 91201; phone: 818-695-5000; Internet: www.dreamworks.com

✔ **MGM (Metro Goldwyn Mayer):** 2500 Broadway St., Santa Monica, CA 90404; phone: 310-449-3000; Internet: www.mgm.com

✔ **Miramax Films:** 375 Greenwich St., New York, NY 10013; phone: 212-941-3800; Internet: www.miramax.com

Four-walling has a ceiling

Four-walling refers to distributing your film yourself without the aid of a professional distributor. I don't recommend this route because it's time-consuming and expensive. You have to pay for your own 35mm film prints, place ads in newspapers and magazines (which is not cheap), and make your own posters. You also have to contact individual theaters and convince them to show your film. Usually, only art houses and small theater chains will consider a film that's not represented by a major distributor — and you usually rent their theater and split the profits with them.

- ✔ **New Line Cinema:** 116 N. Robertson Blvd., Ste.200, Los Angeles, CA 90048; phone: 310-854-5811; Internet: www.newline.com

- ✔ **Paramount Pictures:** 555 Melrose Ave., Los Angeles, CA 90038; phone: 323-956-5000; Internet: www.paramount.com

- ✔ **Sony Pictures Entertainment:** 10202 W. Washington Blvd., Culver City, CA 90232; phone: 310-244-4000; Internet: www.sony.com

- ✔ **Twentieth Century Fox:** 10201 W. Pico Blvd., Los Angeles, CA 90035; phone: 310-369-1000; Internet: www.fox.com

- ✔ **Universal Studios:** 100 Universal City Plaza, Universal City, CA 91608; phone: 818-777-1000; Internet: www.universalstudios.com

- ✔ **Warner Bros.:** 4000 Warner Blvd., Burbank, CA 91522; phone: 818-954-6000; Internet: www.warnerbros.com

- ✔ **The Walt Disney Company:** 55 S. Buena Vista St., Burbank, CA 91521; phone: 818-560-1000; Internet: www.disney.com

The best foreign distributors

Although setting up your own domestic distribution by dealing with individual TV networks, home video, and theatrical studios is possible, I don't recommend this approach for foreign distribution. To get your film distributed successfully overseas, you need a qualified and competent foreign distributor who can track your film's sales, speak the languages, and benefit from the relationships with the foreign buyers that they deal with on a regular basis. There are also complicated tax and delivery requirements that are a major headache for an independent filmmaker and should be left up to the expertise of a foreign distributor.

The following are the top ten distributors that distribute films to overseas foreign markets. Foreign territories usually license video, television, and theatrical rights:

- ✔ **Alliance Atlantis:** 121 Bloor St. East, Ste. 1500, Toronto, Ontario Canada, M4W 3M5; phone: 416-967-1174; Internet: www.allianceatlantis.com

- ✔ **Crystal Sky Worldwide Sales:** 1901 Avenue of the Stars, Ste. 605, Los Angeles, CA 90067; phone: 310-843-0223

- ✔ **Curb Entertainment:** 3907 W. Alameda Ave., Burbank, CA 91505; phone: 818-843-8580; Internet: www.curbfilm.com

- ✔ **Film Artists Network:** P.O. Box 93032, Hollywood, CA 90093; phone: 818-344-0569; Internet: www.filmartistsnetwork.com

- ✔ **Fries Film Group:** 22817 Ventura Blvd., Ste.909, Woodland Hills, CA 91364; phone: 818-888-3052; Internet: www.friesfilms.com

- ✔ **Miramax International:** 99 Hudson St., 5th Flr., New York, NY 10013; phone: 212-219-4100; Internet: www.miramax.com

- ✔ **New Concorde International:** 11600 San Vicente Blvd., Los Angeles, CA 90049; phone: 310-820-6733; Internet: www.newconcorde.com

- ✔ **New Line International:** 116 N. Robertson Blvd., Los Angeles, CA 90048; phone: 310-854-8511; Internet: www.newline.com

- ✔ **Nu Image — Millennium Films:** 6423 Wilshire Blvd., Los Angeles, CA 90048; phone: 310-388-6900

- ✔ **Showcase Entertainment:** Warner Center, 21800 Oxnard St., Ste. 150, Woodland Hills, CA 91367; phone: 818-715-7005; Internet: www.showcaseentertainment.com

Demystifying Distribution Contracts

After you settle on a distributor, you must sign a contract. Distribution contracts can be long, detailed, and confusing. When you get to this stage, I suggest that you contact an entertainment attorney or someone versed in distribution contracts. You don't want to lose your film and profits to a distributor because you didn't understand the distribution contract.

The following are some of the things a distribution agreement addresses:

- ✔ **Grant of rights:** What media rights is the domestic distributor taking — TV, theatrical, home video? A foreign distributor representing your film overseas usually takes all rights.

✔ **Term:** For how long does the distributor have the right to distribute your film? It can be up to 25 years. If it doesn't fulfill a certain amount of net sales, you, the filmmaker, should have the option to cancel the agreement (in writing, of course).

Whatever deal you strike with a distributor, decide on a minimum dollar amount that it has to reach in net sales (meaning that you pocket those dollars). If the distributor doesn't reach that number in two years from the date of signing, then all distribution rights revert back to you, and you can find another distributor. I usually use a number like $200,000 to $500,000. If you don't reach that, it's time to move on.

✔ **Territory:** Is it for the whole world or just certain territories? Usually with a foreign distributor it's all territories except the United States and Canada, which is usually taken by a domestic distributor.

✔ **Delivery requirements:** What picture elements do you need to provide? A 35mm print? A video copy? Do you have publicity photos, artwork, actor and crew agreements, and an accurate credit list ready to hand over to your new distributor?

✔ **Accounting terms:** You need to have access to the distributor's books regarding the collection of sales on your film. How often do you have access to those books?

✔ **Gross and net dollars:** Look for the definition of *gross receipts* and *net receipts* (after agreed-upon expenses are paid) that will be split between the distributor and you, the filmmaker. You can find further definitions of *gross* and *net* later in this chapter.

✔ **Statement terms:** Does the distributor have an obligation to provide you with producer's statements of any and all sales on your picture? Usually, the distributor provides monthly statements the first year, quarterly the following year, and annually thereafter, but this is negotiable.

✔ **Payment terms:** When is the distributor obligated to pay you your share of the profits from your picture? It's usually after defined expenses (marketing and distributor's fees). Determine the allocation of gross receipts — what's paid out and when. Also determine if there is an *advance* paid (upfront money to acquire the rights to distribute your film).

✔ **Marketing expenses:** This category includes prints and advertising costs, film-market expenses, the costs of making the film trailer, and so on. Put a cap on marketing expenses — meaning that your distributor can't spend beyond that point. Prints and advertising usually cost between $50,000 and $100,000 on an independent film.

✔ **Proof of copyright:** The distributor wants to ensure that you are the original owner of the property.

In perpetuity is a term that's used in distribution contracts. It means "forever," ensuring that the distributor has the rights to your film forever — unless you put a term on it. Agreeing to a limited term, such as ten years with a renewal clause, is to your advantage.

Errors and omissions insurance: Covering yourself against "Oops!"

A distributor can purchase *errors and omissions insurance* (E&O) after it decides to distribute your film. E&O protects you and the distributor from being sued by any third party, if someone says that you stole his idea, slandered him in the film, or used something of his in your film without permission.

Usually, a distributor makes sure that no such liabilities exist in your film before it takes it on. If it has concerns, it'll ask you to cut out the offending or questionable material. A distributor will usually pay the cost of E&O (see Chapter 4), which can run around $6,000, and then deduct it from your profits.

Keeping an eye out for creative bookkeeping

Bookkeeping is another reason why you need to have an attorney review your distribution agreement for your film. Distributors can be very creative in their bookkeeping, and your film could end up never seeing a profit — no matter how many sales your distributor makes. Expenses have to be clearly defined in your distribution contract. A distributor can charge excess overhead costs and other hidden charges if you aren't careful.

When you receive a contract from a potential distributor, it will contain definitions of *gross* and *net*. Your attorney must look over these definitions carefully. *Gross* is all the monies that come in on your film; *net* is what's left after your distributor takes its expenses. Make sure that those expenses are clearly defined. A distributor's expenses consist of:

✔ **Distribution fee:** For a foreign distributor, 20 percent to 30 percent is standard off the top of all gross sales. With a domestic distributor, the fee could be an advance, such as $500,000 paid up front to you to acquire distribution rights to your film, with royalties paid on a percentage of the sales (this is negotiable). Or the distributor may want a *complete buyout* (a flat fee paid with no royalties and the distributor ends up owning your film).

 ✔ **Market expenses:** For foreign distributors, these expenses include overseas film-market costs; for domestic distributors, they include conventions or film markets.

 ✔ **Promotional flyers:** For handing out to buyers (design and printing costs).

 ✔ **Posters:** To hang up at the film markets (design and printing costs).

 ✔ **Trade ads:** To create buyer awareness of your film (design and advertising costs).

 ✔ **Movie trailer:** To help sell your film to buyers (creative and editing costs).

 ✔ **Screening cassettes:** VHS viewing cassettes or DVD screeners of your film provided to potential buyers upon request.

 ✔ **Travel:** For you to attend an overseas market with your foreign distributor.

Always put a cap on expenses. Clearly define the amount of expenses the distributor can deduct against the sales on your film. After the defined expenses are recouped (including the distribution fee), you'll begin to share in the profits.

Chapter 20

Exploring and Entering Film Festivals

In This Chapter

▶ Understanding the benefits of entering and attending film festivals

▶ Finding film festivals that suit your film

▶ Submitting the right materials

---

*Y*ou've finally completed your film, and you can't wait to win some awards for all your hard work. Film festivals are the perfect place to get your film noticed and perhaps gain some recognition for it. This chapter provides first-hand information about entering and (hopefully) winning film festivals, along with how to choose the best festival and the right category for your film. I also give you some hints about getting a discount on the festival entry fee or even getting the fee waived.

Being accepted at a festival such as the Sundance Film Festival is as important as winning. (It *is* a nomination.) An award or acceptance at a prestigious festival can give you and your film credibility. In this chapter, you find a list of the top ten festivals where you can enter your film and compete for award recognition.

Film festivals are also a great place to network and even commiserate with fellow filmmakers on the trials and tribulations of getting your film completed. If you attend the festival in person, you'll have a chance to talk with agents, distributors, and other people you wouldn't normally have a chance to hang out with informally in Hollywood or elsewhere.

Demystifying Film Festivals

A film festival is a festival to send your film for possible acceptance with other films. It's a place to compete, be judged, and either place, win, or lose.

A film festival is also a spot to meet new friends, watch films that may never make the mainstream market, and make some business contacts that could help further your career.

Film festivals are springing up like weeds all over the world. With so many out there, you're bound to find at least one that will screen your film, regardless of how good or bad it is. Any recognition from a film festival is better than no recognition at all. Check with your next-door neighbors and see if they're planning a film festival of their own. If they are, enter it. You may have a good chance of winning — especially if you've lent them a cup of sugar or your lawnmower lately.

Most film festivals are run by committees. A film-festival committee consists of a festival director and the organizers, volunteers, and judges. Often, festivals hire judges who are skilled industry craftspeople and can recognize the talents of their peers. Some of the higher-profile festivals involve well-known actors, producers, and directors as judges. These judges are familiar with the process of filmmaking and look for expertise in story structure, direction, acting, editing, and the picture as a whole as well.

Along with the excitement of watching your film with an audience and gauging the reaction, networking is a very important part of attending a film festival. You never know what new friends or business contacts you're going to meet. After all, you'll be around your peers — people who love film as much as you do.

Because many filmmakers are now making their films with digital video cameras, many film festivals are now accepting finished product on videotape — which is screened utilizing video projectors — as opposed to film.

Film festivals are often endorsed by the state or city in which they're held, such as the Palm Springs Film Festival and the Santa Barbara Film Festival. The festival promotes tourism and revenues for the city. Some festivals are run by nonprofit organizations.

Film festival recognition adds to your credibility as a filmmaker. If you win just one film festival, you're officially known as "an award-winning filmmaker."

Knowing the difference between a film festival and a film market

Many up-and-coming filmmakers get confused by the difference between a film festival and a film market. A *film festival* is a *competition* of films vying for recognition in the form of awards and acknowledgment. The visibility that filmmakers get and the networking they can do open up the possibilities for finding a distributor, if they don't already have one.

A *film market* is a business convention that showcases films for sale to buyers looking for film product all over the world. At a film market, the films already have representation with distributors that are soliciting the films to domestic and international buyers for the TV, home-video, and theatrical outlets. The Cannes Film Festival has a film market that parallels the festival but is a separate entity.

MIFED in Italy, the American Film Market in Los Angeles, and the Cannes Film Market in France are the three main worldwide film *markets*. See Chapter 19 for more information about film markets.

Understanding the benefits of entering film festivals

Besides being a great place to check out what other independent filmmakers are doing, a film festival serves two main purposes:

- ✔ Showcasing films
- ✔ Helping filmmakers find potential distributors for their films

Also keep in mind these other benefits to entering and attending film festivals as you wonder whether your film is good enough to enter:

- ✔ **They give you the opportunity to network with other filmmakers.** You can meet your peers and share stories and misadventures.

- ✔ **They provide a forum in which you can meet business contacts.** Agents, attorneys, distributors, and studio executives are much more approachable in a festival environment.

- ✔ **They give out cash and prizes.** I don't know anyone who's ever complained about winning cash or prizes. Prizes from festivals are often film related, such as free laboratory services, camera and editing equipment, and film books and magazines.

- ✔ **They give out statuettes and certificate awards.** Being able to display an award or any type of accolade for your hard work is always nice. An award also gives you and your film credibility.

- ✔ **They offer panels and seminars that you can learn from.** Many festivals have credible filmmakers and entertainment-industry guests who offer invaluable insights and answer questions.

- ✔ **They can help generate publicity for your film.** Your film could get written up in the local paper of the festival or even get a review (hopefully a good one) from one of the major trade papers like *The Hollywood Reporter* or *Variety*. Local news and entertainment shows may interview you on camera and ask you about your film.

✔ **Festival parties are fun — and you can network, too.** People (especially agents and distributors) are often more relaxed and approachable after a few drinks and some good music. Just don't drink too much and make a fool of yourself by dancing on the tables. You want your *film* to be judged — not *you!*

Don't be intimidated by film festivals. Your film may be the little gem a particular festival is looking for. Anyone can enter a film festival as long as he or she pays the entry fee and submits the film under the festival's rules. Anyone can win, too!

Psst!: Secrets to Entering and Winning Film Festivals

The secret to entering film festivals is what I call *entry etiquette*. Winning is beyond your control, but following some basic rules I describe in this section brings you closer to that win.

Don't take it personally if your film doesn't make it into a festival. With many festivals receiving thousands of submissions annually, a film can easily be overlooked.

Refraining from sending a work-in-progress

Even though some festivals accept works-in-progress, you're just donating your entry fee to the festival when your film doesn't get selected because it isn't finished. I've made this mistake before and want to warn you to avoid it. Wait until your film is completed — including music and sound mix — before you submit it for consideration. Many filmmakers eager to make the deadline for the big festivals like Sundance and Toronto end up sending a work-in-progress. But the festival selection committee rarely gives an uncompleted film the benefit of the doubt. It will be viewed alongside completed films and most likely lose out. Submitting a work-in-progress wastes your time and money — and the festival's time as well.

Even if you think that your work-in-progress is a masterpiece, don't submit it. If it's not accepted, you ruin any chance of it being accepted in the future when it's actually completed. Rarely will a selection committee view a film it's already judged, even if it's been totally revamped.

Entering the right festivals for your film

Your film is in the can, and you can't wait to send it out and start collecting invitations to all the great film festivals. But wait: You have to choose carefully which festival is best to enter. You can start by going to www.filmfestivals.com for up-to-the-minute information about film festivals, including entry details and deadlines. You may even want to call or e-mail each festival you're considering and ask if your film is appropriate for its festival.

Going to a film festival's Web site enables you to get updated information and even download an entry form immediately. Note that most film festival Web sites have the extension .org, *not* .com; many festivals are nonprofit organizations.

So how do you decide which festival is right for your film? Think about your intended audience. If your film is a mainstream piece that *Star Wars* or *The Lord of the Rings* audiences would love, it isn't exactly Sundance Film Festival fare; Sundance often looks for off-beat or controversial films. If your film's about an escaped convict who kidnaps grandmothers, it isn't going to be accepted at a children's film festival — unless it's a comedy, and the heroes are an odd gang of misfits.

The following is a list of ten top film festivals, in order of popularity, to consider submitting your film to. The list is a compilation of my favorites, including first-film and independent film–friendly festivals and a family festival dedicated to those rare independent family-produced films.

- ✔ **The Sundance Film Festival** takes place in Park City, Utah, in January, with an entry deadline in early October. This is the festival of festivals, established by actor Robert Redford and named after one of his favorite classic films, *Butch Cassidy and the Sundance Kid.* (That's why he's often still referred to as the Kid.) Sundance has become one of the toughest festivals to get a film accepted at. The festival is overloaded with submissions, and a film has to have a sophistication that Sundance audiences and judges have become accustomed to. The festival favors independent films. If your film gets accepted for screening, that's almost as good as winning — being accepted carries a lot of merit. But it's a tough one, so don't rely on Sundance to be your film's festival premiere. Internet: festival.sundance.org; phone: 310-394-4662.

- ✔ **The Toronto International Film Festival** takes place in Toronto, Ontario, Canada, in September, with an entry deadline in April/June. This festival has been around since 1976 and is considered the second most popular among the elite film festivals, after Sundance. Films are judged on artistic values and subject matter, similar to the Sundance Film Festival. Independent films are especially welcomed. Internet: www.e.bell.ca/filmfest; phone: 416-967-7371.

✔ **Telluride Film Festival** takes place in September in Telluride, Colorado, with an entry deadline in May/July. The festival is for real movie lovers and accepts all types of films as well as experimental, first-film, and artsy styles. Telluride accepts projects finished on videotape as opposed to film, using video projection. However, they prefer to screen a DVD instead of a VHS cassette of your project (the best quality and cheap to ship!). Internet: www.telluridefilmfestival.com; phone: 603-643-1255.

✔ **Worldfest Houston** is in April, with an entry deadline in January. It accepts digitally finished videos transferred to DVD for best image quality, as well as the traditional 16mm and 35mm film prints for projection. The festival accepts a wide array of styles, from wide commercial appeal to experimental short films. Internet: www.worldfest.org; phone: 713-965-9955.

✔ **Cannes Film Festival** takes place in May, in the breathtaking city of Cannes, France, with an entry deadline in March. The Cannes Film Festival is in the elite company of Sundance and Toronto. It carries a different sophistication and is run with the international elegance of a European gala event. The festival accepts higher-profile films, especially with an international flair. Internet: www.festival-cannes.fr/default2.php; phone: (33-1) 45-61-6600.

✔ **American Film Institute Fest** takes place in November, in Los Angeles, California, with an entry deadline in June/July. The American Film Institute's fine reputation offers credibility to any film that is accepted into the festival. If you win, it doesn't hurt your credibility, either. The festival accepts most styles of films, especially independent. Internet: www.afi.com/AFIFEST; phone: 323-856-7707.

✔ **Slamdance Film Festival** takes place in January, with an entry deadline in October/November. Slamdance was created in 1994 to catch the spillover of films that don't get accepted into Sundance. It's very much a festival for independent filmmakers and first-film entrants who find themselves left out in the cold — even though they have a film that an audience would appreciate and enjoy. Internet: www.slamdance.com; phone: 323-466-1786.

✔ **Palm Springs International Film Festival** is in January, with an entry deadline in November. Established by the late Sonny Bono, Palm Springs has fast become a festival favorite. In the quaint city of Palm Springs, the festival enjoys the closeness of Hollywood but is just far enough away to find its independence. It accepts independent and mainstream films. Internet: www.psfilmfest.org; phone: 760-322-2930.

✔ **The International Family Film Festival** takes place in April, in Santa Clarita, California, with an entry deadline in March. Organized by the people who ran the former Santa Clarita International Film Festival, the

International Family Film Festival is a great festival that recognizes films for families and children and is a great outlet for the family-film filmmaker. Most other festivals don't screen many family films. Internet: www.iffilmfest.org; phone: 661-257-3131.

✔ **Dances with Films** takes place in April, in Los Angeles, California, with an entry deadline in February/March. Also known as the "Festival of the Unknowns," this festival boasts that it features films with no-name directors, actors, and producers. It was originally established to get away from the politics of other film festivals. It's very first-film friendly and welcomes independent films with great stories. Internet: www.danceswithfilms.com; phone: 323-466-1786.

A program called Gorilla, by Jungle Software (www.junglesoftware.com), is a complete production-management software package for independent filmmakers that includes a database of film festivals. The program lists addresses and contact information for more than 125 film festivals.

Deadlines and entry fees are subject to change, so always visit the festival's Web site or call ahead. Questions are usually answered quickly via e-mail.

Entering the appropriate genre and category: Door #1 or door #2?

After you've selected the right film festival, you have the dilemma of entering in the correct genre and category. If you choose incorrectly, you could blow your film's chances of winning or placing. Some festivals allow you to enter several genres for this reason — very helpful if you can't decide exactly which genre your film fits into. Is it a comedy, drama, science-fiction, or fantasy? A combination of several genres? If you don't know your film's genre, who does?

Usually, the judging committee won't correct your mistake if you enter under the wrong category. It has too many entries to weed through. If you're undecided, call the festival and ask its opinion. You can also screen your film for friends and ask what category they feel your film falls into.

Along with knowing the genre your film falls under, you have to choose the correct category, which is usually one of the following:

✔ **Animation:** Utilizing traditional drawings, stop motion (like Gumby and Pokey), or digital computer-generated images.

✔ **Commercial:** A 30-second to 1-minute commercial that's purpose is to sell a product or idea.

✔ **Documentary:** A behind-the-scenes nonfiction (sometimes controversial) production that shows the real side of a person or event.

- ✔ **First feature:** Your first attempt at a feature-length film (at least 90 minutes) with a cohesive story.

- ✔ **Independent film (low-budget):** A feature-film length production produced with limited funds and independent of a major studio or distributor.

- ✔ **Public Service Announcement (PSA):** A 30-second to 1-minute commercial making a statement about health issues, environmental issues, or any subject matter that promotes a better society.

- ✔ **Short film:** Usually under 30 minutes. Encapsulates a complete story with developed characters within a shorter running time.

- ✔ **TV movie:** Usually slotted within a two-hour time period on a TV network. Produced specifically for the small screen (TV) keeping in mind the TV censors with regard to subject material.

- ✔ **TV program:** Usually runs within a one-hour time slot. Can be a variety program (such as *America's Funniest Home Videos*), a reality show (like *Survivor*), or a one-hour drama show.

Some festivals accept screenplay submissions as well. So if you have an unproduced screenplay that you're proud of, submit it to the appropriate festival. I entered my original screenplay *Undercover Angel* in the Santa Clarita International Film Festival (now called the International Family Film Festival), and it received an award certificate. I then put the award logo on the screenplay to show that it was an award-winning script, which gave the screenplay credibility and raised interest in the project. (The film was produced successfully a year later!)

FAB-ulous recognition

The Film Advisory Board (FAB) is an organization dedicated to recognizing quality films for children and family. FAB has acknowledged many studio pictures, including *E.T.: The Extra-Terrestrial* on its reissue. Films do not compete against each other; rather they are recognized on their own merits and, if worthy of a FAB award, receive recognition. There is no deadline date — films are looked at year-round. The Film Advisory Board does have an annual awards dinner at the historic Roosevelt Hotel in Hollywood every year. You can find information about FAB at www.filmadvisoryboard.org

The Telly Awards, founded in 1980, are similar to FAB in that entries do not compete against each other. TV commercials, films, and TV programs are judged on individual merit and receive an award if the judges feel that the film or program has a high standard of excellence. All genres are accepted as long as they have not been broadcast on a major network. For more information about the Tellys, check out www.telly.com.

Writing a great synopsis of your film

Just like when you had a carefully prepared pitch to sell your film idea to an investor or distributor (Chapter 3), you need to pitch an intriguing synopsis of your film that will convince the festival screeners to consider your film for their festival. If you write a boring synopsis, they will anticipate a boring film.

Picture perfect: Selecting the best photos from your film

Photos from your film are an important marketing tool. Film festivals will request still photos from your shoot to use in their brochures and marketing materials — should your film be accepted. A picture always draws the reader's attention to an article and helps the reader to understand and remember the material more than with no photograph.

Make sure that you have photos taken on the set. Submit photos that best represent your film, such as an interesting confrontation between your actors, or something that causes an emotion in the viewer. If you have any name stars, then make sure they're in the photos.

When you send photos from your film to a film festival, be sure to label each photo with the name of the film. Identify the scene and the actors in the photo. If the festival people decide to publish the photo in their publicity ads or festival program, they need to have this information clearly marked.

Choosing the best format

Only a few years ago, if you completed your film on videotape (as opposed to cutting on film for release in theaters), you were out of luck when it came to having a festival show your film. If a festival accepted your film for screening, you had to provide a 16mm or 35mm film print. Many independent filmmakers were knocked out of the game because their finished projects were on tape only. You can always transfer your finished video product to film, but that process is lengthy and expensive. Because you're taking a smaller video image and enlarging it for the big screen, the picture quality may suffer by magnifying grain and imperfections, depending on the quality of the original footage.

Now that digital filmmaking is coming into its own, many film festivals have video projectors that can project virtually any form of video on which you submit your film. New filmmakers can now receive equal consideration regardless of whether their project is finished on videotape and then burned to DVD or submitted on traditional 16mm or 35mm film stock. If you finish your production on videotape as opposed to film, you have a variety of different video formats that you can transfer onto for screening purposes:

- VHS and Super VHS (½-inch videotape cassette)
- Digital video disc (DVD)
- Mini-DV (miniature digital video cassette)
- DVCAM (digital video camcorder, similar to mini-DV)
- BetaSP and DigiBetaSP (professional-grade broadcast video cassette)
- ¾-inch cassette tape (¾-inch tape in cassette)

DVD is the favored format when using a video projector. A DVD is as good as your original in picture quality if it's transferred digitally. Burning your projects onto DVDs is easy and inexpensive. Shipping a DVD also costs much less than shipping other formats.

Entering without a box

The traditional way of entering a film festival consists of filling out an entry form and mailing it in with your film submission (usually in the form of a VHS screening cassette) along with your entry fee and supporting materials (still photos, synopsis, and so on). A new company, Without a Box, is working on simplifying the film festival submission process for the filmmaker.

Without a Box (www.withoutabox.com) is a unique service that creates a direct link between the filmmaker and the film-festival circuit by allowing you to submit your film entry online to hundreds of film festivals of your choice worldwide. You still have to send the actual screening tape, but Without a Box is working on a way to fix that, too. Online submission is especially invaluable when you're submitting to more than one festival.

Without a Box collects all the necessary information from you and then inputs it into the entry forms of all the festivals you want to enter. Your information is customized to each festival's distinct entry form. This saves you from entering the information on individual entry forms for each festival you want to enter.

Without a Box offers support services, including a staff to answer your questions via e-mail or phone. You can also find festival entry discounts and product deals if you become one of its 20,000 members (and counting). The service enables you to do a vast search on the site to find the most suitable festival for your film, enter multiple festivals, upload scanned publicity photos from your film, and track your film submissions. Check it out with a free 60-day trial or two online submissions — it's a $79 yearly fee if you decide to join. The film-festival resources are still accessible even if you don't join — you're only charged if you use the submission service for Without a Box.

Getting an entry-fee discount

Pretty much every film festival in the United States charges an entry or submission fee, which can range from $20 to $200. Then, if you win, some festivals charge you extra to purchase the award statuette or certificate! Some film festivals offer entry discounts to students and independent filmmakers. Calling and asking about available discounts is a good idea.

Some festivals reward you with an entry discount if you submit your film early. The discount is usually mentioned on the entry forms or festival Web site.

Entering more than one film

If you want to submit more than one entry, treat them as individual submissions. If you send several films, it looks like you're more concerned with quantity rather than quality. Also the support materials for each film could get mixed in with the wrong submission if they come in the same shipment. Mail them in separate packages. Don't put your eggs in one basket — put them in different baskets!

Part VI
The Part of Tens

The 5th Wave   By Rich Tennant

LITTLE-KNOWN FACT: Most of the movie stars' handprints in the cement sidewalk in front of Grauman's Chinese Theatre were put there AFTER the cement had dried!

In this part . . .

Y ou find helpful tips, secrets, and priceless advice
that can save you a lot of time and trouble and help
you make your film a success. You're given tips for discovering new talent, ways to avoid Murphy's Law, and ideas for
publicizing your film to gain recognition and maybe even
attract a distributor. You also find out how to stay up to
date with the best entertainment magazines and
newspapers.

Chapter 21

Ten Tips for Discovering New Film Talent

. . . .

. . . .

Discovering new talent can be a fun position to be in. You could be the catalyst that launches someone's acting career. Marilyn Monroe, Sandra Bullock, Dustin Hoffman, and Meryl Streep were all discovered — and you can bet that someone is taking the credit for discovering them. This chapter shows you how to root out unknown talent.

Studios often conduct casting calls, looking for that special someone to play a leading role. Daniel Radcliffe was discovered after an extensive worldwide search for the perfect Harry Potter. Emily Mae Young, the little girl featured in the Welch's Juice commercials, had never starred in a feature film until my mother saw her on the commercials. I hired Emily for my film *Undercover Angel,* and she went on to win several best-actor awards (which weighed more than she did!). After my film, she was called in for auditions with big-time directors, including Ron Howard and Martin Scorsese.

Viewing Independent Films

Watch independent films for actors whose performances you admire. Contact the production company that produced the film and tell them you enjoyed the actor's performance and want to find out how to contact his or her agent. If the actor is a member of the Screen Actors Guild (SAG), the actor's union that represents over 120,000 performers, you can call the guild for the actor's contact number (usually the agent or manager). The SAG phone number to locate an actor is 323-954-1600.

One way to track down an actor is to first get his correct name from the film's credits, and then try searching on the Internet. Many actors nowadays have their own personal Web sites and can be found by typing in their name with the .com extension or by locating them with an Internet search engine, like Yahoo! or Google.

Going to See Local Theater

No matter what city you're in, you can go to the local stage show and discover great talent. Just make sure the actor is able to tone his acting performance down for your film because stage actors tend to *project* bigger (speak loud and over-enunciate so the theater audience can hear them) than trained film and television actors do.

Most theater plays have playbills that provide information on each actor featured in the production. You also may be able to request a binder or folder with each actor's headshot, résumé, and contact information. One of the many reasons actors do stage plays is to attract film-industry people (someone like you) who may hire them to act in a film.

Attending Actors' Showcases

Showcases are different from stage plays, in that it *showcases* actors' talents specifically for industry people, such as casting directors, directors, producers, or independent filmmakers like yourself. The performances are usually short vignettes by the individual actor or by pairs. Go down and see a showcase (almost every city has one) — you're bound to find some natural talent. Backstage West (www.backstagewest.com) lists showcases and actors' events. Or check with local stage theaters in your area, where they often post upcoming showcases and performances.

Visiting Acting Schools

Almost every city or small town has an acting school, or at least a drama department at the local schools or colleges. If you're in a big city like Los Angeles, New York, or Toronto, you'll have no problem finding actors through the educational system.

Talking to Agents and Managers

Agents and managers have done the hard work for you by finding and representing talented actors, many of whom may be new to television or film. I've worked with agents who are eager to get their new clients out working, gaining experience, and getting videotapes of performances to show off the actors' talents.

Most cities also have modeling agencies, which are another good place to find local talent. Many aspiring actors start out modeling first. You could be the one to give them their big break!

Searching the Academy Players Directory

The Academy of Television Arts and Sciences publishes *The Academy Players Directory* every six months. The directories consist of four books divided into actor types:

- Leading men, younger leading men
- Leading women, ingénues (supporting women)
- Characters (comedians/comediennes)
- Stunt performers (men and women) and children

These directories are usually purchased by casting departments, directors, studio executives, and independent filmmakers looking to cast their own films. Each issue is $75 and can be ordered by calling 310-247-3000 or going to the Web site at www.playersdirectory.com. *The Academy Players Directory* is also available online.

Schmoozing at Film Festivals and Markets

Film festivals are often attended by actors whose films are being showcased (see Chapter 20). Film markets (see Chapter 19) offer an informal environment to catch people relaxed and in a schmoozing mood.

Many actors attend the various film markets and festivals for the sole purpose of meeting filmmakers who can use them in their next films.

Walking Down the Street

I'm not talking literally finding someone "on the street," unless you hit them with your car or bump into them on the sidewalk. But you can often find actors in common everyday places. A great place to meet actors is at a photocopy place — actors are always photocopying their résumés. A photo retouching store or printer that does headshots (especially in Los Angeles, New York, or Toronto) is a great place to find actors, too.

I found my leading lady for my film *Undercover Angel* while dining in a local neighborhood restaurant. I found someone's purse at my table and a few minutes later saw a woman looking around like she'd lost something. It turned out this was her purse — and she turned out to be Yasmine Bleeth (of *Baywatch* and *Nash Bridges*). I sent my script to her agent explaining how we met, and the rest is history — she starred in my film!

Holding Talent Contests

Clubs, theaters, and TV programs sometimes hold talent contests. Find out where these contests are being held and go down to meet people waiting in line. If you have a comedy club in your town, go down on amateur night, and you're sure to discover some great comedians.

Starring Your Family

Maybe your star is right in your own family. I put my mom in my film *Undercover Angel* as the landlady (besides if I didn't, I was afraid she'd send me to my room), and she did a great job. How about your brother, sister, or dog?

Maybe *you* have that star quality — so why not cast yourself? Ed Burns cast himself in his film *The Brothers McMullen*. Mel Brooks starred in a lot of the films he produced and directed, like *Young Frankenstein, Blazing Saddles,* and *High Anxiety*. Plus, if you star in your film, you can give yourself top billing!

Chapter 22

Ten Ways to Get Publicity for Your Film

In This Chapter

▶ Publicizing your film

▶ Creating an awareness of your film

You made a film and now you want people to know about it. Some people think publicity is to stroke a filmmaker's ego, but the real purpose is to get your name and film out there — to create awareness through repetition. When you see a commercial for a soft drink, suddenly you're thirsty. You see a pizza commercial and consider ordering one. In this same way, you want to create awareness for your film so that distributors and audiences will flock to it. Publicity can also give you credibility as a filmmaker and get you more work. It's amazing how people accept you when they see your name in print.

Generate publicity only when the timing is right. Usually the best time is when you've scheduled a *screening* (projecting your film in a theater) for your film, whether it's for a general audience or one specifically for entertainment industry guests, such as distributors and home-video and TV buyers.

Sending a Press Release

A *press release* is a one-page announcement of a publicity event for your film that you can fax to your local newspapers and TV stations. Use a clever heading to catch a reporter's attention. The release should also have the words *For immediate release, please* (it never hurts to be polite) so they know it's timely and important. It should state what, where, when, and why. This way, your press release for a screening or other publicity stunt allows the press and the rest of the population to show up at the proper time and place.

Doing a TV or Radio Interview

Promoting your film on a local radio station or on a cable-access program is a great way to create exposure. You can even run a short clip from your film on a local TV show or news program. The opportune time to do interviews is when you have a screening of your film planned.

Getting a Review from Local Film Critics

When you're planning a screening of your film, contact local film critics in your town and invite them to the show.

If you can't afford a screening, you can also mail videocassettes to the local critics and ask them if they'd consider reviewing your film (see the following section). If you get a great quote from one of the reviews, you can use it on the video box cover, posters, or newspaper advertisements for your film. As a courtesy you may want to ask permission to use a particular quote.

Sending Out Viewing Cassettes

After you've completed your film, you need to make screening dubs to send to distributors and potential buyers. You can even send a VHS cassette (or DVD copy) to your local newspaper and see if it'll do a review on your film. Even if you plan a screening, you still need to send viewing cassettes or DVDs because many distributors or buyers won't attend and will ask for a viewing copy instead.

Attending Film Festivals

Enter festivals to start creating awareness of your film. If your film places at a festival, you can then contact your local newspapers and TV news programs and notify them of your award-winning film.

Here's a crazy idea: Organize your own film festival. Enter your film (don't let anyone else enter) and award yourself first prize for best film. Then send a press release to newspapers and local TV news. Even if people find out it's your own private film festival, it still makes for a funny news story.

Setting Up a Web Site and E-mail Distribution

Set up a Web site for your film (you can purchase software programs that guide you easily through the process, or you can hire a professional to set up your site). A Web site can be a promotional site letting people know the details of your film (storyline, cast, fun details, and so on). You can direct distributors to your site if they're considering picking your film up for distribution. If you set up the Web site before you make your film, the site can provide information for potential investors and also for actors you're considering. For an example of a film's Web site, check out the Web site for my film *Miss Cast Away* at www.misscastaway.com.

You can also send e-mail messages to a select group of people, telling them about your new film and any publicity events you're planning. Send messages to potential distributors, studio acquisition people, as well as home-video companies and TV network executives. Be sure to target your mailing list — you don't want to be considered a *spammer* (someone who solicits over the Internet to people who don't request mailings from them).

Printing Buttons, T-Shirts, and Other Premiums

Promotional products, called *premiums* or *giveaways,* such as buttons, T-shirts, mugs, pens, key chains, and hats with your film's logo, create great publicity for your film. (People rarely throw away something that has any type of value to it.) You can give these away at shopping malls, at your premiere screening, or at film markets and film festivals. Most cities have promotional product and apparel companies; check out your local Yellow Pages under "Advertising — Promotional Products."

For my film *Undercover Angel,* I created Mr. Dodo stuffed animals and sent one with each screening cassette of the film (see Mr. Dodo at www.mrdodo.com).

I've used a company called Sichel that does custom-embroidered jackets and clothing. Give the company a call and request a catalog at 818-255-0862. If you want a great deal on T-shirts, try the $2.95 Guys at www.295guys.com.

Planning a Publicity Stunt

A *publicity stunt* is anything that draws attention to you or your film. Choose a publicity stunt that isn't dangerous or illegal (you don't want to get arrested — that's the wrong kind of publicity!). A costumed character giving out flyers or delivering a video copy of your film to a film executive or distributor is okay. Sending a singing telegram with a copy of your film to a potential distributor works, too.

A more expensive publicity stunt is having a prop plane fly a banner advertising your film. A cheaper way to go is to hire some beautiful models to give out flyers on your film or sell tickets to a screening.

When I was a teenager, I shot a film when the circus came to town and wanted to create some publicity for the screening. My friend Gary Bosloy volunteered to dress up in a gorilla suit and run around the neighborhood. Someone called the local radio station and reported that a gorilla was loose, and everyone assumed it escaped from the circus that was in town. I then called into the radio stations and local news programs and told them it was a publicity stunt to promote our film. This stunt got us free publicity!

Holding a Screening Party or Charity Event

If you can afford to rent a screening room or theater, consider setting up a premiere to introduce your film to an audience. The audience should consist of potential buyers for your film, including distributors and TV and home-video acquisition people.

Your screening can also be a charity event where all proceeds go to a specific charity. A charity screening creates positive exposure for your film and helps a good cause at the same time.

Placing an Ad

Consider placing an ad in the newspaper to announce a screening of your film. If you want to see the response to your film with a paying audience, this is a way to go. However, advertising in a newspaper costs considerable money, so you may only want to run a small ad so you have a better chance of making a profit on your screening.

Chapter 23

Ten Ways to Avoid Murphy's Law When Filming

"*E*verything that can go wrong, will go wrong." Welcome to Murphy's Law — the curse of any project. But you don't have to be a victim of Murphy's Law if you plan ahead. If you anticipate disruptions and know how to problem-solve, you'll be prepared to handle Murphy's Law, or even keep Murphy away.

In regards to planning, my dad used to say, "You can't go right doing wrong, you can't go wrong doing right." I always have a plan A and a plan B — and even a plan C. Think through all the possibilities that could hold up your production and then plan for them. It's like puppy-proofing your house — you have to think of everything the puppy could get into and lock those things out of reach. Every time I forget to take my lunch off my desk, the dog always remembers. Avoiding Murphy's Law is like buying insurance. Ensure your production by planning ahead for those things that will go wrong.

Testing the Camera and Film Stock

Before you begin shooting your film, test the camera. If you're shooting film, shoot some test footage and send it to the lab to check for scratches and steadiness of picture, and to make sure you don't have fogging from a light leak in the camera.

Having a checklist and checking it twice

Make a checklist of all the items and equipment you'll need, along with any important reminders (like giving your Aunt Sally a credit for letting you shoot in her apartment for one scene). You can start the list way ahead of schedule and continue to add things until the day of shooting.

Don't rely on your memory — no matter how good you may be at remembering things, you'll always end up forgetting something. It's like going to the grocery store. You make a grocery list so you know exactly what you need and don't end up forgetting something.

Testing your camera is really easy if you're shooting with a video camcorder (analog or digital). Just shoot some video and then play it back on a regular TV to make sure the image looks okay.

Scouting Locations for Noise

Planes, trains, and automobiles: Not good news for your sound takes. Make sure the location is quiet enough to record sound on your shoot. If you're shooting a scene that's supposed to be taking place on the shores of a desert island, you don't want to find out the first day of shooting that you're in the fly-zone of a major airport. The roar of planes taking off and coming in every few minutes can make it extremely difficult to get a clean audio take (see Chapter 12). Same with train tracks. If you must shoot near train tracks, find out the train schedules so you can be forewarned when recording dialogue.

Watching the Weather Channel

If you have an outdoor shoot scheduled, watch the Weather Channel (or go to www.weather.com). If torrential rain is predicted, you'll know to plan for your indoor cover set ahead of time. (A *cover set* is an indoor scene that you're prepared to shoot in the event that your outdoor scenes are rained out.)

Having Backup Locations and Actors, Too

Take nothing for granted. You could lose a location because of the owner changing his or her mind, charging you more than what was agreed upon, or disturbing the neighborhood. If you don't have a backup arranged, you could waste a lot of time trying to find a new location.

Have a backup for actors, too. In Los Angeles, I've had my share of flaky actors who were late or forgot to show up on set.

Using a Stunt Double

Don't take a chance with your actors. Always use a stunt double for any type of action that could potentially disable your actor. Even if a stunt seems pretty simple, you don't want your lead actor spraining an ankle and hobbling around the rest of the shoot. Very few actors in Hollywood do their own stunts. Jackie Chan is one of the few who does, but he's apparently broken almost every bone in his body in the process!

Keeping a First-Aid Kit or Medic on Set

Be prepared for injuries — whether a simple knee bruise, a cut finger, or something more serious — by having a first-aid kit on set. Even better, have a medic on set if you can afford one (especially if your film has stunts or pyrotechnics). And always make sure you have the phone number and directions to the closest hospital.

Recognizing that Cell Phones Don't Work Everywhere

Check out your locations beforehand to make sure that cell phones work in the area. If it's a remote area and you don't pick up a signal, make sure you have access to a land phone. You always need communication to and from the location.

Mapping Out Directions

Always have maps drawn up and distributed to cast and crew so no one can say he or she didn't know where the location was. In addition to the visual map, have the directions spelled out from all directions.

Some people are visual and can read maps just fine; others are better at following written directions. You can get maps or step-by-step directions from Web sites like www.maps.com or www.mapquest.com. You can also e-mail these maps to cast and crew.

Providing Plenty of Parking

You don't want your cast and crew driving around the block for 20 minutes on the first day of your shoot. Plan ahead and find a parking lot that your team can use while at this location. If everyone has to park a distance from the set location, arrange to have a mini-bus shuttle everyone from the parking lot to the set.

Setting Security Overnight

Pay a few extra dollars to have someone stay with the equipment at your location if you're shooting there the next day. Maybe someone on your crew, like a production assistant, would be willing to sleep on a couch or in a tent. Don't ever leave your equipment like your lights and camera in an unlocked vehicle. (Try not to leave them in a vehicle, period!) Someone will be sure to steal something if it's left unattended — Murphy's Law, you know. I've even had a clapboard and chair stolen off my set.

Powering Up Ahead of Time

Here's a bonus tip to guard against Murphy's Law. When you scout your locations, make sure they have places to plug in your lights and equipment. Otherwise, you'll need to budget for a generator to run all your electrical devices.

Even if the location has power, the location owner may request that you bring your own power and not tap into his or hers.

Chapter 24

The Ten Best Filmmaking Magazines and Newspapers

In This Chapter

▶ Subscribing to entertainment periodicals worth reading

▶ Finding out what's going on in Hollywood

*I*f you want to be a successful filmmaker, you need to tap into the entertainment industry, and the best way to do that is to subscribe to some of the following trade papers and magazines. You can't hope to pick up all of your knowledge just from hearing it through the grapevine.

Always double-check subscription rates before sending in your payment.

The Hollywood Reporter

The Hollywood Reporter is one of the two top trade papers in Hollywood. Subscription prices are $175 for 52 weekly issues and $229 for 255 daily issues. The *Reporter* keeps you up to date on anything and everything on that's happening in Hollywood — from the latest studio deal to the current deals of the movers and shakers you need to know about.

P.O. Box 480800
Los Angeles, CA 90099
Phone: 323-525-2150
Web site: www.thehollywoodreporter.com
E-mail: subscriptions@hollywoodreporter.com

Daily Variety

Daily Variety, along with *Weekly Variety* (which comes out once a week and recaps the news from *Daily Variety* for the prior week), is considered the top periodical next to *The Hollywood Reporter.* A yearly subscription to *Daily Variety* is $279. *Weekly Variety* is $259 for a yearly subscription. This paper contains news stories and current events including weekly box-office grosses.

P.O. Box 15878
North Hollywood, CA 91615-9434
Phone: 323-857-6600
Web site: www.variety.com
E-mail: variety@espcomp.com

Backstage West

Backstage West is for actors, filmmakers, and film and stage crews. This paper comes out once a week, and features classified ads, casting notices, and related articles of interest to actors and filmmakers. A one-year subscription (51 issues) costs $95 if you're on the East Coast, $89 if you're on the West Coast, and $145 if you're up there in Canada, eh.

P.O. Box 1992
Marion, OH 43306
Phone: 800-745-8922
Web site: www.backstage.com
E-mail: bcks@kable.com

Premiere Magazine

Premiere Magazine tells you what's happening in the world of entertainment and is a little more on the gossip side than an industry paper. A one-year subscription (10 issues) costs $12 in the United States or $20 in Canada.

P.O. Box 55393
Boulder, CO 80322
Phone: 212-767-5400
Web site: www.premieremag.com
E-mail: subscriptions@hfnm.com

Entertainment Weekly

Entertainment Weekly has entertainment news and stories similar to *Premiere Magazine.* The decision of whether to subscribe to this one or to *Premiere* is really just a matter of personal preference. A one-year subscription is $29.95.

P.O. Box 60001
Tampa, FL 33660-0001
Phone: 800-828-6882
Web site: www.ew.com

People Magazine

People Magazine is full of fascinating stories that could inspire a screenplay, whether by triggering an original story in your mind, or by helping you track down someone written about in the magazine so you can write their life story. Promotional rates are around $2.09 an issue for 52 issues. You do the math (okay, I'll do it — that comes to $108.68).

P.O. Box 60001
Tampa, FL 33660
Phone: 800-541-9000
Web site: www.people.com

American Cinematographer

Find out more about camera techniques and secrets with *American Cinematographer* magazine. Each issue unravels the mystery of how photography and effects were done in popular films. A one-year subscription runs $29.95.

1782 North Orange Dr.
Hollywood, CA 90028
Phone: 800-448-0145
Web site: www.theasc.com
E-mail: subscription@theasc.com

DV Magazine

DV Magazine (which stands for *Digital Video Magazine*) is a great technical magazine that keeps up to date on digital technology. This magazine includes equipment reviews and great articles offering technical tips and essential information for the digital-video enthusiast. A one-year subscription (12 issues) costs $19.99.

P.O. Box 1212
Skokie, IL 60076
Phone: 888-776-7002
Web site: www.dv.com/magazine
E-mail: dv@halldata.com

MovieMaker Magazine

MovieMaker Magazine is geared toward the independent filmmaker. This magazine has articles and up-to-date information on lab deals, insurance, shooting techniques, and new equipment. The magazine also keeps the filmmaker informed on film festivals and includes interviews with top moviemakers. Sign up online for subscription rates starting at $9.95 for one year (4 issues a year). Canada is $26 for 4 issues.

2265 Westwood Blvd. #497
Los Angeles, CA 90064
Phone: 310-234-9234
Web site: www.moviemaker.com
E-mail: subs@moviemaker.com

Your Local Newspaper

Check out local newspapers for unique stories and events that may not reach a national readership (there's less chance of a Hollywood producer seeing the same story) that you could turn into a commercial screenplay.

The Hollywood Creative Directory

The Hollywood Creative Directory isn't a periodical but a reference guide. Depending on the particular edition, they're updated several times a year. A must-have for writers, producers, directors, and crew. Copies are available in book form (the printed directories listed below are all $59.95) or online (www.hcdonline.com). Directories include

✔ *Hollywood Creative Directory* (updated three times a year): Lists names of producers, studios, and network executives. The directory also lists current production credits for all production companies, TV networks, and studios.

✔ *Hollywood Representation Directory (Agents & Managers)* (updated twice a year): Lists agents and managers and their contact information.

✔ *Hollywood Distributors Directory* (published every winter): Lists distributors and contact information.

Index

• *C* •

NOW AVAILABLE!

FOR DUMMIES™ Videos & DVDs

Save 15% when you order online at:
www.collagevideo.com/dummies15

Basic Yoga Workout FOR DUMMIES

with Sara Ivanhoe

An Easy-to-Follow Yoga Practice

Instructor Sara Ivanhoe offers step-by-step instruction of the 12 essential yoga postures. This workout shows you proper technique, as well as tips on modifying postures for your fitness level. Today, many people use yoga to help alleviate back pain, reduce stress, and increase flexibility.

VHS - 45 Mins. $9.99
DVD - 70 Mins. $14.98

Beyond Basic Yoga FOR DUMMIES

with Sara Ivanhoe

An Easy-to-Follow Workout

The *Beyond Basic Yoga Workout For Dummies* is the next step for anyone who has enjoyed *Basic Yoga Workout For Dummies* and is ready to enhance their practice with 12 more postures. This workout is a little more advanced than the basic yoga program but still features the *For Dummies* format.

VHS - 45 Mins. $9.99
DVD - 55 Mins. $14.98

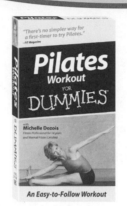

Pilates Workout FOR DUMMIES

with Michelle Dozois

An Easy-to-Follow Workout

Instructor Michelle Dozois offers step-by-step instruction of 18 popular Pilates mat exercises to help you strengthen and lengthen your muscles, improve your posture, and tone and tighten your midsection.

VHS - 40 Mins. $9.99
DVD - 60 Mins. $14.98

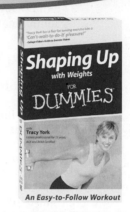

Shaping Up with Weights FOR DUMMIES

with Tracy York

An Easy-to-Follow Workout

Instructor Tracy York offers step-by-step instruction of 12 key strength-training exercises and makes it easy to work out at any level. This workout incorporates both upper- and lower-body exercises to help tone muscles and burn more calories per day, which leads to fat loss.

VHS - 51 Mins. $9.99

Basic Ab Workout FOR DUMMIES

with Gay Gasper

An Easy-to-Follow Workout

Instructor Gay Gasper demonstrates her top 10 exercises to tone and flatten your tummy. Throughout this workout, she gives you more advanced options for the exercises so you can start at any level and then advance as you become more fit.

VHS - 45 Mins. $9.99
DVD - 55 Mins. $14.98

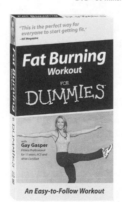

Fat Burning Workout FOR DUMMIES

with Gay Gasper

An Easy-to-Follow Workout

In this workout, instructor Gay Gasper offers step-by-step instructions of the 10 basic exercises that make up any aerobic routine. She incorporates both high- and low-impact choices in an effective workout to help you burn more fat, use more calories every day, and meet your fitness goals.

VHS - 45 Mins. $9.99

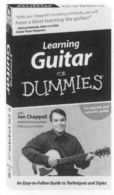

Learning Guitar FOR DUMMIES

with Jon Chappell

An Easy-to-Follow Guide to Techniques and Styles

Instructor Jon Chappell provides step-by-step instruction of all of the skills you need to become an accomplished guitar player! By simply watching the instructor onscreen and following along, you can learn to play songs — without reading music.

VHS - 75 Mins. $12.98
DVD - 75 Mins. $16.98

To Order Call: 1-800-546-1949

Distributed By
Anchor Bay Entertainment, Inc.
1699 Stutz Dr., Troy, MI 48084
© 2002 Anchor Bay Entertainment, Inc.

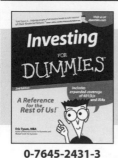

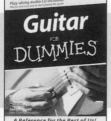

FOR DUMMIES®

A world of resources to help you grow

TRAVEL

0-7645-5453-0

0-7645-5438-7

0-7645-5444-1

Also available:

America's National Parks For Dummies
(0-7645-6204-5)

Caribbean For Dummies
(0-7645-5445-X)

Cruise Vacations For
Dummies 2003
(0-7645-5459-X)

Europe For Dummies
(0-7645-5456-5)

Ireland For Dummies
(0-7645-6199-5)

France For Dummies
(0-7645-6292-4)

Las Vegas For Dummies
(0-7645-5448-4)

London For Dummies
(0-7645-5416-6)

Mexico's Beach Resorts
For Dummies
(0-7645-6262-2)

Paris For Dummies
(0-7645-5494-8)

RV Vacations For Dummies
(0-7645-5443-3)

EDUCATION & TEST PREPARATION

0-7645-5194-9

0-7645-5325-9

0-7645-5249-X

Also available:

The ACT For Dummies
(0-7645-5210-4)

Chemistry For Dummies
(0-7645-5430-1)

English Grammar For
Dummies
(0-7645-5322-4)

French For Dummies
(0-7645-5193-0)

GMAT For Dummies
(0-7645-5251-1)

Inglés Para Dummies
(0-7645-5427-1)

Italian For Dummies
(0-7645-5196-5)

Research Papers For Dummies
(0-7645-5426-3)

SAT I For Dummies
(0-7645-5472-7)

U.S. History For Dummies
(0-7645-5249-X)

World History For Dummies
(0-7645-5242-2)

HEALTH, SELF-HELP & SPIRITUALITY

0-7645-5154-X

0-7645-5302-X

0-7645-5418-2

Also available:

The Bible For Dummies
(0-7645-5296-1)

Controlling Cholesterol
For Dummies
(0-7645-5440-9)

Dating For Dummies
(0-7645-5072-1)

Dieting For Dummies
(0-7645-5126-4)

High Blood Pressure For
Dummies
(0-7645-5424-7)

Judaism For Dummies
(0-7645-5299-6)

Menopause For Dummies
(0-7645-5458-1)

Nutrition For Dummies
(0-7645-5180-9)

Potty Training For Dummies
(0-7645-5417-4)

Pregnancy For Dummies
(0-7645-5074-8)

Rekindling Romance For
Dummies
(0-7645-5303-8)

Religion For Dummies
(0-7645-5264-3)

Available wherever books are sold. Go to www.dummies.com or call 1-877-762-2974 to order direct

FOR DUMMIES®

Plain-English solutions for everyday challenges

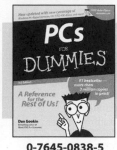

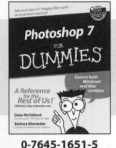